W9-BNO-100

CRITICAL AC
The Best Travel Writing Series

"Travelers' Tales has thrived by seizing on our perpetual fascination for armchair traveling, including this annual roundup of delightful (and sometimes dreadful) wayfaring adventures from all corners of the globe."   —*The Washington Post*

"*The Best Travel Writing 2007* is a globetrotter's dream. Some tales are inspiring, some disturbing or disheartening; many sobering. But at the heart of each one lies the most crucial element—a cracking good story told with style, wit, and grace."
—*WorldTrekker*

"*The Best Travel Writing 2006*: Here are intimate revelations, mind-changing pilgrimages, and body-challenging peregrinations. And there's enough to keep one happily reading until the 2007 edition."   —*San Francisco Chronicle*

"There is no danger of tourist brochure writing in this collection. The story subjects themselves are refreshingly odd. . . . For any budding writer looking for good models or any experienced writer looking for ideas on where the form can go, *The Best Travel Writing 2005* is an inspiration." —*Transitions Abroad*

"Travelers' Tales, a publisher which has taken the travel piece back into the public mind as a serious category, has a volume out titled *The Best Travel Writing 2005* which wipes out its best-of competitors completely."   —*The Courier-Gazette*

"*The Best Travelers' Tales 2004* will grace my bedside for years to come. For this volume now formally joins the pantheon: one of a series of good books by good people, valid and valuable for far longer than its authors and editors ever imagined. It is, specifically, an ideal antidote to the gloom with which other writers, and the daily and nightly news, have tried hard to persuade us the wor
are in my view quite w
book is a vivid and del
is in essence a wondro
inseparable part of its
so much hard work as

THE
BEST
TRAVEL
WRITING
2008

TRUE STORIES
FROM AROUND THE WORLD

TRAVELERS' TALES

THE BEST
TRAVEL WRITING
2008

TRUE STORIES
FROM AROUND THE WORLD

Edited by

JAMES O'REILLY, LARRY HABEGGER,
AND SEAN O'REILLY

Travelers' Tales
an imprint of Solas House, Inc.
Palo Alto

Art Direction: Stefan Gutermuth
Interior design and page layout: Melanie Haage using the fonts Nicolas Cochin, Ex Ponto and Granjon.

ISBN 1-932361-54-5
ISSN 1548-0224

First Edition
Printed in the United States
10 9 8 7 6 5 4 3 2 1

The Sailor

My old friend is a sailor
From the crew of many boats.
In his face shine the answers
Taught by visions and horizons
Lit with precious understanding.

He's learned so many nameless lessons
From the risings
And the settings
Of the sun—this vagabond in me.

"What you see in me is you," he says,
"For we never see each other—
Only ourself who is the other.

"And the sense of one and other
Cannot stand before the vision
In the mirror
One could think to be another."

—Moro Buddy Bohn, *Kin to the Wind*

Table of Contents

Publisher's Preface

I read Steinbeck's *East of Eden* recently, a marvelous book with more well-wrought themes and characters than a dozen Oscar winners, and it got me to thinking, naturally, of Paradise. It's what we're all after, one way or the other, under many a flag—salvation, enlightenment, self-realization ("Be All You Can Be," as the U.S. Army correctly exhorted), fulfillment, nirvana, heaven. From saint-in-training to suicide bomber, it's what we do as humans, looking, looking. Some of us search in church and temple, some in the affections of others, possessions, power, drugs, asceticism, duty, service. Then there are those who seek paradise in travel, as do the writers in this book. From Joel Carillet's opening story, "Red Lights and a Rose," which takes place in Bangkok, the stories roll around the world until Rolf Potts brings it back to Thailand in the closing piece, "Death of an Adventure Traveler." Of course all these stories reveal the essence of place, but equally they reveal the essence of the traveler and the heart of the stranger.

Travel is surely one of the best ways to explore the territory of the spirit. While I think we can all agree with sages through the ages that our spiritual home lies within, that realm is nonetheless fog-shrouded by the routines of daily life, which slowly numb us to the miracle of being. As Steinbeck writes early in his book, "And it never failed that during the dry years the people forgot about the rich years, and during the wet years they lost all memory of the dry years. It was always that way."

We get stale if we stay home too long: travel creates motion, a fine breeze that reveals the contours of our insides, our errors of judgment and wishful thinking, and the possible path of our future selves. Even a stroll around the block can do the trick, for a while anyway.

Listen to Mary Patrice Erdmans walking the Way of St. James in "Gods Who Smell Like Goats" (the same passage rang the chimes of Sara Wheeler, as you'll see in her Introduction):

> I went to walk and to clear my head. I
> went because of the wretched monkey of
> yearning that never lets me know what
> exactly it is I am yearning for. Along the
> way, the innocent faith of an eight-year-old
> came back to me as I walked without a map
> or knowledge of the language across the
> foggy mountains, blue asparagus fields, and
> enigmatic silent villages of Spain.

Thus is she refreshed, reminded of who she is, living in the present like a child. Travel releases us to rediscover this in the very motion of the voyage, in the mirror of other cultures. The outward journey always turns us inward. Then we get home, we rejoice for a while, the fog rolls back in, and we forget the beauty of home, we forget the beauty of friends and families, and we need to be reminded by the face of a stranger.

While paradise is within, it is our nature to roam. We are born to look for paradise outside until we remember that it was inside all along: here, there, everywhere, as above so below.

The frontis poem by Moro Buddy Bohn is from *Kin to the Wind*, his unpublished tale of wandering the world without money as a young troubadour. The discoveries he made about life, the friendships he formed, the adventures he had, are pure testament to the message of his poem and to the power of travel—not only are we kin to the wind, we are kin. In each other's faces are ourselves, and our salvation.

—James O'Reilly
Palo Alto, California

Introduction

SARA WHEELER

This sprightly new collection gives the lie to those wearily familiar mantras that all the journeys have been done, that globalization has robbed travel of meaning, that travel writing is dead. It shows that the open road still beckons, for better or worse, just as it always did.

I love *The Best Travel Writing 2008* most for its thematic range. It is metaphysically global. The subject shifts from the voyage between broken-ness and redemption in Joel Carillet's piece on Bangkok, to that hard-won path between resentment and acceptance in Matthew Link's story about home-schooling adrift on the Pacific. Cloudy issues of faith lie at the heart of Margo Berdeshevsky's take on the Philippines, while Jennifer Baljko describes the vertiginous reality of *castellers* in Catalonia. When I started out as a writer, it seemed to me that travel offered the perfect vehicle. In this anthology I marvel again at the elasticity of the genre.

Unlike their predecessors a generation or two past, these contributors have had to confront the distinction between travel and tourism (because, of course, there was no mass tourism until relatively recently: the nature of travel has changed.) This new lot are writers who travel, rather than travelers who write. There is a difference. Broadly speaking, they instinctively concentrate either on the personal or on the particular, and integrate modern realities into whatever it is they want to say. "Even on a cruise," Kevin McCaughey writes in "Heroes of the Caribbean," "it's possible to experience real travel." What will a changing climate do to the places so lovingly conjured in the book? We do not really know. But I hope they will still be there for the yet-to-be-born generations of travel writers.

Like all proper writing, these stories leave images that linger. The "fresh-faced nun" poking her head out of the door in the Santa Clara convent, Carrion de los Condes, in Mary Patrice Erdmans's Spanish tale (I like the way Erdmans talks of "the wretched monkey of yearning." I know that simian devil); sunset on a dusty highway in "the withered heart of Why" in Dustin Leavitt's heart-breaking parable of Mexican despair and hope. All the world is here, and all its rich complexity. Like many before them, some contributors ruminate on notions of "home," and the paradox implicit in the concept. One longs to leave home for the desert, another longs to get back to her desert home. And, like life, these narratives are not all coconuts and honeyed sands, as Richard Goodman discovers in Tortola. "All life is a journey," Homer tells us in the *Odyssey*, perhaps the oldest travel story in the world. (Though at my age, I prefer the *Iliad*'s "All life is battle.")

In these pages one learns again that travel writing is about more than travel. Exotic or banal, eventful or becalmed—whatever the trip, the writers here make it their own. To quote Apsley Cherry-Garrard, author of *The Worst Journey in the World*, possibly the greatest travel book ever written, what counts, on the page and in the moment, is "the response of the spirit." The journeys writers make are slip roads to the private colonies

of the imagination. Yes, writers have now been everywhere. But the eye that looks inward always sees a new
landscape. Happy Travels.

❧ ❧ ❧

Sara Wheeler's books include the bestselling Terra Incognita:
Travels in Antarctica, *and* Travels in a Thin Country: A
Journey Through Chile. *She has also written biographies of
the travelers Apsley Cherry-Garrard, one of Captain Scott's men,
and Denys Finch Hatton, the white hunter, and Karen Blixen's
lover, played by Robert Redford in* Out of Africa. *All her books
are published in the United States by Modern Library. She lives
in London, England, and is currently writing a book about the
Arctic.*

❧ ❧ ❧

Red Lights and a Rose

Our freedom to love others is an astonishing thing.

I WAS THINKING ABOUT PARADISE, A WORD SO OFTEN flippantly tossed around in churches and mosques, at Club Med resorts, and on Norwegian cruise liners. The word could be powerful, but we've made it soft.

It was 1 A.M., an hour before closing. A bottle of Heineken hung from my left hand and a pen from the other. And on the stage before me were six women wearing black high-heeled shoes and black thongs, dancing as if they thought paradise were far away indeed. They danced with remarkable indifference, each clutching her respective pole, moving their knees and hips with the same tired pep as an old Volkswagen about to break down. One woman kept her hand around her navel, self-conscious of her stretch marks. For her, the pole was a shield she used in a vain attempt to hide herself.

1

This was anything but an erotic sight. It was more like witnessing a subtle form of torture.

Is paradise a place we stumble upon only after death, where, if we are to believe some Muslims, seventy-two virgins await, ready to indulge us in sensual pleasures?

"Pretty Woman" played on the sound system and I finished what was left of my beer. An American businessman-type with a Texas drawl sauntered in and found a seat. Now four of us guys were in a room with eight girls, six on stage and two sitting among us. It didn't take long for the Texan to find the prettiest of the bunch, a woman in her early twenties who had quit her job as a bank teller about two months before. She was not here because her family was poor; she was here because she wanted to be rich and men like the Texan would pay well to spend the night with her. She was quiet, polite, and intelligent, and I had no difficulty imagining her working in a bank. But now she looked so small next to this big man. Her dark eyes stared straight ahead—straight into the wall—as he put his arm around her and began to caress her shoulder. I thought of a quiet animal caught in the claws of a hawk, too frightened to move as it prepares to be swallowed. But she was here voluntarily.

Is paradise, if we are to believe some Christians, largely an individual enterprise where, by simply believing in Jesus but otherwise going about our lives as we normally would, we will find ourselves in celestial glory after we die?

Back on the stage another woman, Ann, was about to rotate off. A twenty-seven-year-old mother who speaks Thai, three tribal languages, and a few words of English, she had been working here one and a half years to earn money for her extended family, most of whom live in a poor village seven hours north of Bangkok. I had asked

Ann if she likes her work—I knew some women did—
and she replied with a tired smile that said she did not.
She danced and prostituted herself only because provid-
ing for the needs of her family was her top priority. Her
seven-year-old daughter remains in the village, in the
care of her grandmother.

The lights were dim and the music loud, yet it was
conducive to note taking (in Asia to write a book, I was
taking a lot of notes about a lot of places). Just before
Ann stepped off the stage and returned to my table so
that we could continue our conversation, I made a note
to ponder the idea of paradise as "right relationships."
Later, back at my hotel, I would write, "Paradise is not
indulging in selfishness, it can't be bought with money,
it can't be had without including the poor. It will not
descend so long as we sit on a couch watching television,
or stand among pews singing songs. We enter into it neither by driving planes into towers nor by hoarding store-
houses of grain. It is deeper than 'feeling good.' And it is
wider—much wider—than personal salvation."

This was my second night in Soi Nana, a square
three-story structure with the feel of a frat house. Or
was it more like that ride at Disney World, Pirates of
the Caribbean? Yes, that was it, Nana reminded me of a
Disney World ride: Pirates raucously chasing screaming
women, people living out of bounds, with ogling eyes,
on a quest for ill-gotten treasure. Yo, ho, ho, a pirate's
life for me! But here many of the swashbucklers were
upper middle-class businessmen from the West, strolling
in and out of clubs with names like Spankys, Lollipop,
Carousel, DC-10, and G-Spot. And at less than two dollars, which covered your first beer, it was considerably
cheaper than Orlando.

Over a three-day period I would visit several clubs in Nana, all of which were pretty much the same. They were like trash compactors, all of us pressed too tightly together, fighting the heat and humidity, sensing that intimacy was strangely recyclable here. It was a raucous environment indeed, with so much careless movement that hearts were easily broken. At least this is how I read the looks on the faces of several women, and later what I would hear them say.

And yet it was here, in a minefield of flesh and dreams, where black cats prowled on sheet metal awnings in search of geckos, where satellite dishes pulled in ESPN that overweight German tourists watched as girls nestled compliantly into their girth, where sound systems belted out the likes of Billy Ray Cyrus so that girls could rock their bodies to the rhythm of "Achy Breaky Heart"…it was here that I stood on the verge of discovering something new about paradise.

With few exceptions, Nana was not a place of desperation. It was something more playful and ambitious than this. When the ladies weren't sitting with patrons they were often in the back room giggling together, as though they were kids enjoying a late night at a friend's house. There was an atmosphere present that would have had an appeal even if everyone had been fully clothed.

Nor was Nana merely a place where money was exchanged for sex, since hundreds of women brought their dreams to work. They sought a quality Western man, someone with whom they might live happily ever after. And so a clearly demarcated border between business and friendship did not exist. It was easy to see why men who might not seek a prostitute at home might do so here. The girls radiated playfulness and innocence, and made you think you simply had a friend. You never knew when you'd be met with real affection.

But, you never knew a lot of things, and vision is difficult when the lights are dim. There was something unsettling about all this flesh, as if it had been so exposed that it managed to become ghostly. The music was the most real thing here, or at least the clearest, and so I tethered myself to it in an effort to see well. The musicians and I were old friends, friends I hadn't heard from in ages, and I listened to every word they had to say because they reminded me of a place and time that tonight I couldn't afford to forget. Music is rarely as potent as when it is heard in a strip club.

In its moral ambiguities and brokenness, Nana was a place where you saw everything in a new way. Flesh wriggling on poles was an unusual teacher, not the kind that demanded rote memorization of facts and figures but one that instead employed the Socratic method, asking questions of the student to which the student had to craft an answer. And the women were not merely teachers from afar. They often came over to sit awhile. They were scantily clad, sometimes naked, but many of them were keen on leaving sex behind and simply sharing a story and hearing one in return. The place was all about human connection—its possibilities, failures, and dangers—and this is precisely why I sensed that something of paradise was here, just waiting to take shape.

I recalled my first visit to Bangkok four years earlier. I don't remember her name anymore, but she was a go-go girl in Patpong, another adult entertainment district, and it was there that we met one night and sat in a corner of a club. She was completely nude, as were the other thirty-some women in the room, and I think this may have been why her eyes were so striking—with no clothes, the body was left unadorned, and her eyes, so earnest and intense, contained a power they otherwise might not have. I could think of only one parallel in my experience: looking into the eyes of a Saudi woman, who was fully draped in black fabric except for a slit at the eyes.

She was in her mid-twenties and had seen many men, she said, but I was different—why? I fumbled over an answer. It might sound strange, I told her, but after watching so many men who did not seem loving enter these doors, I decided to enter them as well, and invite someone out for dinner. "Would you like to join me for *pad thai*?" I asked. She said yes, but her shift wouldn't end for three more hours. After about one hour, she was called to take the stage, where she would join three other ladies to (there is no delicate way to describe this) shoot bananas from her vagina and then pop open bottles of Coke, also with her vagina. For the last hour her eyes had looked broken—broken, but not defeated—and now they begged for trust. "Please don't go," she pleaded, "I come back soon." Of course I would wait, I said. Then she stood up to leave. With her eyes looking at the stage, she appeared nervous, perhaps even pained, and for several moments she didn't move. When finally she did take a step it was not toward the stage, though she would be up there in only a few seconds; rather she turned back toward me. She leaned close to say something, her eyes still begging.

"Please don't watch," she whispered.

Walking around Nana now, four years later, I remembered her and wondered how her body and spirit had fared with the passage of time. But while I could still remember her eyes, I knew I wouldn't be able to recognize her even if she were still in the city. I couldn't even remember her name. I hoped that if I were to meet someone again tonight that I would remember her—her story, her name, her face—for many years to come.

It was about midnight, in a sea of bubbliness and hardness and crassness, when I met Fon. She was dressed in jeans and a white t-shirt, had a tattoo emblazed on her right arm, and sat on a stool at the door to a club, urging men to peek through the curtain and enter. She snagged my arm as I passed.

"Come inside!" she screamed, just as all the other girls outside all the other clubs would scream. But Fon seemed particularly obnoxious.

Tired, I said I was on my way home and needed to sleep. But she persisted, "No problem, five minutes, drink one beer."

"No, really," I said, "I'm almost out of money. I've got to go home."

"No problem, I buy," she responded, and then slipped into the club. She emerged a moment later with a cold Heineken and an extra stool.

"Really, I don't have money to buy that drink—I will *not* buy that drink," I said, suspecting some catch in her offer. But she was clear: the drink really was her treat.

We exchanged biographies. She was twenty-four years old, from Phuket, and had been living in Bangkok for two months. Her boyfriend had died three years ago in a motorcycle accident. As for the tattoos, she got the first at the age of fifteen and now had a total of five, all of which she pointed out to me. The last one cost a whopping 7,000 baht—the equivalent of $175.

Fon was an enigma, not because of her generosity—
three times this week I would invite prostitutes to dinner
to hear their stories, and each time they would insist on
covering the bill—but because talking to her was like trying to start a cantankerous car, one that might turn over
but then croak a moment later. She was not quiet, nor was
she unsocial; she simply chose to be difficult. "Who are
you?" I wanted to blurt out several times. But I will never
know. And maybe neither will she. Kind one moment but
caustic the next, she was incapable of prolonged conversation and kept much of herself locked away.

The conversation wasn't the smoothest, but after
some time it suddenly fell headlong into a jarring pot-
hole. "Do you want to fuck me?" she snarled. I winced
at both the question itself and her tone, which really
was vicious—like someone maliciously running fingers
down a chalkboard. She was admirably blunt, but I had
no idea what she was actually saying. Was this a test, or
an invitation? Was it the voice of a wounded woman
who wanted to be attacked so that she could attack
back? Whatever it was it didn't even intimate love. It
screamed of its absence.

"No," I said, suddenly feeling more worn out.

At 2 A.M. Nana closed. The neon lights were extin-
guished and the people—giggling and screaming ladies,
all sorts of men—spilled into the street, where they
plopped down at food stalls or hailed taxis. The area
swelled with energy—something like the halls of a high
school on the last day of the year when the final bell
rings—and it was contagious. I let the rush of people
go ahead of me because I wanted for just a moment to
experience Nana void of its people. When the crowd had
passed and it was just Fon and me left in the courtyard,

what I noticed most was the litter strewn on the ground. And I felt that not all the trash was visible because some of it had walked out, buried in the hearts of all who had spent time here. I knew that more wholesome venues get trashed as well, but here the litter made me think that joy does not come cheaply, and if it does come cheaply it will not likely stay. I thought of the words "sex industry" and felt keenly that the emphasis here was on industry. I thought of a construction worker wearing his work boots, factories polluting the sky, and laws trying to regulate it all. I thought of a wilted flower, a poisoned spring, nature in decay. And I thought how ugly is the floor of a place that sees innocence as a marketable asset. The whole environment was an odd mix, a troubling mix, a place that if not now would later call out your tears to cleanse yourself. And maybe in some odd way you'd even feel that your tears came from someplace else, that because they were not entirely your own they were not merely personal property, that they were meant not only to cleanse yourself but also in some very small way to bathe things like this trashy courtyard.

Fon asked if I was hungry—I was—and recommended a family-run food stall a couple blocks down. We ordered hotpot and pulled meat and vegetables onto our plates as a downpour swept through the area. When the rain passed Fon invited me to see her apartment, which wasn't very much farther down the street.

The first thing I noticed when she opened the door of her one-room efficiency was the bed, neatly made and occupied by a stuffed animal. It was Tweety Bird. The walls were decorated with posters of Western boy bands and Leonardo DiCaprio. On a Buddhist altar beside the bed were two open bottles of Strawberry Fanta, some peeled fruit, and joss sticks. And for an entertainment system she had a portable CD player and tiny speakers. Sitting down next to Tweety, Fon pulled a shoebox full of pirated CDs out from under her bed. "Do you like Enrique Iglesias?" she asked.

Fon was a rough personality—tattoos, a stud in her tongue, a callous sneer reflecting her many, many sexual encounters with men. But her room was that of a child.

I met Fon for a late breakfast about noon the next day. The night before we had talked about my love of news, and this morning she presented me with a copy of the *Bangkok Post*. She also offered to let me stay at her place free the rest of the week rather than spend money on a hotel. "I wouldn't bother you because I work nights when you sleep," she said, "and I sleep in the day while you away. Really, no problem."

I didn't see Fon the rest of the week—I had thanked her for her offer but needed to stay across town—but two days before my scheduled departure from Bangkok I wanted to return and say goodbye. But how?

Michelle, a backpacker from the Seattle area whom I had first met three months earlier at the Thai-Cambodian border, helped me out. We met for dinner and I told her both Fon's story and my wish to say good-bye in a memorable way. "Take her a rose," Michelle suggested without much thought. It was a beautifully simple idea, and Michelle urged me to make the hour commute back across the city to follow through with it. "Trust me, she will remember a rose."

It was almost midnight when I arrived at Nana. A young girl—she couldn't have been more than twelve—was selling roses at the entrance to the complex. It almost seemed right that a child—someone who had an innocence about her, who might remind us of another way—was selling something as fragrant and tender as a rose. I walked up the steps, took a left on the second floor, passed several clubs, and was soon at Fon's. Someone else was sitting at the entrance though, and I asked her if Fon was around. The woman looked at the rose and smiled, then tore into the club to find her.

When Fon came out she looked surprised. Her face turned tender, and for a moment the tattoos looked like they didn't belong to her. Her eyes were vulnerable and her movement almost graceful. "I wanted to say good-bye before I leave Bangkok tomorrow," I said. "And I wanted to give you this rose."

All around us Nana roared. The music didn't stop, nor did the screams and giggles and whispered invitations to adjourn to a hotel for an hour. And it struck me that Hell and Paradise do not always have a large no-man's land between them, and that at times they may even share the same space. The vision of Paradise held by some Muslims—women available for sensual pleasure—suddenly looked as shallow as a muddy puddle. And the vision held by some Christians—personal salvation, just "me and God"—appeared emaciated and tragic.

At least this is what I thought when Fon took her rose. We stood together in the midst of noise and brokenness, but I also sensed that, at least for a moment, we stood together in the hope that right relationships are possible.

That is to say, we stood together at the door of paradise.

❧ ❧ ❧

Joel Carillet is a freelance writer and photographer based in Tennessee. His work has appeared in a number of publications, including The Christian Science Monitor, Washington Report on Middle East Affairs *and, perhaps oddly,* Chicken Soup for the Tea Lover's Soul. *"Red Lights and a Rose" was excerpted from his unpublished memoir,* Sixty-One Weeks: A Journey across Asia, *and was also a Grand Prize winner for Best Travel Story of the Year in the second annual Solas Awards (BestTravelWriting.com). His biweekly travel column, "Reflections on the Road," along with other stories and photos, can be found at jcarillet.gather.com.*

CAMERON M. SMITH

~ ~ ~

Ice Ghost

Alone on the North Slope.

I KNEW THAT POLAR BEARS TORE APART CABINS EVERY winter, so the first *crunch*—the sound of a large animal stepping carefully in deep snow—stopped my breath. The second crunch tripped a dozen primal alarms, jolting me out of my sleeping bag to stand with the cocked twelve-gauge aimed at the door, the plywood cabin's weakest point. A month before I couldn't have found the gun's safety switch, much less brandished the big Remington like Rambo, but when you go to Alaska, alone, in winter, you learn about guns. It was nearly 40 below, but I didn't move for the next ten minutes as the crunches slowly circled the cabin. *It knows I'm trapped. It's patient. I have to do something. I have to act.*

When I'd arrived in Barrow to begin my month-long winter expedition on the North Slope, everyone—from visiting sea-ice scientists to native hunters—had warned me about polar bears. And everyone had different advice: they hunt at night, they hunt in the day…they don't go inland, they go inland all the time…you can deter them with a warning shot, no, they don't care about guns, they just keep coming. The only consensus was that polar bears were smart—smarter than a lot of people.

One Inupiat hunter, Billy Leavitt, swept aside all speculation as we tore down an ice road in his battered pickup. The 60-below wind-chill roaring through his window cooled Billy nicely but just about froze me solid.

"Nanuq—the polar bear—does what it wants," he explained, smiling as he spoke in the long vowels and soft consonants of Native American English.

"You can't predict it. Nanuq doesn't speak. If it wants to eat you, it don't matter what kind of gun you got. It's not in the world of man."

Billy gestured at the flat white landscape rushing by.

"If you go out there, you're in the polar bear's world. You just got to live with that."

"Out there" was Alaska's North Slope, a windswept flatland that expanded for miles before knuckling up or dimpling down here and there. The nearest mountains, or even hills, were a hundred miles south. But up here, three hundred miles north of the Arctic Circle, where Alaska was drawn to its uttermost northern tip, the land was flat and open, cloaked by snow most of the year. In the short summers the snow soaked into the tundra and countless shoelace streams trickled into countless shallow lakes. To the north the land ramped down to the Arctic Ocean, its surface frozen for much of the year. I'd come to explore this wilderness alone in winter, dragging a sled containing my food and other supplies. My

last expedition, to Iceland, had been three years before—
too long. I needed to get out. I needed to breathe again,
to fight for my life again.

I have to act. But I was paralyzed, imagining the polar
bear crashing violently through the doorway like they
crash into seal dens. Death would come faster if I didn't
resist. *I have to act. It could be waiting for me to come out.
But I have to act. Are you prepared to kill? Yes.*

In record time I dragged on my clothes and cracked
the door, squinting against the snow light and wind
before leaping outside. Knee-deep in a drift, I sighted
down the gun's fat black barrel, swinging it from side
to side. Nothing. No bear. Only blowing snow. Blood
roared in my ears. Cold knives carved into my face. I
edged around the corner of the hut, still sighting down
the barrel. Nothing. Then I saw prints in the snow.
Laughing, I let the gun barrel swing down. Caribou
tracks. Caribou! *Paralyzed by herbivores!* I went inside to
make breakfast.

Later I headed out for firewood, part of my daily routine. There wasn't a tree within 300 miles, but the little
hut overlooked an Arctic Ocean beach where driftwood
piled up in summer. Tramping down to the snowed-
over beach, I stopped to turn full circle, scanning for
polar bears.

Wood pointed out of the snow here and there like the
prows or rails of sinking ships, twisted and splintered by
shifting sea ice. This wood had journeyed far, entering
the Arctic Ocean either from Siberia or one of the great
Canadian rivers that drain forested lands hundreds of
miles east. Some pieces came free easily; others were per-
manently frozen in, curving down through the snow like
tusks. I used an ax to hack out the wood and chop it to

pieces. Sometimes the ax bounced off the icy wood with a clang, as though I'd struck metal. Bent over the work, I felt uneasy, watched like prey. I began to behave like an herbivore, compulsively popping up to scan for predators. Kneeling to examine natural wonders—a crack in the sea ice, or a galaxy of glittering snowflakes blowing like a stream of stars funneled between two snowdrifts—I always felt watched. I didn't feel more comfortable as time passed. A bear could be watching me, learning my patterns. Each day I felt more vulnerable. I was terrified of becoming complacent. Exercising vigilance for my very life charged my spirit. I was alive again.

But I was an infant in this brutal world, where a breeze might corkscrew the temperature down to 70 below, which is about 140 degrees below room temperature and freezes exposed flesh in seconds. My food froze before I could get it to my mouth. My heavy boots, and drifts of deep, ash-fluffy snow, demanded a new gait. And Nanuq was always in mind, subtly factoring into every decision. I was re-learning the basics: how to eat, how to walk, even how to think.

My master for this re-education was Cold itself, a ghost, defined only as the absence of heat energy. Great heat is tangible, pressing like stacks of smothering blankets. Great cold is its opposite, a vast absence, the earth's blanket stripped away, empty space in arm's reach, ready to brand and sear, wither and cripple. All accomplished simply by an absence of energy. Cold is death, either approaching or upon you. You calculate every action to elude it. I wore gloves in my sleeping bag, ready to hop out in any emergency—like the hut catching fire, or a polar bear tearing down walls—without losing my fingers.

Fiddling with sound recording equipment, or my tripod and cameras, I learned how to work with my back to the wind, how to windmill my arms to drive blood back into my fingers, and how to run in place with the Remington slung over my shoulder.

In the evenings the driftwood blazed and popped in the hut's little iron stove, collapsing into piles of irregular cubes with pulsing red cores and blackened corners. They radiated pure bliss into my opened palms, warming my blood and then my very heart. Some of the wood burned cool, hissing and spitting salt-water, the pale green flames edged with white.

After a week alone I began dragging my sled back to Barrow for more film and supplies. From a jetliner this land was a featureless white blur, but on the ground I found it endlessly varied.

Sometimes I crossed fields of sastrugi, waves of snow arranged in orderly ranks, one after another. To cross them I trudged up one side and then loped down the other before the 200-pound sled could bomb down and break my legs.

Sometimes I traveled on sea ice, my boots crushing a million ice flowers—spiky, two-inch crystals that stuck up in bristling clusters. Cracks in this part of the frozen ocean were small, only inches wide, but shot as far as I could see. They formed when the moon drew at the sea beneath the foot-thick ice.

I also crossed frozen lakes, the black ice, six feet thick and hard as bottle-glass, screeching under my crampons. I often knelt to examine shapes that seemed to move beneath the surface. Through the thick, irregular lens of frozen water, spectral gray bubbles wobbled if I moved my head from side to side, and I did this to keep them in their surreal, drunken motion. Some were big as balloons, others like marbles. Deeper forms were blurry. In some places, multitudes of star-white points clustered like rising soda fizz. And there were isolated specks, lonely as interstellar dust. The surface of the space-black ice was often broken by inch-wide cracks that shot and jagged like lightning bolts hurled from the sky and caught in the ice. Most of the cracks were filled with snow and the broad gray slots dropping into the ice looked like curtains or gray guillotines. Occasionally the scenes would be obscured as a gust-driven swarm of sparkling grains slid across the ice.

I knew that each bubble and crack, each ripple in the ice, had a story, was information. But this was an encyclopedia I could not read. I didn't know the language. I hadn't observed enough.

Once I spent ten minutes gazing into the ice. Had I been on a mission to devour miles and make records, to compare myself with other people or turn this wilderness into a racetrack, these treasures would have gone unnoticed. I would have trampled over them while columns of numbers—representing calories, miles traveled, ounces of fuel consumed, miles yet to go—ticked and streamed through my mind. I'd played that game before, dragging my sled like an automaton across the lifeless, 100-mile-wide expanse of Iceland's Vatnajokull ice cap. It had been a good challenge, serving its purpose, but I had a different quest, now—to learn the language of the ice. So if I traveled slowly, I didn't care, and it took me nearly three days just to haul my sled twenty miles back to Barrow. By luck, Billy Leavitt picked me up just outside town and drove me in.

"It's too warm this year," he said. "When I was a kid it would be 70 below even before the wind-chill!" I couldn't imagine it.

Standing in a hot shower, almost incapacitated by ecstasy, I dimly wondered how the native Inupiat had adapted to this land. Hundred-below windchills, blinding billows of drift snow, the world's largest land predator...what were these folk? How could I understand them? An opportunity at some glimpse of understanding arose. I learned that the Inupiat Messenger Feast, Kivgiq, would take place over then next few days, and that I could attend. Kivgiq was a social, economic, and cultural gathering of native people from across the Arctic. I couldn't miss it. Rather than re-supply and rush back out, I stayed in Barrow for the three-day spectacle.

A thousand or more natives from across Polar Alaska and Canada had gathered—children, adults, teens, and the elders, who told the legend of the Messenger Feast.

When the Inupiat were young and learning to live in this place, life was hard and they hunted all the time. But when they knew how to live, Eagle Mother taught them to drum and sing and dance, and how to build a large feasting house. She told them to invite neighbors to listen to the songs, and dance to the drums. The invitations were delivered by Messengers, who also made requests of the invitees: here is what the sponsor of the feast, respectfully, wishes from you.

Drums—fifteen at a time—beat slowly, directing the subtle movements of dancers' bodies, a shoulder shrug, an arm or wrist gently turned. The slow beat was the invitation to let go, to be taken by the spirit of the dance. After a time, suddenly, like a bomb, the pace and volume increased—*BOOM BOOM BOOM...BOOM BOOM BOOM*—accompanied by wailing and chanting, as the dancers were taken, stamping their boots hard, locking their bodies in stiff postures of shock or terror. Sometimes there were sweeps, syncopated paddling

motions, the communal pursuit of a whale. Sometimes
arms were hauled joyfully towards the chest, pulling
in a whale, sustenance for a whole village, starvation
staved off for another season. There were pantomimes
of hunger and plenty. Conflicts were acted out and resolved. And there was always respect for the land and its
animals, the gravitational center of this culture around
which all else revolved.

These performances were as important to Inupiat
survival as any harpoon or kayak; they were instructions
for a proper life. *How did they survive here?* I'd asked.
It was a question only a wholly urbanized person could
ask. How did they survive here? Easy. Keep your population low. Don't mow down your resources. Manage the
plants and animals so their populations will be healthy
for your descendants, as your ancestors did for you. Be
respectful of the land. It is not rocket science.

And have a sense of humor! Some of the greatest applause at Kivgiq came for "Eskimo Elvis," a dancer out-
fitted in a caped jumpsuit, sunglasses, and pompadour.
"E" rocked the crowd with a fusion of Inupiat and Elvis
moves complete with a karate-kick ending that sent the
crowd through the roof. Kivgiq ended with solemnity, but
laughing was just as important. Life is short, after all.

Soon I was pulling my sled again, south and east
from Barrow, out for more lessons. Thirty-below tem-
peratures left my facemask caked with ice by the time
I crawled into my tent in the evenings. The snow
crunched and squeaked underfoot, as if I were crushing
styrofoam blocks with my boots.

One day I spotted a Thing ahead. I couldn't identify
the shape, but it was an object in the snow, its outline
different from anything else in the snowscape; although

there were plenty of regular shapes here, like the legions of sastrugi, this one didn't belong. It stood up from the snow, whereas most everything here seemed to lie low. And the color wasn't right; it was an off-white, almost yellow. When the color registered, my most primitive alarms were tripped again—*polar bear!*

But it didn't move, and soon I was close enough to see that it was wood, and then the shape resolved into a dogsled. I stepped closer. It was almost entirely swallowed up by the snow. The wooden walls were peeling, and rusty nails bent out here and there—someone had salvaged pieces from it. I wondered when it had been abandoned, and why. Was it months ago, years? Decades? A hundred years? In this dry environment, wood might easily last that long. And this thing might be here for centuries more. It reminded me that we humans come and go, while the things we build remain long after we've moved on, like ghosts.

One morning a stiff wind drove the temperature down to 70 degrees below zero. The wind rushed through my face, bypassing skin and muscle to directly attack the bone. It felt as though a screwdriver had been jammed between plates of bone in my skull and was prying them apart. Stunned and gasping as though I'd been punched in the face, I crouched with my back to the wind, raising my neoprene frostbite mask and lowering my goggles. I could only function here when completely insulated from my environment, like an astronaut on the moon. In this sense, my appreciation for the environment was filtered. It was different than when climbing on rock, for example, when my fingertips were a direct interface with the natural world, taking in, as Craig Childs has written, "a limitless flow of information" from every

crack and crystal. And it was different from scuba diving, when my entire body was submerged and in contact
with fickle currents and temperature gradients. In the
Arctic my body was insulated from these sensory in-
puts and learning was slower. It was all right, though. I
would come back. There were riches here.

On my twentieth morning in this frozen world the
Earth rolled another fraction and the rind of the sun
flooded up and over the snowy horizon, a syrupy slash
of bloody red and molten copper. Turning from the roil-
ing blaze, I saw that the snowscape was now an irregular
checkerboard of hues. A million wind-scalloped hollows
brooded watery green, cold cups patterned regularly
between battalions of small wavelets and whips of wind-
blown snow that stood up a little, their peaks catching the
light and glowing as if lit from within. The snow radiated
a misty pink and the expanse of delicate shades leaping
away from my boots in all directions seemed so buoyant
that the entire snow-capped tundra might just rise and
gently float away, an immense flying carpet. For a moment I forgot the cold and the wind and allowed myself
to believe that I was in a magical place.

I recalled the wonders of the past weeks. I'd watched
a herd of caribou trample the snow to get at the tundra
beneath, and I'd been entranced by the lunar stare of a
snowy owl perched on a distant hummock of snow. I'd
come across dozens of arctic fox trails, frantic scatters of
paw-prints that bounded across crystalline snow before
abruptly changing direction, or commencing gigantic
loops.

Once, I'd heard the Arctic described as a "wasteland."
Having walked slowly here, having taken time to kneel
and wonder at the wolverine and caribou tracks, or lem-

ming nests, I knew that this was the evaluation of someone who had been here but had never really opened their eyes. Perhaps they had flown over in a jet, or torn along the surface in a snowmobile. But nobody who'd taken the time to walk here, to get down on their knees and learn, could call it anything less than a thriving biome. Cold, yes, but without question thriving—crackling like the ice under my boots, electric with life.

≈ ≈ ≈

Cameron M. Smith has traveled from the equator to the Arctic, reporting his experiences in many magazines, including Archaeology *and* South American Explorer, *and in the book* They Lived to Tell the Tale: True Stories of Modern Adventure *from the Legendary Explorers Club. He will return to the North Slope in Winter 2008 to fly a paraglider over the tundra, and in Winter 2009 to scuba dive beneath the sea ice. His blog, amphibianadventures.blogspot.com, covers his recent travels. "Ice Ghost" was a Grand Prize winner for Best Travel Story of the Year in the second annual Solas Awards (BestTravelWriting.com).*

❦ ❦ ❦

The Unquenchable Sea

An unusual journey as a child marks him forever.

WHEN WE WERE OUT AT SEA ON *BUNGO RYE*, WE kids always wanted to jump into the crystal Pacific when it was calm. Dad would haul out the sea anchor: the big round canvas tarp connected by a ring of ropes like a parachute connected to the boat. Its drag would stop the boat from moving forward. He lowered it into the water, then the steel ladder that hung just above the water's surface, dipping into it at intervals as the boat gently rocked with the movements of our bodies. We yelled and leapt into the flat water, its coolness surrounding our unwashed skin and hair that had gone all greasy in the salt air.

But down on the water's surface, the sides of the bowl rose up completely over our heads, making us feel even more insignificant than usual. Looking into the ocean un-

derneath was even worse. Lines of white sunlight streaked
down into the invisible space for miles. It felt exactly like
we were up on top of a tall building, ready to plummet
to the depths without any support, like in a falling nightmare. We could literally see down forever, and this water
was as deep as it comes. We could have all been swallowed
up, pulled down to the unknown bottom, boat and all,
and nothing would have made any difference. No coast
guard would know nor any news organization find a
trace. We would become another vague sea myth, another
voyage gone into the one-way oblivion.

Dad would stand up on deck as we swam, looking for
sharks. He'd have a huge black automatic rifle cocked in
his arm. It was kept under the couch downstairs, next to
the oversized military fatigues he told us we all needed
to put on in case we were approached by an unseemly
ship, and the crew needed to look like it was made up
of men, not mere children. My father would stand there
on deck shirtless, as he usually was. The salt-and-pepper
pattern on his head sneaking its way on to his burly
chest. His eyes would scan the horizon like a macho
robot, searching for figures coming at him in the water.
He was prepared, practically hoping for the worst.

The first time he did this on our inaugural voyage, I
heard Dad's arm cock the rifle as we stood behind him,
dripping with pure saltwater from the sea. "Stand back,
you kids. I'm gonna do a practice round."

I saw him cradle the gun like John Wayne, the hero
of so many of his favorite movies. His eyes were fixed
squarely on that ominously raised horizon. The rifle
went off with a huge crack, and it sounded like an ear-
splitting echo ensued, although I couldn't see how in the
immense vastness around us. My stepsister Rikki and I

were closest to him, and we both jerked back and Rikki gave a yelp when the bullet case flung back at me, hitting me on my bare chest. A bright red mark formed.

Dad turned around with a smile plastered on his face. I looked at him carefully. "Oh, I got hit by a bullet case," he mocked. "Does it hurt?"

I pretended to be indifferent. He laughed and turned back around, triggering another round into the far away ocean. This time I made sure to stand back.

Even on our first voyage on *Bungo Rye* I already knew exactly what to be wary of, and it wasn't Jaws. It was the immeasurable, impassive ocean, and my father when he was joined along with it.

I became a wanderer of the globe at an early age. That's because I grew up on a sailboat. More exactly, I grew up on my father's boat. It was his trip, his voyage, his fantasy—the rest of us were just along for the ride.

For five years, from the ages of twelve to seventeen, I lived on the waves of the Pacific, attempting to keep my equilibrium. There were five of us aboard a fifty-two-foot cutter, the *Bungo Rye*: my dad's girlfriend, her two blond daughters who were close to my age, myself, and my father, the captain. We did home schooling, we fought, we swam, we got sick, we met strange and fantastic characters, we were swept up in rough seas, we missed home, we fell into places on a map we never knew existed. We were real sojourners, the old-fashioned kind, without a home, without a final destination.

Ever since my dad had grown up hanging around the docks and old ships of Mystic, Connecticut, looking up to the sailors around him rather than his own absent, alcoholic father, he had known that was his calling: the endless, unquestioning sea. Shortly after my mother perished in a flash flood in California, my dad sold his insurance business, commissioned a sailboat to be built in Taiwan, and we all flew to Hong Kong and set sail.

But who takes off onto a million miles of water, without first contemplating their own death in vivid Technicolor? I guess my father had to find his own soul floating out their somewhere. Between two crests of transparent breaking waves, he would catch the glimpse that was his own life, in its entirety from start to finish. He would then see it for what it was, clearly and evenly and without judgment. Then it would submerge itself again, blending and sinking into the immeasurable oceans of the planet. All the planning, the labor, the willing, the phenomenal backbreaking hassle to get out onto that sea, it would all come to a conclusion right then and there.

And he would be alone out there, just him and the waters that are God. And I hope—I assume—he would at last be at peace. I'm guessing that this is what it was all about in the end.

I could tell you about the several countries we spent time in, how they were all different, the myriad humid, teeming islands a thousand miles from everything with exotic names like Espiritu Santo, Mindoro, Manus, Babelthaup, New Britain. But that would take away from the real star of the picture—the great, mysterious Pacific Ocean herself. My father's true mistress.

When you have been traveling out at sea for a long time in a small vessel, it feels exactly like you are on a spaceship journeying between two distant stars. No safety net, no explanation. And no uplink to Houston. You are com-

pletely raw and open to the planet, and your life is a mere
particle flooded by the sea itself. There seemed to be no
reference to direction, and no end to anything. You could
almost tangibly feel the curvature of the earth unfold
in front of you and drop off into empty space. Humans
aren't really supposed to see such things literally—only
in dreams. I had read the book *The Voyage of the Dawn
Treader* by C.S. Lewis as a child, where a magical boat
journeys to the end of the sea to find where the world
ends. Oftentimes, I thought I was on the same boat.

The perspective of the open ocean from surface level
can freak out even the oldest and saltiest of old salts. The
horizon rises up at the seams above you, creating what
yachties called "the giant fish bowl." You are at the bottom of it, nearly submerged. The rim could have been
several hundred meters away, or several hundred miles,
it was always hard to tell. Sometimes, in the changing
light, it appeared quite reachable and benevolent. Other
times, I sensed it went to eternity, and the horizon just
sat there, eyeing me from a zillion miles away, not paying attention to our plight or our voyage or our lives.
Dad told us the horizon was roughly twenty-five nautical miles on all sides of us, but even with this numerical
constraint, it still shifted before my eyes—expanding
and retracting as it pleased, without regard.

I would sit at the stern and gaze at the watery trail that
Bungo Rye left in its languid wake behind her, expecting
to see some sort of breadcrumb trail left by Hansel and
Gretel. But like those ill-fated travelers, our own path
behind us slowly faded and joined the rippled surface of
the rest of the water, as if continually erasing the fact we
had ever been there in the first place. There could be no
turning back. The earth literally illustrated the fact to

me as plainly as it could, right before my eyes. The path was always forward, perpetually ahead, and the rise and fall of the bow of the boat was never ending, plowing ahead methodically, everlastingly, like the pendulum of a cuckoo that refused to ever give up.

I could see my father's strange attraction to traveling across the space of it, this unquenchable sea. But to me, it felt like a dangerous love affair.

Dad spent a lot of time teaching us the basics we'd need to know if he fell overboard or died at sea. He was strict and serious about it. We had to know how to navigate, how to sail the boat without an engine, how to survive for months out on the ocean if need be. We practiced lifeboat drills and man-overboard drills, and my step-mom Sherri made sure we were always tethered to the boat by harnesses and lifelines. We kids knew how to chart a rough course with the satellite navigator, and drew points on a chart and joined them with lines to track our progress, like a colossal game of dot-to-dot across the Pacific Ocean. We knew how to take up and down all the sails, and to furl if the winds became strong. We knew what a squall looked like, and how to recognize it barreling toward us and how to sail through it. We knew that channel sixteen on the ham radio was for S.O.S. There was no fooling around. This was reality in its elemental form.

Strange things happen at sea. Dad would tell us the strangest things happen early in the morning, or near the equator. This was near where we hit the doldrums, which Dad had told us stories about—where ships in olden times would languish for months, drifting around the wandering currents, where modern yachties' motors would fail, and all that would be found of them was an empty boat with no sign of life. Or stories where the husband falls overboard one night, and the wife doesn't know how to sail, so she floats around until someone finds her, and she's half-crazy, a vegetable. And we knew that most of these nautical urban myths were actually true.

Once when we were sailing from Micronesia down to Papua New Guinea, we hit the latitudes of the doldrums near the equator. These were the fated regions Dad had warned us about, where the great sailing ships of yore would aimlessly drift for months without a flutter of the sail, and the crew would slowly starve to death or go insane. We suddenly went from an ocean to a rippleless ice skating rink. The water was so shiny, you couldn't tell where the horizon ended and where the sky began. It was like living in a seamless, glass world. A languid swell did try to rock the boat, but it didn't seem to have enough energy to care. The only breeze present was from the forward motion of the boat, propelled by the motor—which luckily didn't break down.

We slowly came upon forms in the water, and as we approached, we could suddenly see miles and miles of what looked like toothpicks in the water. A whole forest of huge logs had somehow washed out to sea and ended up in purgatory here. Dad knew exactly what to do and carefully turned port and starboard and port again, weaving our way through the maze of floating hazards. Thank God we hadn't come upon them at night, or we may have very well hit one and busted the hull of the boat or tore the propeller off. And then what?

But somehow, through all the miles of the ocean and obstacles therein, this is what my father did: He kept us alive.

Sure, we may have felt like accessories to his oceanic dream, like mere crewmembers, indentured servants who were paid in food and board and at times treated with disdain. Like we had been punished for some vague crime by being ripped away from the life we knew, our friends, our family, and set to roam the sea *ad infinitum*. Our selfish teenage thoughts, our closed interior world being forced to join to an exterior vastness, our need to survive it at all costs.

It wasn't until years later that I understood this living vision of my father's, this alien, phantasmal world of liquid space he set out to somehow exist upon, was extraordinary. Not so much that he had actually conquered it, but that this form of ocean was present in the world in the first place. The unending water was a myth that was more real than reality. And I saw that the boy I was was a mythical being as well, traveling on a vessel with sails, floating across the face of the planet, touching the empty sky with an outstretched hand.

Whether my father knew it or not, he had given me the great ocean, and he had given me life in its purest form as well.

≈ ≈ ≈

Matthew Link is a writer, editor, and filmmaker living in Manhattan. The former editor-in-chief of The Out Traveler *magazine, he also worked personally with guidebook pioneer Arthur Frommer at* Budget Travel *magazine. He publishes* The Rainbow Handbook Hawai'i, *has written for numerous magazines, and has appeared on many television and radio shows. His documentaries have aired on PBS stations and at international film festivals. He has traveled to over sixty countries and Antarctica, but Africa is his all-time favorite destination, and, he hopes, his future home.*

PETER WORTSMAN

<del>☙ ☙ ☙</del>

Holy Land Blues

A wayward pilgrim finds the seamy and sublime in the
Promised Land.

THROUGHOUT THE THREE-HOUR-AND-FIFTEEN-
minute-long flight from Vienna to Tel Aviv,
following in Theodor Herzl's tracks, I nursed the illusion of rebirth. It was 1975 and the romance of Zion
hadn't yet hardened into a grim reality of tit for tat.
Longing to escape from what, in my mythic take of the
moment, seemed like the great rubble heap of Europe
to the fragrant orange grove in the desert, I felt giddy
with expectation. This sentiment was further reinforced
by the comportment of some of my fellow passengers. A
curtain separated the plane's rear cabin from the rest, like
the women's section in an Orthodox synagogue. I heard
muffled whispers and sighs and was dying for a peek,
when, at cruising altitude, the curtain was pulled back

and the stowaways, Russian emigrants hidden for security reasons, let out delirious exclamations of rapture and relief. Processed in the human clearinghouse Vienna had become in the twilight of the Cold War era, the Russians were on the last leg of their exodus.

I was on an exodus of my own. I'd spent the fall and winter in Vienna researching my parents' severed European roots and the unhappy history that had sent them packing, all of which I hoped to sandwich between the covers of a book. The German woman I was seeing, a former child prodigy, took her cello to bed, which made for an oddly wooden *ménage à trois* in which I'm afraid the bulky instrument got the best of it. To make matters worse, the Viennese police paid me an unannounced visit one morning at 3 A.M. to investigate my activities, whereupon the neighbors stopped talking to me. The cellist took up with a conductor. And never being able to get my coal oven to work quite right, I slept alone with earmuffs and a ski cap and pecked at my work-in-progress on an Olivetti portable with fur-lined leather gloves. So much for the chilly charms of Herzl's Vienna.

We experienced some turbulence en route to Tel Aviv, but nothing compared to the hubbub that erupted when, to the rousing background notes of the Israeli national anthem, the captain announced that we were flying over Eretz Yisrael. The entire plane, the Russians and myself included, spilled to the right for a heart-thumping, tear-filled first glimpse of the Promised Land, whereupon the aircraft tipped and the captain clamored for us to return to our seats lest our lopsided enthusiasm send the plane into a tailspin. The ensuing panic detracted somewhat from the stirring effect. And though the landing was smooth enough, I nevertheless felt shaken off-balance, fighting off nausea, and foreboding.

Tel Aviv. My hotel was hardly a Hilton but the room was airy and the price was right. A mild sea breeze came as a welcome relief from the lonely chill of a Viennese winter, Israel already being well into a balmy Middle Eastern spring. On my very first night I was awakened in the dark by a distant rumble, and fearing a terrorist attack—an occasional disruption of daily life at the time—I leapt out of bed and, naked but for the bed sheet wrapped around me, Biblical style, bounded into the hallway. My neighbor's door was ajar and the light was on.

"Was that a bomb?" I cried out with dark misgivings.

"*Vot* bomb?" came the ironic, Central European accented reply. "*Sat vas chust* an Arab alarm clock!"

Stepping closer and peering in through the door, it took me a while to locate the speaker amidst the smoke and clutter. On the floor sat a man of indeterminate age with a sharp face and gray chin beard, a cigarette balanced precariously on his lower lip, surrounded by open trunks and suitcases, fingering their contents. "I'd ask you in for a cup of tea," he shrugged with what might best be described as a sneer spiked with a smile, "but I'm afraid there's no room and no tea."

"Loud noises make me jumpy," I said, "I just got here."

"*Velcome* to the Promised Land," he chuckled. "I've been in transit all my life, never bother to unpack. Let the bastards bury my remains in a steamer trunk," he shook his fist at the window, "it's cheaper than a casket."

Hakarmel Market, Tel Aviv. Like an abacus, the bobbing Adam's apple protruding from the long skinny

neck of the *shoichet*—the ritual slaughterer—kept count
of the kill. Deadpan, he grabbed pullet after pullet by
the throat with his left hand, muttered a prayer, and
passed a sharp knife quickly across with a rapid thrust of
his right, efficiently dishing out death without a wasted
gesture, though one of the headless carcasses squirmed
on the ground before falling still.

The fruit vendor in the next stall, his face as rough
and ruddy as the citrus he sold, sliced and crushed giant
Jaffa oranges in a hand-operated press. It was Friday
morning and business was brisk in preparation for the
Sabbath. A spilt trickle of orange juice blended in the
mud with a steady stream of chicken blood. A stray dog
sniffed at this sea of an unsettling shade of red. The fruit
vendor kicked the dog. The dog whimpered.

Later that day, Sabbath eve though it was, no milk
and honey awaited me. Having neglected to make
arrangements in advance for Friday night dinner, I
risked going hungry. Rabbinic law, the law of the land
in Israel, prohibits any form of transaction involving
remuneration construed as work on the Day of Rest
(which, according to Jewish custom, starts the night
before). A couple of restaurants remained open all the
same for tourists and agnostics, but cash was not accepted. The waiter at one such establishment, whose
English was even more rudimentary than my Hebrew,
pointed from my Timex to a calendar. It took me a
while to catch on to the customary accommodation to
the law: I could leave my watch in hock and pay up
at sundown, Saturday, when the country reopened for
business.

"Can I see the menu, please?"

"Chicken," muttered the man.

My stomach squirmed, a visceral replay of the dancing headless carcass—"Got any gefilte fish?"

"Chicken," he reiterated.

"Chicken," I nodded, my hunger more pressing than
my disgust.

Patiently I waited, but no food was forthcoming. The
waiter just sat there, fingering my watch, looking up
every now and then to cast me a quizzical look. Then
it dawned on me that I was supposed to fetch my own
plate of cold chicken, potatoes, and peas that I only now
noticed languishing in a halo of flies on the kitchen
counter.

(Toward the end of his short life, dying of TB in
Berlin, Franz Kafka fantasized spiritual rebirth in
Palestine, where he dreamed of opening a little restaurant with his lover, Dora Dymant. She would cook
and he would serve, dreamed he—a Sabbath waiter, no
doubt, with ample time for reflection.)

Jerusalem. Who can resist the magnetic lure of the
Wailing Wall? Every lane and alleyway in the noisy lab-
yrinth of the Old City inevitably leads to this sacred cul-
de-sac where, on adjoining plots, Solomon erected his
temple and Mohammed hiked up to heaven. Muslims
flock to the Dome of the Rock, the golden-roofed
mosque built above, to mark the spot where the Prophet
ascended to heaven to meet his maker. Jews cling to the
cramped plateau below, where the lone western wall left
of their ruined sanctuary hugs the absence to the east, a
wall surrounding nothing. Every Jew reconstructs his
own temple from scratch.

The merciful shade of its ancient bricks proved a
soothing balm. Religiously unobservant though I be, my

head felt light and my legs went wobbly leaning against the symbolic parapet of my people's dispersion. *Home at last*, I thought. Greatly stirred, despite myself, I shut my tear-filled eyes and tried to meld with the mortar of Zion, but I was disturbed by a tap on the shoulder.

A bearded old man in black hat and long black coat held out a *talis* (prayer shawl) and a set of *tephillim* (leather phylacteries), urging me to put them on and pray.

"No, thank you," I gently shook my head, "I'd rather mark the moment in my own way." Shutting my eyes again, haunted by the eerie, high-pitched, tongue-trilled religious rapture of Sephardic women in their roped-off cordon of worshipers, I strained to reestablish contact with this sacred rubble heap lovingly preserved in memory for millennia by my scattered ancestors here on the world's Lower East Side. Can a locale crystallized into a concept and dragged clear across creation reacquire a physical reality? Surely we've shed enough tears to irrigate the desert, I pondered, and sank to my knees, prepared for an epiphany.

But before I could resist, the old man had already flung a prayer shawl over my shoulders and begun to bind the leather thongs like manacles around my forehead and knuckles. He rocked and chanted, motioning for me to follow suit. Rising reluctantly, I moved and moaned in the requisite ritual manner, the spell of sanctity broken.

Holiness eluded me at Solomon's doorstep, but I found a glimmer of it in the squint of a sunburnt old kibbutznik in an orange grove in the Galilee, where I volunteered to help out with the harvest. "*Mah-ze?* What's this?" he asked by way of a riddle, plucking a grapefruit from an overhanging branch and crushing it in his pow-

erful right fist. Perched on a ladder propped up against a
tree he himself had planted in his youth, it might as well
have been Jacob's ladder and he a patriarch. Smile lines
crisscrossed his wizened face. A narrow-brimmed blue
cap pulled down low over his bushy brow blocked out
the sun. "That's no juice, my friend," he grinned with
fierce pride, "that's my sweat!"

Perhaps it was my figurative predisposition primed
by all those years of Hebrew School. Something Biblical
must have seeped in after all, though the moral was
jumbled a bit. Everywhere I turned, parables and riddles
hung ripe for the plucking. So, for instance, by some odd
climactic fluke, the sunset split down the middle over
the muddy waters of the Red Sea, at the Gulf of Aqaba
where Israel and Jordan abut, blushing pink on one side
of the border and glowing golden on the other (I can't
remember which was which).

Eilat. We literally bumped into each other on a crowded
bus. She was standing directly in front of me by an open
window, a poster girl for Israel in a short, tight-fitting
khaki-colored skirt, whipping me in the face with her
fluttering black mop of hair.

"Sorry," she smiled, making no attempt to tame and
bind the savage mane.

"My pleasure," I smiled back, inhaling her scent.

The bus was headed for Nueba, a beachfront oasis
of palm trees on the coastal strip of the Sinai in the territory Israel had captured from Egypt in the Six-Day
War (and has since returned). At the time, Israeli youth
flocked there to let it all hang out. Ophrah was going to
meet her platoon-mate, Ziporah, and graciously invited
me to join them.

An Iraqi Jew, Ophrah had dark coffee-colored skin and glistening onyx-colored hair, just as I imagine the Queen of Sheba. Her friend Ziporah, of Yemenite extraction, was no less alluring in an afro that framed her deep brown face like the shade of a palm tree. Heads turned on the beach when the two shed their army uniforms, stripping down to scant bikinis. Is there any sight as sexy as a sun-baked Sabra straining the minuscule triangles of a bikini!

Meanwhile, lining the beach, the males of the species flexed their biceps and whistled catcalls, disconcerted at the effrontery of a foreigner consorting with not one, but two of their nubile fillies. Smiles flashed, winks fluttered, followed by a non-stop volley of lip-smacking come-ons, sassy put-downs, and swift repartees. Largely illiterate in Hebrew and hardly Mr. Universe material, I followed with awe and wonder.

Can this be the same people that languished, pale and anemic, in the dark ghettos of Eastern Europe and *mellahs* of the Middle East? What happened to the sallow-skinned, stooped *Yeshivah bochers*, the haggard yellow men who wiled away lifetimes in ill-lit prayer *Stibln*, pining for the metaphysical Sabbath bride to take their hand and lead them to a spiritual union in an imagined Jerusalem? What happened to the timid maidens and bewigged matrons cloistered behind shutters in Bialystok and velvet curtains in Fez?

Reborn like brash phoenixes out of the ashes of Auschwitz, having shed all Freudian inhibitions and the baggage of guilt, Herzl's pale brainchildren joined with their tanned Oriental cousins to once and for all times unleash the long sublimated Jewish libido. Once let out there was no zipping it back up. A little farther up the beach, naturists shed all and dallied in the dunes. Nueba was Eden minus the "don'ts." No skulking deity to chaperone the party. How I longed to go native and join the fun! I'd have gladly given all the book learning I'd amassed for a freewheeling spirit and a competitive physique.

Still, I could not help but notice the effect this unabashed spectacle had on the black-cloaked Bedouin who stood by, bemused, like shadows separated from their own bodies and the land that belonged to them and to which they belonged, eking out a subsistence living peddling trinkets and cold drinks to the interlopers, where they had once roamed freely.

Were we Jews not wandering desert nomads once, and are we not Bedouin in business suits still, dream-driven children of the wind? I thought of all the itinerant peddlers in my restless lineage, and of myself who feels most alive in transit. Was Herzl, the peripatetic prophet of Zionism, not the most compulsive nomad of them all!?

Having imprudently neglected to cover my head until it was too late, I contracted a pounding headache. A Bedouin woman draped in black from whom I bought a cap whispered something in Arabic to Ophrah and Ziporah that made all three of them giggle.

"What did she tell you?" I asked Ophrah.

A proud smile lit up the lovely Sabra's mahogany features. "She said, 'Black is beautiful!'"

The darkness and the absence of posted street names in Ophrah's Eilat neighborhood and my deficient Hebrew made it difficult to pinpoint the address she'd scribbled on the inside flap of a book of matches soaked in sea water. Needless to say, I arrived late. The coffee was cold. So was Ophrah's welcome. The photograph of a soldier boyfriend, whose existence she had failed to mention, hung on the wall beside an army-issue Uzi.

"So tell me, Ophrah," I asked, feeling flustered, frustrated, ill at ease, far more *meta* than physical, "what does it mean to you to be Jewish?"

"There's my yardstick," she gestured with a proud grin at the firearm on the wall. "This is my land," she stamped her shapely sandaled foot, raising a cloud of red clay-colored dust. "That's the border," she pointed a finger out the window toward Aqaba, whose lights flickered in the distance, the condensation of a golden sunset. "Anybody crosses under my watch, I measure their grave in the cross-hairs."

Back in Tel Aviv I fell ill, addled by the same ball of fire that the Egyptian Pharaoh Akhnaton recognized as the supreme deity, that swirling bundle of gases that kindled a loquacious shrub, etched the headlines into rock, and led a stuttering tour guide with a lousy sense of direction and his complaining entourage on an extended budget sightseeing tour of the Sinai—hotels and meals not included. I fathomed too late why Muslims and Jews cover their heads.

Feverish and semi-delirious with sunstroke, not wanting to return to my seedy Tel Aviv dive, I accepted the gracious invitation of paternal cousins thrice removed to convalesce at their apartment in a posh suburb. As I languished on a couch in the living room, Liuba, a still handsome woman in her late fifties, paused on my prompting from her housework to reflect on the fragments of a shattered old world left behind. She told me of the day she came home to her Warsaw apartment house, forewarned in the lobby by a well-intentioned neighbor not to mount the steps to the apartment, where her father had swallowed the cyanide capsule he kept close at hand in anticipation of his imminent arrest. Of going into hiding with forged Aryan identification papers. Of working as a nurse in a German military hospital and looking out one day to see the Ghetto in flames and burning women and children leaping out of windows. Of squelching her tears, lest she reveal too much, while the Poles pointed and laughed. She told me of the handsome young SS surgeon who one day out of the blue declared his love, proposing marriage, where-upon she fled in the night, never to return.

To the remembered ruins of Solomon's fallen temple Liuba added the rubble of her own incinerated youth. I never asked, though I was sorely tempted, if, given the hostility of neighbors on all sides, Israel did not some-times feel like a gilded ghetto. Soothed by her chicken soup, vaccinated by her sadness, I soon recouped my strength and recommenced my exodus.

In Jaffa, I sat in an Arab café, sipping Turkish coffee, smoking an occasional cigarette for conversation's sake, while gnawing at green olives big as fists.

In the northern hill town of Safed, from whence, the true believers say, the Messiah will one day emerge, I too was dazzled by the ethereal blue light that sparked the wild reverie of the Kabbalists, though this time I made sure to wear a hat.

On a hilltop in Haifa, I sat cross-legged on a low stone parapet, peering down through the lush ver-dure of a public park, flirting with the blue eyes of the Mediterranean, reflecting on my hybrid Semitic and Teutonic roots transplanted in Anglo-Saxon soil stolen from the Manhattan Indians. But something distracted my eye. It took me a while to fathom that the fuzzy pink patch in the clearing was no cluster of desert fruit but a latter-day Adam and Eve actively engaged in the pursuit of knowledge. The leaves both framed and camouflaged this Holy Land peepshow upon which I gazed with a thoroughly unholy thrill. I was roused from my voyeuristic thrall by a high-pitched cough from the throat of a white-bearded gnome, round and red as a medicine ball, who walked up and declared: "From the cross of the young gentleman's legs, if I may make so bold, I can tell he is looking for love. The knees cry out your need. Permit me to introduce myself." Whereupon this Jewish Santa Claus plucked out a wrinkled, tea-stained business card, one side of which was inscribed in Hebrew, the other in English, *S.J. Friedlich, Matrimonial*. "I've got a long list of available brides, all of good family," he pandered, practically salivating, so eager was he to drum up business.

"I'll think about it, thanks," I said, taken aback, indeed stunned—had he not caught me with my pants down, so to speak, and bared the loneliness of my loins? About to pocket the card, I might well have called him the next day or the day thereafter had he not plucked the card back out of my grasp.

"If not now, when?!" he shrugged, replaced the card (no doubt the sole facsimile) in his vest pocket, and slunk away in a muttering huff, probably scaring off Adam and Eve, for when I looked back the clearing was clear.

The fresh water springs falling from the cliffs of the Judean Desert over the oasis of Ein Gedi on the western shore of the Dead Sea might just as well have been a mirage. This is the lowest populated place on earth and surely one of the hottest. A dip in the Dead Sea hardly helps. The bather emerges unrefreshed, body coated with oil slick and salt brine like a fugitive sardine. Parched and unforgiving though the surrounding desert is, humanity has been seeking out this fertile nook to refresh the spirit at least as far back as the fourth millennium B.C., as an unearthed sacrificial altar of a Chalcolithic temple attests. In caves nearby, John the Baptist's ascetic brethren, the locust-eating Essenes, fled civilization such as it was to submit to the elements and scratch their impressions on papyrus scrolls. Jesus could have strolled the oil slick of the Dead Sea without a spill, had he not perfected his act on the Sea of Galilee.

The youth hostel at Ein Gedi lacked most creature comforts. A lone ceiling fan in the lobby scattered flies and spread the heat thick as honey. Come nightfall, sleepless guests and staff spilled outdoors to mingle, soaking up a dark illusion of coolness.

It was here that I witnessed and participated in a sacrificial rite. Among the female lodgers was a German blonde who worked in the kitchen. She was big-boned and a bit ungainly, though not unattractive, and was surrounded every night by a swarm of admirers, other employees of the hostel. Taunts and teases with insinuating undertones were carelessly hurled and unskillfully rebuffed.

What began as seemingly playful flirting intensified little by little into something more serious. Like a storm cloud, the circle of lust shifted about from the brightly lit hostel entrance to an unlit corner of the patio, where paws grabbed and were slapped back. But just as things threatened to get out of control, the seemingly passive object of everyone's desire turned the tables on her aggressors, making clear with the flick of an imperious index finger that she—not they—was pulling the strings. With growls and groans of protest and a flutter of arms, those not chosen scattered like whimpering dogs in search of another bone.

"Why don't you try your luck?" Yossi, a dishwasher who slept in the bunk above mine, egged me on one night, as the circle dilated and contracted and I found myself sucked from its periphery ever closer to the center of attraction. "She's not my type," I shrugged, unaware that the German woman and I were standing back to back. Whereupon she whirled about. "*Komm, Liebchen!*" she commanded and I followed. Accompanied by a chorus of catcalls, we strode out into the Biblical Wilderness of Ein Gedi, where David hid out from the wrath of Saul and John the Baptist cleansed his soul through self-denial, in the pursuit of knowledge.

Though I only stayed a month or so, my visit to Israel actually wrapped itself up a year later at a belly dancing club on the south side of Chicago. The show had already started as I tiptoed past the tables and elbowed my way through the crowd. The sagging ceiling, the dense cloud of cigarette smoke, the press of bodies around me, and the remoteness of the exit door all served to multiply the claustrophobic feel of the place. As the dancer's hand cymbals clashed and the mustachioed oud player plucked and strummed his instrument, I tried to keep my cool.

Like every other member of the mostly male audience, my eyes were riveted to the ripple and roll of the dancer's rhythmic gyrations. The belly dance tames the libido, elevating teasing lust to an art form, just a twitch short of ejaculation.

At the end of the first dance, I followed the lead of the man to my immediate right, stuffing dollar bills into the elastic band of the dancer's skirt as she brushed by. Not stuffed in firmly enough, my tribute fluttered and fell.

"First time?" my dollar-dipping mentor inquired. "My brother's a bit shaky, too, eh Sayeed," he grinned, motioning with the tip of his cigarette at the unsmiling man to my left, the latter as lean as the former was fat.

Sayeed said nothing, he just stared.

"Sayeed doesn't talk much," his brother explained, "ever since he stepped out of an Israeli jail."

I didn't ask what he'd done.

"Where are you from, my friend?" asked the garrulous one.

"New York," I coughed, the cigarette smoke aggravating my asthma and malaise.

"Jewish?" He practically spat out the question, the ash of his cigarette tumbling in an avalanche.

I nodded.

"Better leave now!" he advised, as silent Sayeed clenched his teeth.

I backed off slowly, grateful that the laws of guest-friendship precluded a knife in the back.

In Israel, meanwhile, the flaming sword of the cherubim stationed east of Eden has been replaced by tanks and suicide bombers wrestling for the deed to the tree of life. A new wall is going up to buttress the weeping stones of the old one, on both sides of which the earth opens her mouth daily to receive Abel's blood. Rebirth is on hold for the foreseeable future.

≈≈≈ ≈≈≈ ≈≈≈

New York-born nomad Peter Wortsman has peddled his itinerant impressions to The Boston Globe, Los Angeles Times, The Washington Post, *and* World Hum, *among other newspapers and web sites. He is the author of* A Modern Way to Die, *a book of short fiction, and two plays,* The Tattooed Man Tells All *and* Burning Words. *He also does translations from German to English, and his rendering of the travel classic,* Travel Pictures, *by Heinrich Heine, will be published in 2008 by Archipelago Books.*

❧ ❧ ❧

I Read Walden Once

You are never far from home as long as you are alive.

MARCO CORNERED ME AT THE BAR WHEN WE GOT off the water. "Sugi, you're tired of the tourists. You want to go to the jungle," he said as he handed me a shot of Pisco. "The Tambopata is running."

Marco was an Italian kayaker following the river seasons around the world. We were guiding river trips out of Cusco, but Peru's water was running out, so he was headed north. He spoke very little English, but his Spanish was impeccable. He was solid on the water and he was the only man down there who treated me with respect. I was done with the Cusco scene and in a moment of insanity, told him I would go.

We were drinking with one of two guides who had been to this particular river. It's too far, too unpredictable, too hot, too wet; the place will ravage you. But Leo had been (though he said he would never go back) and he drew us a map of the 300-ish kilometer section on a napkin. With that napkin in a ziploc bag, Marco and I headed to Putina Puncu at 3 P.M. the next day. Onion bags disguised our two crafts (a cataraft and a kayak), everything we owned, and food for roughly two weeks.

The thick, lush forest rose at a low angle into gray clouds. I sat in my cataraft, half rigged, waiting for Marco, wondering what I was doing there. The Tambopata River rocked my boat. I was surrounded by locals...staring. First there were hordes of children, then just men. The bank was littered with garbage. I had sat there nearly four hours watching one person after another come down to defecate in the river. Women did their laundry, bathed their children, and dumped their trash. Flies buzzed through the coke bottles and condensed milk cans.

A man with an official look to him had shown up and told us we needed a permit. Who needs a permit for a river that no one runs? He told us that we could go one hour upstream to a town where we could pay and they would turn a blind eye. Maybe. So Marco left on the back of a motorcycle with this "ranger." He would meet me on river-left past the last footbridge a few miles down. It was supposed to be one hour of class I-II riffles to this footbridge. So I strapped on the kayak and went alone.

Gladly, I pushed off the shore and headed around the bend out of town. Condors circled and landed on the rocks in the river before me. Plain brown birds opened their wings and exposed a huge pair of red-and-orange eyes. River otters played in front of my boat. The air was thick, sweet, and loud with life.

With my head thrown back, I was marveling at the green roof above me, when suddenly this jungle tunnel reverberated with the boom of water. The river dropped away and I couldn't stop. I slammed into a rock and wrapped my boat. I had a rope, but no one to throw it to. In and out of the boat, pushing and pulling against raging water, I could free it only to wrap it on the next exposed rock. My short breaths through tears and panic were desperate, paralyzing.

Four hours later I got to the supposed place where Marco would meet me. It was dark. He was not there. I couldn't get my stove to work. I pulled the boat out of the water and tied it with two ropes to a tree whose trunk was a good fifteen feet in diameter and whose top I could not see. I put up my tent, crawled in wet and collapsed. The jungle screamed at me as the last bit of light left me in the dark. Marco was not there and I didn't know what to do. Stay put till morning? What if he didn't come?

Eventually I fell asleep with my light on, but bolted awake when Marco and the ranger arrived at 2 A.M. I didn't get out of my tent. All Marco said was that he got the permits. I thought he might come talk to me, but he just put up his tent and went to bed.

The next morning the river sounded soothing. I guess I had forgiven it since it was the only thing familiar in this screaming, wet place that stank of decomposition. It turned out that while I had been flailing on the water, Marco and the ranger crashed the motorcycle into the river. After I recounted my travails with the stove, Marco made the long trek back to the village for a new one.

Trapped in the white bubble of my tent, I felt the sweat drip down my eyelids and onto Henry David Thoreau's

Walden. A visceral longing for my desert home developed there in the dank, skyless snarl. I wanted the sky
that my dad works like a red ant against, where he can
watch a storm build for hours and flood east over the
mountains before it swings north and sweeps over his
fresh cut hay. With no way back, I clung to Thoreau's
words, fooling myself that I had a choice. I *chose* to go
on, despite the unknown, to "drive life into a corner and
reduce it to its lowest terms." It started to drizzle and I
ate one bite of bland bread at a time.

I had no reason to be certain that I would get out of the
jungle. Ever. I adhered to the familiar and clung to the
little things like stuffing my sleeping bag or breaking
down my tent, but especially rigging my boat. I found
the most familiar thing in the jungle was myself. I ques-
tioned why I was sitting alone in a tropical rainforest
scared out of my gourd, driven downstream. I noted
in my journal at 11:25 P.M. that, "I have abandoned the
minute and taken flight. I left the simple pastoral life
of a family ranch on the Oregon high desert, because I
sought the world. Surrounded now by the stuff of lore,
I am flabbergasted at my inclination to go backward,
against the trend of mankind." I was discovering my
wings and roots were both mighty from a lifetime of
battle. I felt splayed as I watched the mosquitoes bounce
against the tent wall. I hadn't considered the battle before, because I didn't realize I was rooted. I had only
ever been concerned with my wings. Suddenly I realized
I was flying in Peru with my roots raw and dangling.
As Thoreau considered every place a possible site for a
house, I knew exactly where my house needed to be, on
the southern rise of the north forty acres, the same dis-

tance from my parents' house as my parents' house was from my grandparents' house.

I lay there under the weight of the water downstream and contemplated Thoreau wedging his feet down through the mud till he came to hard bottom and rocks in place. He called that reality. The jungle's clay soil seemed bottomless. There was no room for me there amidst all that other life on top of life. The forest wailed and closed around my tent. Something was eating holes in the netting. If Thoreau had a great deal of company in his cabin on the pond, with squirrels and small birds, I didn't know what I had, nor if I should have been grateful like him or if I was right in my terror.

The river braided out around rocky islands where I found clean lines through easy rapids. I was grateful to have Marco downstream. He would look down different channels and tell me if they were clear and deep enough to run. Yet, just as the jungle started to become comfortable, the Rio Colorado, a swollen red tributary on the right, slammed into the left bank of our chattery mountain stream and turned it into a massive red serpent. The river was thick with the crimson clay that is the base of the rainforest. It swelled from maybe 1,000 to what felt like 30,000 cubic feet per second, which can be imagined as 30,000 basketballs all passing a single point every second. It became one mighty current, river wide. The helical flow ricocheting off the banks back to the center of the river obliterated the calm-water eddies that are a boater's refuge. My sixteen-foot raft could have fit twice on the amplified wave faces.

I swung out of control, to the outside of a right bend, when Marco saw the first break in what had become impervious jungle walls. He signaled for me to eddy out too late and I missed the asylum. I slammed into the trees below, grabbing madly at their branches. Spiders bigger than my face darted through the limbs. Two of them fell onto my legs and were washed off by the water that surged over the upstream tube of the cata. I did not let go. It took an hour to pull the raft back up through the current and trees and spiders.

The Tambopata flooded in the sun. It started to deluge at dark. Then it rained harder. I could feel the runoff from the forest gush under my tent. I dug a trench around the tents, which were cleaved into two-foot deep ditches by morning. It sounded like the ocean outside my tent, eating away at our beach. I peered out the plastic window of my tent door into the dark and listened to the waves swat at the beach, like big red claws. We were at the high water mark with nowhere to go.

Misty clouds hung low in the forest and put contrast in the layers of dense green. The white trunks of the trees were like pencil lines, marking the skeleton of the canopy. Condors circled down the river, and we saw gigantic parrots in the trees, as big as condors, with tails as long as their wing spans. The map on the napkin from the bar in Cusco, drawn over a week ago at this point, indicated landmarks of the canyon's beginning and end, but nothing about what was inside. I could hear the sediment in the thick water pull through the net in the floor of my cata and along the big blue tubes. It was a constant low hiss.

We blew downstream all day before we found another tiny pause in the chaos of the bank. Marco grabbed the machete and went to clearing a spot big enough for our two tents. When the heavy blade ricocheted off a piece of bamboo he dropped the knife, speechless as his blood welled slowly to the surface. I ripped off my shirt and put immediate pressure on the cut on the outside of his shin. He sat down and I elevated it over my knee.

We did not exactly have a first aid kit. I had some antibiotic ointment, a couple of finger band-aids, duct tape, and a needle that my mom had sent to me for mending my pants. We had nothing to clean the wound and the only water we had was silty river water that we boiled for drinking. Being a good river guide, I had packed a fifth of vodka.

We were over a week from the most primitive medical care, so we cleaned the cut with some vodka after Marco took a few big swigs and then I taped a dry cotton shirt around it and set him up with dinner in bed. The incident made my thoughts and movements meticulous. The idea of losing Marco was debilitating for me. I checked on him several times in the night. I would stand beside his tent and listen to him breathe. He never asked for anything.

At 6 A.M. we moved downstream to the last known camp above the canyon. Marco went first after we boiled his bandage and redressed his leg. The water was thick and hard to read. I could not see massive pour-overs amidst the snarl of waves until I was on top of them. We knew the camp because the napkin marked a beach on the left above two tributaries coming in directly opposite each other. I walked out onto the rocks and watched upstream and down till it got completely dark. With only a sliver of sky to judge from, I tried to predict the weather. The temperature had dropped a good thirty degrees. The rainforest was supposed to be hot and sticky. I wore my down jacket in the jungle.

For three days Marco and I ate pasta with salami, cheese, carrots, garlic, and onions. We drank coca tea with too much sugar to sleep. I boiled Marco's bandages, which had started to stink, and redressed his wound twice a day to fight infection. We talked about rivers. The big ones: the Zambezi, the Futa, the Slave…maybe in an effort to put the one we were on in its place. We reassured ourselves that we'd seen bigger water. The distinction that we left unsaid was that some rivers carry their water better than others. If large volume rivers are voluptuous, then the Tambopata was morbidly obese.

We stood our ground on the line between the river and usurping jungle. The place was far too complex to trust, and therefore, allowed only sporadic sleep. I confessed my severe homesickness to Marco one night through the walls of our tents. He told me to make my home wherever I go. It reminded me of an old Maasai man who said to me once, *"Melakua ang inchu"*—"You're never far from home as long as you're alive." Your home is in your heart and mind's eye. Home is a place, but it is also the strength you take on your peregrinations. It is roots grounded in place, it is wings governed by no place. I noted the stipulation that home is never far *as long as you're alive.*

At 5 a.m. on the third day the water had dropped negligibly. I could not sleep through the thunderous sound of the river shifting the massive boulders of its bed. Marco and I decided to go. The weather did not look like it would break any time soon. We had left Cusco two weeks before and our food was dwindling. Downstream was the only way out. It is rare to have to operate from the understanding that you have only one option.

I rigged to flip, pulling the cam straps extra tight. I tried to remember everything I had ever learned or been told that might be relevant, chiefly that, even if I flipped, *Never let go of the boat*. There was no indication that the river had ever run higher. On many rivers you can see driftwood and other deposits high in the trees. We *were* high in the trees. A log slammed into the side of my boat, its roots raw and wild, slapping my face.

The light was flat and the forest hung over the water. The rapids were continuous. Dogged current and walloping waves funneled into a mess of holes the size of buildings. The holes and falls swallowed half the river in places. With no choice I read and ran without hesitation. My life depended on my ability to turn fear into focus. My mind and body had to be quicker than the river.

There were no lines in the rapids. I got surfed a few times, sucked back into holes and spun before they spit me out. I bent my oar and heard the metal frame flex and crack. I had never felt surges like I did that day. River waves are usually consistent, but these waves behaved like a sea in storm.

Our precious napkin showed the landmark that would indicate the end of the gorge and the beginning of the flats. It would be a boulder the size of a two-story *American* house and a tributary would enter there on river left. As the river screamed around a left bend, I saw the first rock I had seen since above the Rio Colorado. It was sticking out about three feet. The tributary on river left was blowing its banks. I blasted up on the pillow of water piled on the upstream side of the boulder and slid off it to the right. The river eventually calmed down and flattened out like a fat snake in the sun. Marco started to

play in his kayak. We talked a little and started watching
for birds. The canyon was done.

Our camp that night was the flattest we had. I explored briefly into the woodland barricade, but found
it positively impenetrable. We tried to go in with the
machete, but could not get fifteen feet from the edge.
Plus, we were scared to use that thing, so we stayed on
the black-sand beach. For the first time I didn't feel like
root-balls and bugs were about to overtake me, leaving nothing but my sunglasses or *Walden* sitting there
opened to a page with a single underlined passage: "I
went to the woods because I wished to live deliberately,
to front only the essential facts of life, and see if I could
learn what it had to teach." There is an implication in
"living deliberately" and that is the notion of having
some semblance of control over life. All I wanted was to
survive what the jungle had to teach so that I could get
back to a place that I could comprehend. I didn't have an
answer for Marco when he asked me why on earth I had
been so hellbent to leave the sky-dominated lands of my
home, but I was ready to explore my own place, to live
and work seasons in an ecosystem I could understand.

At 5 A.M. I woke up to the full moon penetrating dense
fog. We had floated four days from the gorge. I listened
to the water, which roared from the slightest distur-
bance, and waited for light so that I could read. I had
made my way through much of *Walden* in my days waiting for the river that wouldn't drop. Thoreau said at one
point, "However intense my experience, I am conscious
of the presence and criticism of a part of me, which, as
it were, is not a part of me, but a spectator, sharing no
experience, but taking note of it." With eyes out of focus

on the cloudy water in front of my boat, my mind was absent from the experience at hand. I could not let go of my familiar home that, juxtaposed with the land slipping by at the speed of water, was both physically and ecologically simple. It was waiting for me at the end of Lower Bridge Road on my family's ranch. The roots I had been oblivious of had latched on like snakes around the home branch.

The fog burned off at breakfast and the jungle was a new place. We dried our tents and our wet clothes for the first time in eleven days. We pushed downstream onto the glassy water of the plains, down a river with so little gradient that in most places there was no perceptible current. A jaguar stood invisible against the texture of the river stones. A two-meter caiman slid off the bank while monkeys with tan faces played in the trees.

Marco jumped on the cata with his kayak at lunchtime. I straddled the back tube like a big blue banana and finished *Walden*. I dangled my feet in the water and let the current play with them where deep rocks disturbed the almost perfect layers of laminar flow. I wiggled my toes and watched the jungle slide by.

Somewhere in the fat part of South America, headed to the Atlantic, I tried to conceive of the incomprehensible nature of that place. It was just a matter of endurance at that point. It was the eleventh day of our journey. Marco and I still found things to talk about, although there was a lot of comfortable silence. His cut was healing and had only minor infection. Our minds had come to a standstill and the jungle seemed bigger and more beautifully complex than before. It did not seem so inhospitable because at least two-dozen different kinds of butterflies were landing on my boat. They were every shade of yellow, orange, red, neon green, and iridescent blue.

We erected our placeless home on a sandy rise beside a massive tree probably deposited by the floodwaters we had come on. It sounded like a war zone with frogs that went off like machine guns on rapid fire. The full moon rose orange off my left shoulder and I fell asleep despite the shooting.

I woke up at first light with the birds. There is nothing lyrical about anything that lives in the rainforest and if that place was awake, so was I. We waited for our tents to dry, because dew in the jungle was like a hard rain in the desert. When we left it was hot and still and I pushed for only two hours before we came to the Tambopata Research Center and a whole string of motorboats. Motors are prohibited on the majority of the Tambopata River. We thought we could hear the faint buzz of an engine over breakfast, but we had heard a lot of things in the forest.

As we pulled up, a cargo boat was getting ready to launch and they agreed to give us a ride to the confluence of the Rio Madre de Dios and the town there. We de-rigged in ten minutes. The cataraft tubes were deflating as the boat pulled away from the dock. The jungle went by like a film. What would have taken us six days pulling only took six hours in the dugout boat carved from a tree that must have been eight feet in diameter. Our captain wore only jean cut-offs and aviator sunglasses. He held a beautiful woman in his lap, her long black hair flowing past the left side of his face.

Marco left immediately on the four o'clock bus, a big beefy four-by-four that looked fit for the jungle. The tires stood above my head. The clearance under the bus must have been at least three feet. Twenty-four hours non-stop to Cusco and medical attention.

I lay under a cotton sheet on the third floor of a hostel and felt almost immune to the sultry heat. The street below seemed busy with sexy women and mopeds for a Tuesday night in the middle of the Amazon rainforest. I would have taken even a flooding river over the engines and horns outside my window.

When the plane took off from Puerto Maldonado we headed out over the Tambopata. It bent back on itself a hundred times, hardly guided by the flat plain of the Amazon. The Tambopata wriggled off to the south and the carpet of rainforest below was green and even like the sea. Its limits were indiscernible.

※ ※ ※

Before turning twenty-four, Sarahlee Lawrence ran over 10,000 miles of the planet's rivers before heading back to Oregon where she makes her home. She has published travel stories about her many adventures, including horseback safaris in East Africa and South America. In 2006, she received the Rising Star Award for nonfiction at the Nature of Words literary conference.

❧ ❧ ❧

The Skeleton Coast

The debris of centuries seems small here.

C AN YOU IMAGINE A MORE PITIABLE FATE? YOUR ship reels broken in the storm. Implacable winds and currents run you aground, but by a miracle, you do not drown. You overcome and drag yourself exhausted onto the sand—and then realize that drowning is not the worst way to go. You cheated death, only to find yourself cast upon one of the harshest places on Earth. You can choose to stay where you are and die of exposure or thirst. Or else you can trek hopelessly into the endless desert, to perish there instead.

All along the Skeleton Coast of Namibia, in southwestern Africa, you see the hulks of dead ships, ancient and modern. You cannot help but reflect on the fate of the shipwrecked sailors. In many cases, what remains of their vessels now stands far back from the sea, partly

covered in sand. Sometimes these relics are almost entirely buried; all you can see is a mast. Countless more,
you think, have vanished altogether. What must have
befallen their crews, in the days before radio and air-
borne rescue, requires little imagination. Sand, salt pan,
and arid mountain stretch inland for a hundred miles.
Away from the sea, there is little or no water—no sustenance, it seems, of any kind. When you see an animal—
which you do, now and then—you are astonished that it
can eke its existence from this nothingness. No human
unused to such a place ever could.

Conditions for visitors, it must be said, have improved
lately. (And I am not speaking of the hulk that, during
an early-twentieth-century spell of diamond prospect-
ing, became what was presumably the remotest brothel
in the world.) The Skeleton Coast is a bit more accessible
than it used to be, and it is beginning to be recognized as
a vacation spot, though other parts of the Namib Desert,
to the south, still get more visitors.

It was chiefly the southern Namib, in fact, that my
wife and I had traveled to see. Landscape photography
is an avocation of ours, and we had wanted to bear our
tripods in homage to the famous, fabulously photogenic
dunes of Sossusvlei. You are sure to have seen the pictures, perhaps without realizing where they were taken.
The sand there is a vivid ocher, and it rises vertiginously
1,000 feet and higher. Strong southwesterly winds sculpt
it into immense longitudinal dunes, with smooth, undu-
lating surfaces and edges like blades. Compositionally
speaking, the setting is perfect: Dry watercourses give
flat approaches, with trees positioned just so, to provide
scale. At sunrise or sunset the dunes cast shadows that
are deep and long, and the color blazes.

Sossusvlei did not disappoint—which, given our expectations, is saying a lot—but much to our surprise, it was not the highlight of the trip. After we saw the red dunes, we flew north, via Swakopmund, on the first leg of a four-day "flying safari" over the Skeleton Coast Park. The southern section of the park, roughly between the Ugab and Hoanib rivers, is open to the public, with a couple of access points by road; and fishermen from South Africa visit the coast south of the park. But the northern section, between the Hoanib and Kunene rivers (the Kunene forms part of Namibia's border with Angola), is accessible only by light aircraft, operated under concession. Our pilot-guides flew us and our companions over the length of the park in two six-seater planes. We hopped up the coast, driving each day by Land Rover from improvised landing strips to explore the dunes and mountains. We slept each night in a different campsite.

From the air, flying low, you are surrounded by breathtaking scenes. The beauty is unrelenting, and almost too much; you experience a kind of aesthetic overload. In the evenings, we were dazed. You don't see much wildlife, though you are low enough to get a good look at what is there: seals and flamingos along the coast, and further inland the occasional oryx (a large antelope that seems able to subsist on nothing). We spotted just two desert elephants from our dune-skimming Cessna. Apparently, these rare creatures like to surf the sands; I have seen them do so on video, but cannot vouch for it firsthand.

The sands of the Skeleton Coast desert are paler than those in the southern Namib. The dunes are not as high, and the sculpting of the wind is less regular. The

patterns are more chaotic and harder to photograph—
yet, to my mind, even more beautiful. The expanse is
awe-inspiring. We drove to high points in the dunes
and, despite the modest elevation, gazed out for what
must have been twenty miles. To the horizon in every
direction, there was nothing but pristine, curving planes
of sand—precise edges that might have been cut with a
scalpel, and surfaces minutely poised at the limit of what
the laws of mechanics allow, before they flow, fall, and
cascade.

There is a wonderfully poetic technical term for that
limit: the angle of repose. Wind blows sand up a dune
and drops it, at the crest, onto the leeward side, until the
angle of the leeward surface to the horizontal exceeds
the angle of repose; when that critical slope is reached,
the sand drops away on the leeward side, leaving a perfectly defined edge, until the angle of repose is restored.

When you disturb the sand on one of those edges, it
moves like a viscous liquid, pouring over the surface beneath. From an edge, say, a hundred feet up, this film of
excess sand may take minutes to move slowly but unstop-
pably all the way down. It is mesmerizing. All the while,
of course, the dunes themselves are traveling down the
wind, in endless pursuit of the angle of repose—six to
ten feet a year, it is reckoned, on average. Though it all
depends: There is so much more to sand than you might
think. The properties of a dune—including its angle of
repose—turn on many different factors: wind, depth of
material, size of the grains, shape of the grains, sorting
of the grains (one size or many), dryness or dampness of
the grains, and so forth.

When conditions are just right, something peculiar
can happen: Sand can sing. Perhaps you are thinking

I was in the dunes too long. (The grains! The grains!) No doubt some said the same of Marco Polo, after he wrote in *The Travels* about the singing sands of the Gobi Desert. Nothing but sand, he said, and yet he heard "the sounds of all kinds of musical instruments, and also of drums and the clash of arms." He put it down to desert spirits. The people who know the Skeleton Coast talk of roaring dunes, not singing sands, but I think they are referring to the same thing.

When the sand has exactly the right characteristics, and when the correctly constituted surface forms part of a bowl with the right acoustic properties, a small flow of disturbed sand can cause a sound that builds almost immediately to a noise like rolling thunder. The phenomenon has been recognized by physicists, but the precise causes are not entirely clear. Indeed, the leading researchers seem to have fallen out over it. An editor of *Physics World* reports that two of the foremost authorities on the matter, once friends, now "tend to avoid one another."

That must be awkward, because dunes roar in only a few places. Our guides in the Skeleton Coast knew of one. They told us to sit with our companions on the edge at the top of the dune in question, and then, on their signal, to begin scooting down, "moving as much sand as you can." The moment we did so—rolling our eyes and thinking, *Do we really have to do this?*—a deep mechanical thrumming started in the dune. The whole thing was vibrating. It felt like a small earthquake. At the same time a great noise began. I took it for a low-flying aircraft directly over my head. It was far too loud to hear each other speak. We all looked anxiously around the sky; I literally ducked. We had moved, so it seemed, just a few shovelfuls of sand. It was the strangest thing I have ever encountered. Take it from me, Marco Polo was right. Drums and the clash of arms.

꼭 꼭 꼭

Clive Crook is a senior editor of The Atlantic Monthly, *a columnist for* National Journal, *and chief Washington commentator and associate editor of the* Financial Times. *Before moving to the United States in 2005, he worked for more than twenty years at* The Economist, *and for ten of those as the magazine's deputy editor. He was previously an official in H.M. Treasury. He is English, born in Yorkshire and raised in Lancashire, and was educated at Bolton School, Magdalen College Oxford, and the London School of Economics. He has two grown-up children, and lives in Washington DC with his wife, traveling companion, in-house Africa specialist, and fellow landscape photographer, Loretta.*

꽃 꽃 꽃

The Winding Road to Joshua Tree

A native from elsewhere wanders home.

EIGHTEEN YEARS AGO, I SET UP CAMP IN THE GOLDEN West, joining the hundreds of migrant workers who made small fortunes by hauling what is now called content out of the television mines that, like Los Angeles itself, periodically cave in without warning. I was satisfied by neither work nor love, but the terrain began to comfort me in unexpected ways.

In Ohio, where I grew up, I never felt at home; I realized at an early age that I did not belong on the shores of a lake that was frozen most of the time, or in a city that always seemed to whisper discouraging nothings in my ear. I guess that's why I always preferred the New York Yankees to the Cleveland Indians (although I felt like a traitor for rooting for them before I moved to New York, the anti-desert, land of nonstop reaction), and why I used to send away for cactuses (I know you're supposed to say "cacti," but I don't like the sound of it) that I could get from places with names like Kaktus Jack's and Desert Botanicals and keep them on a window ledge near my bed. I don't know if my window ledge faced west or not (the gray skies often obscured the sun), but seeing the outlines of my little cactuses against the clouds fueled my fantasies of the never-neverland where the turnpike went, the land where the misunderstood found understanding, the land where Zorro and Bat Masterson and Wyatt Earp wouldn't let anyone hurt you, the land where a girl named Jane lives forever as a Calamity, the land where the only thing anyone or anything really wants is a drink of water.

Once in Los Angeles, I immediately had the sense that I had planted myself at the edge of a desert, and that I was indigenous and could flourish here. I liked the idea of sinking roots into this quicksilver garden, this false greenhouse watered by hijacked rivers and tended by gatekeepers anxious to keep the temple of fame from getting too crowded. Maybe it was the light; the light was different out here—things showed up better, looked more like themselves. Maybe it was the space. Maybe it was in the seamless stretch of sunny days; they were different too, a bright backdrop for a carnival of beautiful creatures who lived phototropic lives, predators who drifted in to drink at the oasis from regions where those who stay behind get old.

Or maybe it was that song in the background, coming from what I soon learned was Joshua Tree National Park, fading in and out, connecting me to some other world, the enchanting tinkle of chimes, from hidden patios up there behind the bougainvillea, rearranged by the Santa Ana winds that swept across the endless waves of sand outside the city, carrying good news.

The song first came and got me when I was on assignment for a local alternative newspaper, attending a workshop facilitated by "the shaman of Beverly Hills," a well-known woman who had written a series of books about women and inward spiritual journeys involving power animals and other primal symbols. The workshop was at a banquet room in the airport Hyatt, down the hall from a meeting of the International Chiefs of Police, who presumably were power animals. Several hundred women were in attendance. After various introductory remarks, the lights were dimmed, candles were lit, and Native American flute-and-drumming tapes began. We were told we were going on a shamanic journey. (As an anthro major whenever I had bothered to, one, declare a major and, two, appear in class, I was not alarmed by this statement and in fact took it with some excitement.) "Close your eyes, get quiet, and visualize yourself going down a hole into the earth," the workshop leader said. "Along the way, take in whatever crosses your path. I want you to follow this path, however it looks to you, to an altar. At that altar, I want you to find something you need from someone you know."

I had not yet been to Joshua Tree National Park, but at the airport Hyatt with my eyes closed, I knew I was deep inside it, traveling down a path marked by ocotillo and sage, crossed by a desert tortoise. As my trance deepened, the path took me to a large sandstone altar that stood under the shade of an ancient and giant Joshua tree. Atop the altar was a small vial of what I took to be water. The sun glinted off the vial, and then from behind the tree my maternal grandmother appeared.

In my family history, she was a woman known for the wonderful and cryptic line, "Life is funny. Oh dear, oh dear." She had died at least a decade before this shamanic encounter at the airport Hyatt, with a letter from me in her hands. It was while living in New Mexico—another desert—that I had found out about her passing. As she approached me in my trance, she handed me the vial from the altar. I took it and started to cry, knowing in my bones that what she had just given me was not a vial of water, but a vial of tears, my own tears, tears I had not shed since my parents' divorce when I was in fourth grade, and from that point on, had pretended that everything was funny and fine when in fact it was rarely either. As I clutched the vial to my heart, my grandmother faded back behind the Joshua tree, reclaimed by the desert. A raven's cry joined my own and then I followed the path back to the surface of the earth, exchanging a glance with the tortoise. Sometimes life is not funny. Oh dear, oh dear.

In an instant, everything had changed. Mary Austen's land of little rain had yielded to me a personal monsoon. I started skipping dinner parties, openings, reordering my life. Joshua Tree National Park had become my church, my temple, my Stouffer's frozen turkey tetrazzini. Week after week I would leave Los Angeles, the Xerox machine of America's dreams, and head for the Mojave, where they all started. I felt at home in this vast space where, if you happened to be near the right dune at the right time, you might stumble across a cosmic joke in the form of a shamanic workshop at the corner of Highway 111 and Bob Hope Drive, a biker with a used bookstore and an espresso machine, a cosmetic epiphany in the form of a shack that peddles thigh cream next to an earthquake sinkhole, or endless miracles of nature such as the reclusive desert frogs that leap out of the sands after a rainstorm.

The more time I spent wandering the trails of Joshua Tree National Park, the clearer it became that the desert—not Long Island, Wall Street, the White House, Madison Avenue, the Home Shopping Channel, or other regions born of mirage—explains the national character: it is the wide-open space that rocket-fuels the American obsession with personal rights, an extreme terrain that both comforts and kills; an underrated scape that is always there but doesn't particularly care if you are; an ever-changing blank slate that does its own kind of business, turning tricks if the tricks are there to be turned, but has no price or any other result in mind. And then, of course, there's Indian bingo.

Soon I was spending so much time there that I found the very Joshua tree of my dreams—the one that looked just like the one under which my grandmother had appeared in my vision—and I visited it often. JTNP became my second home; my friends in L.A. started calling me Chuckwalla Deanne and the friends I made out there started calling me Deanne from L.A. And that's how I learned the cardinal rule of the desert: Don't ask, don't tell. The desert doesn't care who you are, and neither does anyone or anything who lives in it.

☙ ☙ ☙

Deanne Stillman has written for Rolling Stone, The New York Times, Los Angeles Times, GQ, The Nation, Tin House, Salon.com, *and many other publications. She is the author of the* Los Angeles Times *bestseller* Twentynine Palms: A True Story of Murder, Marines, and the Mojave. *This story is an excerpt from her book,* Joshua Tree: Desolation Tango.

❧ ❧ ❧

Castles in the Sky

"Spectator sport" takes on new meaning.

I CLOSE MY EYES, HOPING NOT TO WITNESS IMMINENT destruction. A young child, about five years old, hovers two stories above the ground, barely balancing on top of a shaky pillar of flesh.

I can't resist. Despite the pounding in my chest, I peek through my fingers and watch another boy scamper towards the sky. Pressing his hands and bare feet into the backs and shoulders of men and women with wobbly knees, the lanky ten-year-old towhead passes the balcony where the mayor and other dignitaries stand open-mouthed. The boy climbs higher. The human obelisk sways.

In a few seconds, I'm certain, bodies will collapse upon one another and screams will pierce the crowded Barcelona square, now blanketed in silence.

"What the heck are these people doing?" I whisper to no one in particular. Back home, this would be banned. The insurance liability alone would send shivers down any actuary's spine.

This, though, isn't the United States. This is Catalonia, and here, in a province fiercely protecting its customs, language, and independence from Spain's stronghold, human castle building is as much a sport as an art form.

"This is not just a hobby," Cisco, a *casteller* (castle maker) for about fifty years, tells me later. "I don't think there is anything I have spent more time doing, besides spending time with my wife."

The tradition dates back to the eighteenth century and is loosely tied to a religious dance from Valencia, a city south of Barcelona. Over the years, the custom has morphed into an endurance event requiring a yogi's balance and Cirque du Soleil dexterity. Teams throughout Catalonia, which rests on the shores of the Mediterranean and in the shadows of the Pyrenees, train during the chilly winter months to perfect the technical aspects of *castell* (castle) construction and deconstruction. And, then in the summer and fall, wide-eyed locals pack open-air plazas to see if the spires—much like the Gaudí-inspired ones adorning La Sagrada Familia cathedral—will reach heaven.

An American expat tipped me off about the *castellers*, and with a child's enthusiasm, he urged me to stick around for the weeklong La Mercè party in late September. The *castells* were one of the festival's highlights, and would be worth skipping a beach day to witness, he assured me. I pictured the U.S. equivalent of stuffing twenty frat guys into a phone booth. It sounded quirky. I was intrigued.

Now, instead of sprawling out on white sand, I'm watching children dangle in mid-air. I think I may end up in the hospital with a heart attack, along with the mother of the kid who is hovering a couple stories off the ground.

A few minutes ago, things weren't this stressful. I huddled among the masses in Plaça de Sant Jaume and waited for something to happen. Those in nearby apartment buildings hung out of windows, taking long drags on their cigarettes and Voll-Damm beer. Politicos in suits whooped it up on city hall's second-floor balcony. A father perched his daughter, ice cream cone in hand, on his shoulders. Tourists readied their cameras. Vendors hawked bottled water and balloons. The smell of *bocadillos* (sandwiches) and *pa amb tomaquet* (tomato toast) wafted through the narrow alleyways of the old town.

Four middle-aged men, with bullish physiques and attitudes to match, elbowed their way through the noisy horde. They interlocked arms and formed a tight circle. A dozen other men and women of varying shapes and sizes, in mint green shirts and white pants, slid into the middle of the ring. They crooked themselves under armpits, squeezed against the chests of the burly men and braced for what would be a painful ten minutes.

Along the perimeter, more green-shirted men leaned against the inner circle, and behind them, even more men and women pushed in for support, resting their arms on the arms of the person in front of them. Male spectators, stupefied, were yanked into the mix and crammed into a tightly knit circle that stretched at least fifteen-people wide from the epicenter to perimeter.

A stocky man, taller than the rest, shouted commands. With the *pinya* (the base of the tower), firmly planted, it was time to climb.

Four men with sturdy, athletic frames, crawled on top of the lower level. They tightroped their way to the inner circle and steadied themselves on the shoulders of the men below. They interlocked arms and shouted down to the captain. Hands from the base wrapped around tier two's legs and cupped their butts. I chuckled. I suspected this type of groping wouldn't go over well at summer fairs back home.

On cue, the next round of climbers—men and women with slighter builds—ascended. The four monkeyed up, and, with the precision of ninjas, placed hands and feet on tier two's calves, thighs, and shoulders. Together, the four climbers hoisted themselves up and closed their ring.

A hush fell over the restless spectators. Red-and-yellow striped Catalan flags, draped defiantly down building façades, snapped in the breeze. More *castellers* climbed.

A drumbeat droned. *Throoom. Throoom. Throoom.* Then the *gralles*, a cross between a clarinet and what looked like my sixth-grade recorder, filled in the beat, slow at first. My jaw dropped. This was looking more serious than a frat-boy stunt.

The green-shirted team, or *colla*, hailed from Vilafranca del Penedès, a Barcelona suburb bordered by vineyards. Though not the hometown favorite, the team had a reputation for assembling towers that defied gravity. In the crowd, those in the know knew a 4-of-9 tower—a tower nine-people high with a circumference four-people wide—was a tower that demanded attention, and respect.

The next tier of *castellers*—teenagers, this time—was on the move. Gracefully, effortlessly, hands and feet synchronized in alternating pulley patterns. Right feet bent into the small of the backs of those already standing, just above black cummerbunds. Left knees found standing team members' shoulders. Hands tugged at pants. The teens grabbed each other's arms, simultaneously getting their bearings.

There was no time to breathe. More climbers were right behind them. Boys and girls, barely past puberty, sprinted to the top.

I can't watch. I can't help but watch. I fidget. My heart races as the *timbal*, a small drum, thumps louder, faster. The *gralles* quicken to a Bolero-like crescendo.

The crowd stands still. The little girl on her dad's shoulders stops licking her ice cream cone. Behind me, a camera clicks.

Children, no more than ten, scurry like mice. A tug at the pants above. A clasp of a shirt collar. A mighty heave up the next person's back. Higher into the clouds. Level six. Legs quiver. Weary arms try not to sag. I'm afraid to exhale. Afraid that my breath may cause the human tower of Pisa to lean too far in one direction.

Two kids dash upwards. They hurriedly create a two-person circle. The clock, a few feet above their heads, chimes the hour. City officials on balconies tilt back their heads. A five-year-old, sporting a floppy page-boy haircut, makes his way upwards and squats into fetal position on top of the two kids' shoulders. The *aixecador* is suspended over a nine-person-high shaft of bodies, passing City Hall's second floor. I gasp. I wonder if his mother has already fainted.

All eyes lock on another child—the *anxaneta,* the only person for the ninth tier. The last to climb.

The captain bellows from the perimeter, encouraging the team, in those final moments, to find even more strength. Those in the inner circle grunt. I can't see their faces. I know, though, they are flushed and beaded with sweat, made worse by the 80-degree temperature warming the square. I calculate the base must be holding nearly a ton on their shoulders. Probably more.

The ten-year-old *anxaneta* shimmies up the tower. An air of confidence replaces a brief trace of uneasiness in his soft features.

"I'm not afraid of climbing. I'm afraid of falling," the *anxaneta*, whose name is Marc, says afterwards through a translator. He's been climbing for five years, and has had his share of falls. They're not fun.

"But, when the captain says it's O.K. to go, I go."

A cautious, but quick, combination of tugs and pulls propels him past each level. He gently shifts his weight to compensate for the trembling below. He's so high he becomes a blur.

The *gralles* and the drum escalate to a feverish pitch. I cover my eyes. I peek through my fingers.

The success of the tower—the hope of a people reaching for greatness—rests in this fifth-grader.

The *anxaneta* straddles the five-year-old at the apex. He places one hand on the back of the child. He throws up the other. Victory! He touches the sky.

At that moment, Catalonia shakes off Madrid's economic and political weight. At that moment, Catalonia stands firm, unwavering in a cultural test of persistence, tenacity, and courage. At that moment, Catalonia is free.

Applause fills the urban canyons. Marc descends like a fireman sliding down a pole. Each layer peels off in the same way. The captain wipes his brow and grins a toothy smile. Men hug like brothers. Bystanders cheer in disbelief.

Without thinking, I raise my hands, too, and try to touch the Catalan sky.

≈ ≈ ≈

Jennifer Baljko is a writer who lives in Barcelona. This story won the Bronze Award for Best Travel Story of the Year in the First Annual Solas Awards (BestTravelWriting.com). Her work has appeared in The Christian Science Monitor, Islands*, and in numerous newspapers, magazines, and online publications. She has also contributed to Explorer Publishing's* Barcelona: The Complete Residents' Guide.

❧ ❧ ❧

Heroes of the Caribbean

One guy's truth about luxury cruises.

1. Go

For a long time I scorned the idea of a *Love Boat*-style cruise. From what I heard, all you did was eat. Well, occasionally you called at ports, but only to explore the crooks and grannies of duty-free shopping malls. Then you hurried back on board for more meals, digesting them to evening floorshows by the Can't-Stop-Smiling Dancers.

But then, it was 1994, and I figured I'd done enough real travel. I'd explored three continents. I'd slept under bridges, in brothels, and in a concrete tube at a Czech construction site. So what was wrong with two weeks of adventure-free travel? Besides, what else are you going to do with your seventy-something parents?

2. Escalation

At the modern passenger terminal in San Juan Harbor, I set a bad example by carrying my own bags up the escalator. The elderly couple behind also refused porters, and the husband tangled with his suitcases and toppled backwards. He was wedged on the escalator, so that the steps, while not carrying him up, rolled on, shredding the papery skin of his right arm and leg with their toothy edges. I got down the steps and lifted him. His arm, his shirt, and the glass sidings of the escalator were streaked with blood.

His wife said to me, "You were so brave."

With spots of blood on my t-shirt, and feeling not unlike a hero, I stepped aboard the *Cunard Countess*.

3. Suspicions On the Demographic Make-Up of Passengers

An hour later, exploring the ship's library, a corridor with a few shelves, I met an Aussie. "Apparently," he told me, "some old Yank fell down the stairs and broke his leg." He made no mention of anyone being brave.

There was something off about that Australian, and it wasn't his story; it was his age. He was just fifty. Next to my parents (sorry), and the other passengers I'd seen slow-footing along the promenade, this bloke was a spring wallaby.

4. Fruit Caps

My friend and cabinmate, dragged along to satisfy the pesky dual-occupancy stipulation, was Bilby. He and I were the *only* men under forty sharing a cabin on a ship of 800 passengers. On our first stop, the island of Antigua, we bought cheap sun-protection: a pair of matching rainbow caps. We did not know how queer we looked till we got back to the ship and found a mirror. We stopped saying we were from San Francisco.

5. Other Misconceptions

So we had gay hats and weren't gay. We also thought we would have all the time in the world to do all sorts of things; we were wrong. Every evening the *Daily Programme* was slipped mysteriously under our door. The *Programme* reminded me that sprawled in a deck chaise I'd miss "Informal Meeting of Masonic Brethren" or "Creative Writing with Alma." Moreover, there were films in the cinema, glittery productions every night in the Showtime Lounge, and a band in the Indoor/Outdoor Center. There were shops, exercise rooms, a swimming pool, sauna, library, casino, hairdressing salon, golfing cage, bars, a very mini tennis court, people who demanded watching, and meals, meals, meals.

And then there were the islands. You had to figure out what to do with them.

6. Figuring Out What to Do with Islands

Official shore excursions were for the weak of body and strong of wallet. However, for roughly $60, two parents and two guys in gay hats could create their own enchanting excursion with a local guide. Our guides had names like Cyril, Nehemiah, Henry, or Penguin, and they knew all the best places. On Barbados Penguin showed us the Prime Minister's home. We sat there in the van, with the engine chugging and peered through an iron gate at a medium-sized house.

"Now can you show us where the Secretary of the Treasury lives?" I asked.

7. Food Group #1: Guinness
The effect of a creamy Guinness after a day of govern-
mental home-watching is heavenly, especially when
you're wearing your formal dinner outfit, feeling the
slight pitch of the boat in the cool of a dim lounge. I
liked the Starlight Lounge best. Never crowded, it was
a swanky nightclub/casino at the fore of the boat. I sat
at the blackjack tables every night, drinking Guinness
from foot-tall glasses and trying to make twenty dollars
last hours. The dealers were all British, all in their twenties, all female, all large.

8. Casino Girls
Casino girls? Yes, and by the second week of the cruise,
they'd opened to Bilby and me, upping our relationship
beyond the dealer/gambler level to something like annoyed
familiarity. My favorites were Grinder and Cynthia.

Cynthia was Anglo-Indian, biggish, but well-propor-
tioned. She had the soft features that make Indian girls
so pretty: mellow brown eyes and smoothly curved nose.
She liked us because she liked banter, and it didn't matter how hollow or absurd.

Bilby: "Cynthia, I have a question about the rules.
What would happen if all the cards caught fire simultaneously?"

Me: "Cynthia, I'm going to put this empty coin bucket
on my head now, and I'll tip you two dollars if you say I
look like an organ grinder's monkey."

And Grinder. She was not an object of great beauty,
or any beauty, especially when tucked into the floral
yellow culottes the dealers wore on informal nights. She
was from Bristol, fiercely working class, a sneerer, and
probably a barroom brawler. But I trusted her brutish

sincerity. She was the first and only dealer I've encountered, anywhere, who refused me a seat—for my benefit. The cards were cold. She did it right in front of the other players, not a bit concerned how they might feel about this favoritism. And it was not advice. It was an order, frosted with an accusation of stupidity: "Go to the bar and drink," she said. "Go on. Sod off."

9. Food Group #2: Menu Fare

Menus at the Meridian Dining Room were thrilling. Try an appetizer of mango slices and shredded coconut, followed by clam chowder, salade niçoise, half a lobster with scalloped potatoes and sweet carrots, all topped off by baked Alaska. In actuality, this mass-produced fair was fine, not better. But cruise passengers are sold on the menus, the candlelit tables, the obsequious wine stewards, the waiters in white coats and gloves. They come on a cruise for the semblance of luxury, as upstart sybarites. They step aboard a discount Victorian Age into a cozy corner of imperialism. They journey into a system of ethnic stratification that the world no longer officially tolerates: capable British officers guide the boat; Filipinos carry drinks and change bedding; black islanders vacuum the floors; and Latinos feed you with old-world servitude.

The veneer didn't impress me, but the competence did. On the *Countess*, everyone did his job. The boat was meticulously clean and the crew kind and helpful (even on those occasions when I was especially funny, or tipsy, or both). Day after day, port after port, this 536-foot, 18,000-ton chunk of steel did its thing without sinking.

Even my dealer girlfriends—by far the least responsible workers on the boat—slid the gaming cards with expert hands; and, in addition, at times I found them to be nearly useful sources of information.

Befriending Guinness in the casino, I asked Grinder for tips on the next day's port, Guadeloupe.

"The pisshole of the Caribbean."

Surprisingly, she did not mention...

10. The Fast Fan of Guadeloupe

True, Pointe-à-Pitre is big and crowded, dirty and baking. With its balconies and wrought-iron junkiness, it has the feel of a burnt New Orleans. Still, it was a pleasant change of pace from Antigua and Barbados. We could walk around unmolested by touts and pitchmen. The central market, right next to the dock, functions for locals not tourists. Fish and fruits are cast onto tables or blankets on the pavement. Women in madras cloth and with callused feet twist roots into miniature bundles. Someone screams at a customer in French—a banana deal gone sour. Your nose is perplexed by a stew of smells: curry, mace, body odor, fish, wet dog, leafy greens.

Here, on Guadeloupe, I learned that even on a cruise, it's possible to experience real travel—discovery. Beyond the Place de la Victoire and up toward hills matted with greenery, corrugated roofs, and rainbows of hanging laundry, Bilby and I explored. Without guidebook, map, or sense, we found it.

An electric fan.

There it whirled in an unadorned food shop at No. 16 Rue de Faubourg, its frenzied blades in a bird-cage-thing mounted atop a six-foot pole. It wagged back and forth at junked-up super-animated velocity. The cage bounced, shook, wagged, and wailed at a speed no fan had gone before, a speed no fan could possibly need.

We returned to the boat, ate lunch, considered a nap, a drink, a swim. Then I said, "Let's go back and look at the fan." And that is just what we did.

And so I liked this butterfly-shaped French island, in spite of the contumely I would later hear from voices on the *Countess*. That evening, at the casino, I was playing poker alongside a British throwback with perfect posture and a colonel's mustache. He was telling Grinder that Guadeloupe was ghastly and that the French were daft.

"History," he said. "Imagine. The French trade their entire share of Canada to Britain for Guadeloupe and Martinique."

"I think..." I said.

"Don't be stupid," Grinder warned.

"I think it was a good trade in the long run," I went on. "Canada is Canadian now. But Guadeloupe and Martinique are still French."

11. Time and Other Dangers

For a week I'd lived an ideal if reckless life. I was working out in the gym. I was exploring islands. I was drinking till the early morning hours and getting in with the crew. I had my parents, living and breathing, in a cabin next door to me. I realized that I was in love with my life on this boat and that I didn't want to leave.

The ghastly thing was that seven days of our two-week cruise were gone. From this point on, there would always be less time ahead of us than behind. I was aware of the changing fractions stacking against me with each passing day—halfway through the cruise, four-sevenths, two-thirds—and that awareness strangled my enjoyment.

A cruise, or any journey of defined duration, will always collapse upon itself, and your fellow passengers onto you. Their true personalities leak out. You start to avoid some folk, actively seek out others. Mr. and Mrs. Escalator Accident are old friends. You love the braggart nerd who has seen every episode of *American Bandstand* and who says the rowing machine can't keep up with him. You wonder which dancers are gay. You get close to the casino girls; Grinder really begins to level with you:

"Give me your chips. You're cashing in. We're not keeping the casino open just for you. Go on, off with yuhs before someone else comes in."

12. Closer Still

In the Indoor/Outdoor bar, on the penultimate night, we met Cynthia, our Anglo-Indian dealer. First night off in almost three months, she declared. She wore her black formal dress, shoulders bare. Bilby and I wore tuxes. We sat in a booth, and Cynthia got drunk on Chardonnay and treated us with her 75 percent discount. She asked us if we were gay. "It's just…" she said. "San Francisco. The hats and all."

No we weren't gay, and she was quite pretty, but she talked too much. She knew it, too. She said she drove everyone crazy. Her boyfriend—a boyish Brit who worked in the engine room—corroborated. His name was Mike, and he answered my questions about the boat politely, but his main interest was getting Cynthia to his cabin.

We had more drinks. We heard which of the dancers was sleeping with whom. We heard about the mysterious casino piano player. It was generally assumed by the crew that he was gay, except that, just this week, he'd kissed a Casino Girl, or tried to.

It was 3:00 A.M., and all the passengers had gone off to bed. It was just crew, Bilby, and I. And, at another table, a fortyish Italian woman, and a man with a hand at the hem of her dress. He had a filthy-deep, reddish tan, his tie loosened at the collar, shirt undone two buttons down. This was, we were told, the ship's bread maker, Dieter. He was Swiss and always on the make.

I asked Mike if there was a rule against crew scoring with passengers, and he found this a very funny question.

Around 3:30 came the soft-looking, doughy, mystery piano player, Douglas. Cynthia was drunk now, which was remarkable since she rarely stopped talking long enough to take a swallow of wine. Douglas moved next to her, and ran his fingers over her bare arm, right in front of the engineer boyfriend who paid no attention. I reflected that this action did not seem very gay on Douglas's part. Cynthia moved over to Bilby. She slouched on him good. She wanted to work in America.

"But the only way to work there is to get a green card or marry an American. Do you know anyone that would marry an English girl?" she asked Bilby. "Of course not," she answered herself. "What would a thirty-six-year-old American man want with a twenty-two-year-old English girl?"

But before she could find the gap in that logic, the engineer scooped her up. Goodbye. Gone.

It was just Bilby and I and the sexually indefinable pianist.

What the heck? Far too late for sensible decisions.

Which might explain the blurry half an hour with a bottle of vodka in Douglas's cabin, a triangular nook in the bow. He didn't want to offend, he just wanted to know if we were gay. No? Well, he wasn't either. Then he told us that there were some crazy bars in the

Caribbean, and on a certain beach huge black men sit naked in coconut trees and wave their enormous...

Fifteen minutes later—but after 4 A.M.—Bilby and I headed down the green-carpeted deck to our cabin. The ship throbbed with emptiness. Then, down at the end of the hall, we caught a glimpse of Dieter, the Swiss bread maker. He had the Italian woman pinned to the wall, half behind a fern. They were kissing hard.

Bilby said, "I have a feeling the bread's not going to be very good tomorrow."

13. Degradation

On the last morning, I went to the cardiovascular room to get in one final heart-wrenching session, to sweat out the accumulation of fourteen days of poison. There were a couple of old British ladies on the stairsteppers. They were finishing their first week, and had another to go. I told them I envied them.

Gallantly, I worked the treadmill—full speed, full grade. Then I moved to a stationary bike. One of the ladies took over the treadmill. I had forgotten to reset the controls, and the stop button was worn to invisibility. The lady let out a squeal of alarm. She clung to the rail while the treadmill threw her legs in the air, like a bad dancer doing a reverse can-can. I dashed over, clutched her oldness, and turned the machine off.

She did not act as though I had done anything to help her. Which may have been justified. But two weeks earlier I had been called brave for doing almost nothing. And I'd liked it.

That's the problem with real endings. They fizzle or wither or peter out. Events just don't seem concerned with how to bring an inkling of shape to two weeks of motion.

The ghastly truth was, I was very sad. But that wasn't all. I felt helpless. I was exhausted, demoralized, poisoned from late nights and drinking. But hell, despite all that, the *only* thing I wanted was to...

14. Stay

I could have stayed for weeks, months without boredom. I could have adjusted to sea life. I could have cleaned up my act.

I ran into Mike, Cynthia's no-nonsense engineer, as I was debarking. I asked him where I could find the personnel department.

"I'm going to apply for a job," I said. "*Captain*. Stand on the bridge and go, 'Watch out for that whale!' 'There's an island.' 'Hard astern.' I could do that."

"It's not that easy," Mike said, no humor, all business.

"Well," I said, "How about bread maker?"

"You could probably do that."

❧ ❧ ❧

Kevin McCaughey grew up in Saratoga, California. A week after his eighteenth birthday he flew to Europe, alone and without a plan. Today he is a traveling English teacher, composer, and writer. He can often be found in former Soviet countries. During 2007-2008 he is a Fulbright Scholar in Minsk, Belarus. His web site, English Teachers Everywhere (www.etseverywhere.com), supplies teachers around the world with free audio. He is working on a memoir, tentatively titled Behind the Iron Skirt: Puzzling Adventures with Russian Girls.

꙳ ꙳ ꙳

Flamenco Form

Getting to the heart of the matter—
it's the work of a lifetime.

I AM A TRAVELER IN SEARCH OF FLAMENCO. IN A NIGHT-club in a cave in Granada, I sip Cruzcampo beer and watch and wait for the music to begin. Stools scrape, tables shift, and that narrow room grows crowded. Fellow tourists. British accents. A small stage; a backdrop of wrinkled cloth. In the front row, chic summer cool of the Spanish—young women in tight bodices; men in dark shirts.

This is not my first time in Granada. I passed through thirty years ago, an American student in a hurry to return to classes in France after Christmas in Spain. I had no time to explore the great Moorish palace of the Alhambra, no time to find the music. Now I have returned, deep in middle age, to fill this void in my repertoire of travel. And that afternoon, headed to my hotel, sated from a day within the splendors of the palace, I saw a flyer for the evening's performance: simple, black and white, an address, a time, four names, and the word FLAMENCO. I sniffed treasure, something real, authentic, an antidote to shops with jumbles of bullfight posters, Don Quixote t-shirts, plastic castanets. And in the flyer, I tasted the promise of passion: I may dress like a good girl but I have the soul of a diva.

A man rises and takes the stage. Locks of black hair curl to his shoulders. Pudgy cheeks and jowls. The singer. With his opening wails of *aye, aye, aye*, he wrings the air with grief, his face twisted by the pain of the tale. He sings to the peak of one word, weaves and warbles around the top before riding down the slope of sound to rise again, stretch the air, pulse to another peak, all on that one word. In his voice I hear the cries of the muezzin calling long-ago Moors to prayer, Sephardic half tones, the threads of an Indian raga pulled through centuries of Gypsy wanderings. I do not understand the words but my heart takes the tears, the ecstasy. His head drops at the end of the song. He looks up to the applause as if surprised to see us.

Flamenco was born of a brew of outcasts: Moors and Jews sent into exile, death, and hiding in 1492, the Christian Reconquista of Spain complete. Queen Isabella and King Ferdinand claimed the Alhambra as their own. The Gypsies, who already lived life cast out, took in the newest exiles. Ancient cultures and sacred memories melded a music with strong and complicated rhythms. The uneven beat of the twelve-count—not the familiar 4/4 count of Western time—is common. The names of the song forms are music—*soleás, siguiriyas, livianas, bulerías*—containers for words that hold the anguish of love, loss, exile, hunger.

Two guitarists step onto the stage and sit down. One is tall, gray hair pulled back in a ponytail. The other is roundish with the beginnings of a bald spot. Hands wrapped around each guitar neck, fingers baited to strike, they nod to each other and begin. Single sparkling drops of sound. Tight squeak of finger against string. Filigree of high notes against a wall of bass. Knuckles knock the face of the guitar; wood body, wood drum. Fans of fingers snap open and waves of *rasgueado* break and roll through me over and over and over. I try to enter the music, imitate the clapping, the *palmas*, of the Spanish in the front row, hands perpendicular, fingers spread. But I am clumsy in the attempt, unable to find footing in the uneven beats, like missing the last step on a flight of stairs. The singer's voice enters. Wood and flesh grow the notes, send them forth as pearls flung to the audience. Shouts of *olé* burst from the crowd.

A break at the end of the first set. Guitarists and singer mingle with the summer cool at the front of the room, kissing hello to friends come to share the evening. I go outside for fresh air. Above me, the red rocks of the Alhambra, ramparts lit by moonlight. I had seen their reflection in a courtyard pool that afternoon; rough exterior stones meant to hide, shield, deflect commoners' perception of beauty and wealth within. Mirrored against the gruff red in the surface of the pool, marble pillars webbed together by stucco. And the walls of the Palacio Nazaríes dense with patterns of foliage and flowers that swirl and curl around the script and wisdom of the Koran and flowers and foliage and script and tiles that twine and line memories of the days when Jews and Moors and Christians lived and worked and mused together in Granada before the Reconquista, before the Inquisition.

The poet Federico García Lorca, favorite son of Granada, was haunted by the cruelties of the Inquisition, enraptured with the passion of flamenco. His hometown was his muse, the music his model. Lorca wrote that "Granada is made for music, for it is a city enclosed by mountain ranges, where the melody is returned and polished and blocked by walls and boulders. Music is for cities away from the coast. Sevilla and Málaga and Cádiz escape through their ports. But Granada's only way out is its high natural port of stars. Granada is withdrawn, enclosed, apt for rhythm and the echo, the marrow of music."

The break ends. The dancer takes the center. She is dressed in a simple black blouse and long red skirt. Her hair is pulled back into a tight bun. Lines at the corners of her eyes and mouth do not mar her beauty. She cocks her head to the right, lifts her chin. One hand rests on a hip. The other is raised to the top of an arc above her. The audience is still, poised. With a stomp of heels she announces her beginning and flies into a swirl of skirt and snapping fingers. She lights a staccato of *zapateado* that sounds like a woodpecker gone mad in the forest. Blur of black leather heels and toes. She flings to a stop. Skirt pulled to thigh she spins a slow circle. She stamps once, twice. Her fingers are flowers; her arms snake against the pounding rhythm of heels on wooden stage. The singer joins in. His voice curves around the flick of her hips, shapes the music she dances. She locks him in a gaze that smolders then snaps to face the gray-haired guitarist, who leans into her passion and responds with a roll of chords like a well-muscled bull in the ring. This was what I had craved. This was why I had come. I fill those shoes with her. I fling my soul into her wild and complicated rhythms, into the sensuous arch of her back. I feel the jolt of heel against floor, lick of skirt against legs, heat of music in my own breasts.

The whirling, swirling, snapping, pounding, strumming crest and recede. The audience jumps up, clapping, cheering, shouting, screaming our *olés*. Dancer and singer stand frozen, breathing hard, lost in each other's gaze, then turn to bow to the audience, special nods to the front row.

I walk back to my hotel, beside the river, beneath the ramparts of the Alhambra on the hill above. I have the treasure; how do I carry it home? Will life on another continent destroy what I hold? How will I stop the black press of the mundane? Pat Conroy wrote "...once you have traveled, the voyage never ends, but is played out over and over again in the quietest chambers, that the mind can never break off from the journey." I take heart.

I use my mind and body to continue the journey. The spirit of Granada echoes in the stomp of my heels on the wooden floor of a dance studio in Seattle. My shoes are black leather with a saucy little notch above the heel. I've learned how to flick my skirt on the kick turn at the end of a *paseo*, how to slide my hands against my hips at just the right place in the music. My feet ache from the arc of the shoes. I stepped on my own toe last night. My body struggles against the foreign form of the twelve count—**1** and **2** and **3** and uh **4** and uh **5** and—but I soar when my teacher tells me "That's it! You've got the idea!"

New CDs are stacked in my living room: Paco de Lucía, Carlos Montoya, Gypsy Soul, Sabor Flamenco. I've rented the Carlos Saura video, bought a book called *Song of the Outcasts*, read Lorca's poetry and written in imitation: I have docked within the music and the long reach of my senses has explored its depths. I dance at the fringe of this universe but the treasure holds me captive.

❧ ❧ ❧

Nancy Penrose lives in Seattle, works at the University of Washington, and has been a writer and editor for twenty-five years. She has lived and traveled abroad since age four and writes to explore the territories at the intersection of two cultures. "Flamenco Form" won the Silver Award for Best Travel Story of the Year in the First Annual Solas Awards (BestTravelWriting.com).

≫ ≫ ≫

Key to the City

Sometimes, travel hands you a second chance.

I F THE KEY HAD BEEN PRETTY, I COULD HAVE WORN IT around my neck like jewelry for the last forty years, but it's utterly plain—bronze-colored, round-headed, the kind the Yale company stamps out by the millions every year.

I have kept it anyway, not for its looks, but for what it meant. It was the key to my first apartment, and it opened much more than a front door. It opened a whole city to me. It opened my eyes. It opened my life.

This is the address the key belonged to: No. 1, Makdisi Building, Rue Jeanne d'Arc, Beirut, Lebanon.

I lived there in the summer of 1963, when I was nineteen. Grew up there, is more like it. I fell in love that summer, got—not my first kiss—but the first I wanted, learned to smoke, drank too much Lebanese beer, worked at being sophisticated.

That summer also turned my future upside down. Now I would just say I changed careers, but back then I didn't have one to change. Back then, I just felt lost. Beirut became my comfort.

I had loved it from the start. When my college group stepped out of the plane on our first evening there and started down the shuddering aluminum ladder to the tarmac, the warm, scented air of the city rose up around my bare legs—ankles, knees, thighs, as if I were wading into bathwater. It was the most sensuous thing I had ever known.

No. 1, Makdisi was the address that got us our mail— a mild flood of flimsy blue envelopes from our families in the Middle West to their exchange-student offspring in the Middle East.

There were ten of us, five men, five women, all Minnesota undergraduates working on projects we'd proposed the previous year. I remember only three of our topics: Jim investigated the politics of student groups, Kirsten focused on the rights of women, and I studied archaeology, something I'd dreamed of since I was old enough to read.

The men lived in a dorm on the pine-shaded, seaside campus of the American University of Beirut, always referred to simply as the A.U.B. The women rented an apartment nearby, and the men came over all the time to use the phone.

I was assigned to a small A.U.B. dig in the Bekaa, Lebanon's long central valley, and went down to Beirut whenever I could. As the summer wore on, that was more and more often.

I had arrived in Lebanon believing that archaeology would be what my favorite books had promised me all my life—an endless stream of rich discoveries and richer adventures, Egypt one year, Yucatán the next, and so on and on, all over the globe. But the real thing wasn't like that. All the days were the same, and there was no treasure.

The archaeologists took long midday siestas, to avoid the worst of the sun. I read a lot and practiced smoking. Soon, the best things in my life were listening to jackals howl around the dig house at night—and planning what I'd do next weekend, back in Beirut.

Beirut always wore summer colors—newer buildings in blazing white, older ones in the warm weathered yellows of provincial France, the country's former colonial master. Our apartment was on the ground floor of one of the old yellow buildings. It belonged to a woman whose family owned a jam and jelly factory and who was going to Europe for the summer; her son let us have the place cheap.

The apartment had floors of inlaid tile, a dining-room table that could accommodate all of us, a decent kitchen (we learned to enter it slowly and loudly at night, to give the cockroaches a chance to hide) and a living room furnished with comfortable old club chairs and a gray daybed. The other women claimed the bedrooms, and I camped on the daybed when I wasn't at the dig.

I was helping to excavate the kind of hill that Arabic labels a *tell*—a flat-topped, man-made hill, as opposed to a *jebel*—a natural, roundish, God-made hill. *Tells* look like layer cakes when you slice into them, each layer a mud-brick town—they get older the farther down you dig.

For a few hours each morning and fewer in the afternoon, I stood with the director on top of the *tell* and watched a line of women—farmers' wives and daughters dressed, despite the heat, in heavy skirts and long-sleeved sweaters—filing down into a wide pit and filing back out again. They were hauling dirt.

Each carried a black rubber basket made out of an old tire. One by one, at the bottom of the pit, they went up to the local men who were doing the actual digging, held out their baskets and received a shovelful of earth.

Then they hoisted the black baskets onto their heads and swayed up and out of the pit and over to a refuse tip, dumped out the dirt and started back down again. It was stately—classic, even. And very, very slow.

It had taken ten years of digging to get down to where the Iron Age met the Bronze. The director figured it would take another ten before he got through the last of the villages below.

"Give me a dozen American graduate students," I muttered patriotically into my journal, "and I could knock this thing off in a couple of summers."

Occasionally, I was allowed to jump down into the pit and dig too. Somewhere in an A.U.B. storeroom, there is a clay oven in a cardboard box that my hands lifted free from its grave.

And somewhere, I suppose, is the time-fractured pot I was assigned to glue back together, shard by shard. Gradually, its shape emerged, and I realized it was an amphora, a tapered jar that would have stood about four feet tall. All I had managed to reassemble was its rounded shoulder and part of the neck. It had taken me a month.

"I cannot do this," I finally admitted to my journal. "I cannot spend my life doing this."

The problem was, I didn't know what else to spend it on, and I felt bereft and scared. Years would pass before

I realized that the summer hadn't been a failure—before I saw that it had done exactly what it should have, turning me away from archaeology and onto a path that was a better fit.

These were the summer's real lessons: That no path is permanent. That roads, however chosen, always lead somewhere. That sometimes the hardest lessons stick the best. And that sometimes—if you live—you get a second chance. By the time I understood all that, Beirut would need those lessons too.

When work ended on Friday afternoons, I flagged down one of the old Blue Bird school buses that were Lebanon's Greyhounds and rode south through the Bekaa, up over the coastal mountains and down into Beirut.

If I got a seat on the left side of the bus, there was always a moment when the road curved around a last bend, and I could see the hazy city, with the blue Mediterranean beyond, flowing out into the distance like a land of dreams.

The bus took me to the Bourj, the heart of downtown. Trams, buses, taxis, people—everything in the city started or ended there. The streets were a permanent State Fair, and the busiest were the awning-shaded souks, Beirut's equivalent of Istanbul's Grand Bazaar.

You could get anything in the souks, from baklava to brassieres. I was drawn to the Arabian Nights stuff: Daggers, curved and jeweled and harmlessly dull. Gaudy, gilded sandals, glittering with rhinestones. Hammered brass trays and thimble-sized coffee cups. Tables and chairs inlaid with mother-of-pearl. And Lebanon's trademark silverware, its black handles carved in the shape of resting nightingales.

The crowds were just as varied. On any afternoon, I'd encounter peasant women in jet-black robes that left only their hands and faces bare; old farmers with long moustaches and baggy Ottoman-style breeches; impeccable businessmen in French-cut suits, striding between office buildings, and city women as elegantly dressed and coifed as any on the Champs-Elysées.

There were other differences, of course—dangerous ones that didn't meet the eye. More than a dozen religions were afoot in those crowds, and the tensions between them had already triggered conflicts. But on summer afternoons in the human whirlpool of the Bourj, real war seemed unimaginable.

From downtown, I caught the little tram that ran west along Rue Bliss—named for a person, not my state of mind—to the Moorish arch of A.U.B.'s main gate. Then I walked a few blocks along Jeanne d'Arc to a candy store called Chantilly, ducked around it into a dead-end alley, stepped into our tiny front garden, put the key in the lock and let myself in. It always felt like coming home.

As archaeology faded, my summer took on an end-of-the-world recklessness, something Beirut knew how to cater to. What I liked best were the evenings at our apartment—long salon-like evenings when it seemed as if every person we'd met in Lebanon would drop by for beer and Chantilly chocolate, cigarettes and conversation.

We attracted American expatriates and teachers from the international schools, A.U.B. medical students, people we'd interviewed, and a lot of young Lebanese guys irresistibly drawn to this nest of Minnesota girls.

We were only college kids in wash-and-wear dresses, but those evenings made me feel glamorous and sought-after. They allowed me to think I knew Beirut, and that Beirut had nothing better to do that summer than shine its spotlight right on us.

All this sounds silly now: Beirut was a big city, more than a million even then, and we knew only a tiny corner of it. But that corner felt open and free and safe. It was my first real taste of adult life. I felt intensely alive, and something different happened every day.

One day it was simply a cloud in the sky—an event so rare in a Beirut summer that one of our new friends came over to make sure we didn't miss it.

Another day it was the U.S. Navy's entire Sixth Fleet, stopping by on a training mission. The embassy sent out messages to all the young American women in town, encouraging us to date sailors and help keep them out of trouble.

There were so many uniforms ashore that the streets near the port looked like rivers of white. We dated them in groups. By the end of fleet week, one of my roommates had been out with twenty-three sailors; I'd been out with eighteen. But—in the classic phrase of the time—nothing happened. It was 1963, after all, and the sexual revolution hadn't arrived. None of us slept with anybody.

My most intimate moment, in fact, came when one sailor showed me the last letter he'd gotten from his girlfriend. I had not known until then that nations are defended—and torn apart—by armies of homesick boys. I learned it earlier in Beirut than I would have at home: The Six-Day War would not happen for another four years; Vietnam was lurking in the future, and Beirut's long self-destruction would not begin until the Vietnam War was over.

The guy I fell in love with that summer wasn't among the sailors. Bob was a student from Northwestern, making up a chemistry class at A.U.B. He had black hair and hazel eyes so light that they shone like gold when the sun hit them.

He had grown up in Saudi Arabia, in the sheltered enclaves of Aramco, the Arab-American Oil Company—exactly the kind of expat upbringing I envied. Every time I saw him, my heart turned over. I never knew if his did, but Bob took to dropping by the apartment too, and I spent my weekends trying to be fascinating.

My journal devotes an embarrassing amount of space to the details of this romance—going to downtown discos together, sharing hamburgers at an A.U.B. hangout called Uncle Sam's, our failed attempt to smuggle Marlboros out of the free port, sunbathing on the stony campus beach. One night we skipped through the marble halls of the grand Phoenicia Hotel, holding hands. And once, by our apartment's front door, he kissed me goodnight.

Bob left Beirut before I did, and I went down to the airport with a farewell bottle of champagne and talked a Middle East Airlines flight attendant into taking it to him on board. Just before the passenger door closed for take-off, Bob leaned out and waved goodbye; I never saw him again.

When the rest of us scattered for home, I took my Beirut house-key with me, more as talisman than souvenir. Someday, I promised myself, someday when I had my life figured out, I'd go back, find my old apartment, unlock the door as if I still lived there, hand the key to the startled residents and say thanks.

For years afterward, when the Minnesota winter finally broke and real spring warmed the air at home, there would be a night when I stepped outside and felt the soft, sweet air of Beirut swirl around me again, and I would grieve for the city, missing it, unable to find a way back.

By the time I'd finished a degree in journalism, gotten a job at a newspaper and could afford to return, Lebanon was in the middle of its civil war. When the fighting finally stopped, fifteen years later, the heart of the city had been devastated, and it seemed too late.

Then, early in 2003, some of my old student group got serious about an anniversary reunion in Lebanon. It still seemed dangerous, but we were running out of time. "The way I see it," one man said, making the clinching argument, "it's never going to be safe."

We went back that June. As I'd always intended, I retrieved the apartment key from my jewel box and took it with me.

Amazingly, our old neighborhood hadn't changed much, and the ruined downtown was being resurrected. The old souks were gone, but many of the beautiful yellow buildings had been restored, the sidewalk cafés were back and booming, the crowds were as cosmopolitan as I remembered, and I was just as happy.

Being in the city again gave me such intense déjà vu that I kept forgetting my real age. I remembered it fast enough when I went looking for my apartment: I couldn't find anyone old enough to ask.

I looked for it anyway, but I'd never known more than a few words of Arabic, and while neighborhood residents tried to help, I got nowhere. The next time I tried, I asked an A.U.B. staffer to come along and translate.

Khaled and I walked down Jeanne d'Arc to a cross street called Makdisi, and he pointed to a tall, white building on the corner, its facade a mix of shop signs and modern balconies. He thought it must be that one.

It can't be, I said. It's too new. Too big. It didn't look like that. And it wasn't on a corner.

Khaled asked a shopkeeper. "He says that's the Makdisi building," Khaled said. No, I insisted, it isn't.

We walked up a narrow lane beside it. Midblock, tucked behind the modern building so it was invisible from Jeanne d'Arc, there was a lower building, worn yellow stucco with old green shutters.

Ours was like THAT, I told Khaled. But it wasn't this far back, and it faced the other way. If you took this building and turned it around…

A balding, middle-aged man in a navy turtleneck had come out onto a little terrace on the ground floor and was standing quietly, watching me pantomime turning his building around in the air. He asked in Arabic what I was up to. Khaled told him.

And then the man did something that the Lebanese always used to do: he simply opened the terrace gate and, with a huge smile, welcomed us into his home.

"Come in," he said in English, and we stepped into his living room. It was very plain, with an old tile floor (the pattern looked familiar), divans along two sides, a treadle sewing machine serving as an end table, a few kitchen chairs scattered around, and a large TV mounted high on the wall.

Our host, along with his younger sister, her husband, their four-year-old son and a frail elderly lady—"my auntie," our host said—had been watching an Arabic news report about the war in Iraq. He turned it down a little so we could talk.

No, he said, he didn't remember any building like the

one I described. Neither did his auntie, who had moved over to sit beside me.

She had been a teacher, she confided, in a delicate blend of French and English. As the visit went on, more and more words came back to her. She practiced them, moving her lips silently, before she shyly whispered them to me. It was like listening to lace.

Another wraith-like old auntie drifted in and perched on one of the divans. She said she didn't know about the apartment either and drifted back out.

"My mother will know," our host assured us: She ran a dressmaking shop around the corner and knew everyone in the neighborhood.

By the time his mother appeared, we'd learned how to pronounce each other's names; I'd told everyone about our study group and its reunion trip; we'd all agreed that the Iraq war was a bad thing; they'd offered coffee and tea; Khaled and I had accepted, and the English-speaking auntie had gone into the kitchen and fetched a plate of homemade stuffed grape leaves.

"Eat," she commanded. Plump with lamb and rice, they were the best I'd ever tasted.

Eventually the mother came in, a woman with dyed-black hair, wearing a kerchief and a loose flowered housecoat. She didn't look much older than her son.

But he was right: She knew. And she knew instantly.

Before he'd said anything, she froze, stared hard at my face and rattled off something in fast, excited Arabic. "My mother say she know you directly!" the son translated, and lots of talk broke out.

Khaled translated more precisely. This is what the mother had said about me: "She rented the apartment behind our house forty years ago!"

I was so shocked that my skin tingled. I'm still shocked. I think she was actually remembering one of the other women, but I didn't mind. The important thing was, she remembered *us*. And she remembered the apartment.

Which wasn't there any more. She said the owners—yes, the very same ones who'd owned a jam factory—had torn it down in 1975, just before the civil war started, and put that big white building in its place. The dead-end alley beside our old building had been made into a lane, which was how the replacement ended up on a corner.

I'd been afraid of something like this, but the family's unexpected hospitality took the sting out of the loss. At least it hadn't been war damage.

I dug the old apartment key out of my purse and held it up for them to see. "I was going to open the door and walk in and give it back," I said, and Khaled translated.

Everyone collapsed in laughter. "Now I guess I can keep it," I said. More laughter.

The elderly auntie worked out another of her gossamer English sentences and offered it to me. "You found the key," she said gently, "and you lost the house."

I slipped the key back in my purse and zipped it shut. Yes, I said, and smiled at her. Yes, the house is gone.

But by then it didn't matter. The key had done its old familiar work, as surely as if I'd turned it again in the front door of No. 1, Makdisi Building, all these years later.

It had let me back into a city I loved and permitted me, in that Lebanese family's plain, friendly living room, once again to feel at home.

❧ ❧ ❧

Catherine Watson was an exchange student twice—in high school with American Field Service to Germany, and in college with the Minnesota SPAN program to Lebanon. She has been fascinated ever since by the relationship between "home" and "away." She was the award-winning travel editor of the Minneapolis Star Tribune *from 1978 to 2004 and is the author of* Roads Less Traveled: Dispatches from the Ends of the Earth *and* Home on the Road: Further Dispatches from the Ends of the Earth.

࿇ ࿇ ࿇

Don't Dread the Dread, Mon

What fools we mortals be.

I HAVE A THEORY, SUPPORTED BY A GREAT DEAL OF DATA, that Western women lose twenty to thirty IQ points in the presence of a beautiful African man with dreadlocks. When the dreads are accompanied by good teeth, she can lose up to forty points. Depending on how smart she is to begin with, this can be a real problem.

My first Rasta experience was in a club in Harare's city center. My friend Munya and I had come to see Oliver Mtukudzi perform, and the place was packed. Munya went off to buy beers, and I was left alone.

"Hey, WOOOMAAAN, wot are you doing in my countreeee?" He was by my side the instant Munya left, and he was shockingly good-looking. Tall. Broad shoulders. Beautiful dreads. Not the clumpy, nasty ones that provide sustenance for single-celled organisms, but nice, thin, well-kept ones. And then, of course, the teeth. Knowing my personal weakness, I tried to avert my eyes, but it was the deer in the headlights phenomenon. I just couldn't look away.

"Is Zimbabwe your country?"

"Yes, mon."

"Then why are you speaking in a Jamaican accent?"

"I'm a Rastafarian, this is how we speak. My name is Kudakwashe—it means God's Will."

I would soon find out that the Jamaican accent was very popular among guys with dreads in Zimbabwe. This bothered me. There's no need to change the sound of your voice based on your beliefs. That's just silly. However, if you insist on making the change, at least get it right. Haile Selassie, aka Ras Tafari, was Ethiopian, not Jamaican. These guys are mimicking Bob Marley, which is just shear laziness. Try a little harder, that's all I'm saying.

Kudakwashe wouldn't give up his accent, despite my clever arguments.

"Was dat your husband?"

"No."

"Why don't you come to my house, mon, I want to show you my art."

So here's a guy speaking in a fake accent, who doesn't know that his spiritual guru was Ethiopian, and who wants to show me his "art." I'm no fool. I know that "art" equals penis. I know this guy is a player, and is only hitting on me because I'm a wealthy foreigner. But I can't seem to wipe this stupid grin off my face. I tell myself that he might be the exception to the rule. After all, not every man with dreads in the city of Harare is bad news. Perhaps I've found the one sweet, decent, if slightly dim, Rastafarian. Yes, he's different from the others, and it's possible we'll be very happy together.

I was still basking in the glow of Kudakwashe's teeth when Munya returned with the beers. Munya is a sweet man who always has a smile on his face. But he shot this guy a look of pure hatred. The Rasta scurried away.

"I know that guy, he's always hitting on white women."

"Oh, you know Kudakwashe?"

Munya burst out laughing. "His name's not Kudakwashe, it's Brian. What's wrong with you white girls? You're all so smart and educated, but you fall for the Rasta game every time."

Right. That was embarrassing. No more Rastas for me. I'm too smart for that. I shall not be fooled again.

A couple of weeks later Munya and I went dancing at a different club, on the outskirts of town. We'd been there a couple of hours, we'd both had a few, and we were having a blast. He went to buy round four; I continued to shake my groove thang.

"How do you do that?" said the handsome *non*-dread-locked man, who appeared the second Munya left.

"Do what?"

"Dance like an African woman."

I would have married the guy and turned over my life savings to him right then and there had Munya not returned with our drinks and interrupted the magical moment. I was over the moon. Me, dancing like an African? There was simply no greater compliment possible. I had made it. I could shake my ass like a local. I was hot!

I sailed through the next week, reliving the glorious moment and trying to figure out which of my many dance moves were the most African. It dawned on me that I couldn't possibly be the boring Anglo-Saxon mutt my parents insisted I was; could it be that I had African blood in me? Thereby explaining why I was inexplicably drawn to Zimbabwe? Yes, it was all starting to make sense.

Despite his hacking cough and 102-degree temperature, I dragged Munya out dancing the following Friday, insisting that as a medical professional I knew what was best for him. There was another white chick at the club, which I tended to frown upon because it diluted my novelty value. She evidently felt the same way, because we stuck to opposite ends of the dance floor the entire night. I'm embarrassed to admit that I always felt a bit competitive toward other white women in these situations. I asked myself a series of questions each time. Was I the better dancer? Undoubtedly, especially after last week's confirmation. Was I better looking? Too close to call. She had lovely long, blond hair, but it seemed a bit too blond, if you know what I mean. Was I with a better guy? For sure, because Munya is hot and she was with, oh dear, a Rasta. That knocked her out of the running completely, poor thing. I then felt secure in my title of "coolest white chick" and forgot about her until the end of the night. I nearly bumped into her on my way to the toilet, and it was then that I heard the words which caused my world to come crashing down: "You dance like an African woman." And they were directed at her! Not me! Her!

Any idiot could see that she had no rhythm and danced like a chicken. It was obviously nothing more

than a pick-up line. And I had fallen for it, as she undoubtedly would. I had to face the truth. I couldn't
dance. I was a British-Luxembourger, not African-
American. And I was gullible. These guys were tricky,
dreads or no dreads. I would have to raise my game.

≈ ≈ ≈

*Jennifer Wells is a freelance writer and occasional public health
professional. Her great loves are travel and conversation, usually
over a beer. Or two. She's found mainly in Los Angeles and
Johannesburg, but her heart is in Zimbabwe. She is writing a book
about the lighter side of friendship and life in Harare.*

TONY PERROTTET

⚹ ⚹ ⚹

Mount Rushmore Revisited

One man's monument is another's nightmare.

BLAME IT ON CARY GRANT: THE CLIMACTIC CHASE in Hitchcock's 1959 thriller *North by Northwest,* when he and Eva Marie Saint are pursued by Communist villains across the iconic faces of Mount Rushmore, is an indelible pop culture image. The scene was actually shot in a Hollywood studio, but today the first question that occurs to even the least adventurous visitor is not why the Pharaonic monument was carved, or even how, but: *How can I get up there?* It's not such an irreverent question. In his original vision in the 1930s, sculptor Gutzon Borglum had conceived of a grand stairway for the public leading up to the presidential heads, along with a giant carved tablet that recounted the first 150 years of United States history, but his plan was shelved when they ran out of good granite to carve, not to mention time and money. In fact, since work ended on it in 1941, climbing America's patriotic memorial has been officially prohibited.

Which is why an invitation from the park superintendent to "summit" Mount Rushmore with a "V.I.P. group" is not something you can turn down.

And so, early one crystal August morning, led by clean-cut park ranger Darin Oestmann, I joined five other lucky hikers setting off from the Visitor's Center along a trail through the sweetly-scented ponderosa forest in the Black Hills of South Dakota. My fellow VIPs, I was curious to note, were members of a barbershop quartet from nearby Rapid City—retirees in biker jackets and baseball caps, as well as their manager and his wife, who were scheduled to perform at Mount Rushmore's evening sound-and-light show, and now wanted to harmonize patriotic songs on the presidents' heads.

We proceeded through the forest in silence, listening to birdsong and the cracking of twigs by passing goats, mildly awed by the tangible evidence of history scattered along the path—rusting nails, wires, and lengths of the original air compression pipes used by the four hundred or so local laborers who from 1927 to 1941 followed this route, by wood stair and winch cart, on their Promethean task.

Our guide Oestmann paused on the trail to point out a rarely seen view of George Washington's profile, gleaming in the golden morning light. Mount Rushmore has not looked so good for over six decades. In the summer of 2005, a German cleaning company gave the four presidents their first high-tech face-lift, using 140-degree Fahrenheit water blasted through hydraulic hoses. Sixty-four years worth of dirt and lichens fell from the memorial, including mushroom-like fungi that were over three inches thick. "Now the faces are whiter, and a lot shinier," said Oestmann, who was personally involved in cleaning "about three-quarters of the first president." "You see that dot in Washington's left eyelid?" He pointed to a broken drill bit that stuck in the stone. "You couldn't see *that* before."

This was definitely not your typical manicured tourist path. We scrambled up a few steep boulders, slipped between pine branches near mountains of rubble, then passed the high-security wire fence that now keeps intruders out. Steep metal steps rose into a granite crevice until, directly behind the presidential heads, the sun revealed a carved opening in the heart of the rock—an oblong sliver, looking for all the world like the entrance to the tombs in Egypt's Valley of the Kings. This was the Hall of Records, a vault that Borglum had originally planned as a repository for the Declaration of Independence and other key American artifacts. Worried that future generations might find Mount Rushmore as enigmatic as Stonehenge, the sculptor also wanted information stored on the four presidents—Washington, Lincoln, Jefferson, and Teddy Roosevelt—as well as an explanation of "how the memorial was built and frankly, why."

The Egyptian look was no accident: Borglum had come up with the idea for the Hall of Records in 1935, while watching the hit Hollywood movie *She,* which had an Egyptian theme. The fantasy film included a stairway to the heavens—perfect inspiration for the omnivorous artist Borglum. Sadly, the vault was never finished. Today, it's an ever-narrowing passage that runs about eighty-two feet into the rock, and you can run your fingers over granite walls still honeycombed with drill marks. Still, in 1998, Borglum's wish was partly fulfilled, when the park service placed sixteen text-covered porcelain panels in a teakwood box lined with titanium, and buried the casket beneath a polished black granite capstone—the last work expected to be done on Rushmore.

But the climax of the climb was yet to come. Oestmann led us up the last steep stairway, and we burst from the shadows into a brilliant blue South Dakota sky—on top of George Washington's head, no less, 650 feet above the Visitor's Center and 5,600 feet above sea level. As I wandered jelly-kneed over to Jefferson and Lincoln's brilliant white pates—thankfully, relatively flat rather than round—the sense of space was exhilarating: our view across the craggy, pine-covered Black Hills seemed endless.

In August, 1925, this vista was particularly impressive to Gutzon Borglum, the first time he climbed the raw cliffs of Mount Rushmore to survey its artistic potential. Traveling with guides from the State Game Lodge and his son Lincoln, sporting his trademark Stetson and cigar, the sculptor gazed out on the Black Hills and seemed—if just for a moment—humbled by his under-taking. "I was conscious we were in another world...." Borglum wrote of that moment. "We looked out over a horizon level and beaten like the rim of a great cart-wheel 2,000 feet below. We had reached upward toward the heavenly bodies...and it came over me in an almost terrifying manner that I had never sensed [the scale of] what I was planning." The artist was fifty-seven-years old, an age when many men plan retirement; now he was contemplating an artwork bigger than the ancient

Colossus of Rhodes, on a site that could only be reached by foot trails.

The story of Borglum's fourteen years at the monument, wrestling with nature, government bureaucracy, and his own failing health, has gone down as American legend. (The sculptor died in 1941 from complications after minor surgery, and work ceased on the memorial prematurely; the finishing touches were later directed by his son Lincoln, just before the U.S. entered the Second World War). But that might as well have been yesterday, as we stood amongst the winches and snakes of cable, peering nervously down on the sixty-foot-high heads below, as if these tools were a secret memorial to Borglum the man. Left in perpetuity, they provide a window back to the moment when it all began, when nobody, even the artist himself, knew whether the project might end in humiliating failure. Oestmann pointed out the red plotting points inscribed around Lincoln's eyes, and the green numbers written along his hairline—newly visible since the memorial's cleaning—and he offered to take my photograph perched on Jefferson. "Don't go any further back," he said, as I maneuvered cautiously into position. "That's a sheer drop."

Back to Washington's head, I found the barbershop quartet humbly down on one knee, and they broke into *This Is My Country* as the video camera rolled:

> What difference if I hail from North or South
> Or from the East or West?
> My heart is filled with love for all of these...

It was a grandly theatrical scene, one part unselfconsciously patriotic, one part Fellini-esque—and quintessential Rushmore. Gutzon Borglum was himself a consummate showman, who orchestrated many inaugurations, pageants, and presidential visits at the monument. He would no doubt have approved.

Exotic as it was, for anyone with a sense of history, the reaction to being on top of the Black Hills has to be more textured these days. For Native Americans, Mount Rushmore has an entirely different set of meanings, since it was carved in the very heart of the most bitterly contested landscape in the Western United States. In fact, their foremost cinematic reference for the monument might not be *North by Northwest* but the 2002 film *Skins*, a harsh account of reservation life directed by Lakota Chris Eyres. Its climactic scene depicts a modern Indian protagonist, the disillusioned tribal policeman Rudy Yellow Lodge (played by Eric Schweig) climbing Mount Rushmore and tossing a can of red paint down George Washington's face, leaving a trail like a teardrop of blood.

Mount Rushmore might seem the most stolid of America's historical monuments. What can really change over the decades on those stone faces, which seem to gaze down indifferently on the follies of their countrymen? Quite a lot, as it happens—including a seismic cultural shift that may outlast the recent summer's cosmetic cleaning.

The change has been in motion since 2004, when the first Native American superintendent, Gerard Baker, was appointed at Mount Rushmore. Baker, a Hidatsa-Mandan who was raised on the Fort Berthold reservation in North Dakota, has begun to broaden the cultural programs and lectures at the monument. Two years ago, visitors could learn about Rushmore as a patriotic symbol, as a work of art, or as a geological formation, but nothing about its pre-white history; they would leave having no idea why it arouses such bitterness among many Native Americans. Despite Baker's slow, diplomatic start—he is advancing, he likes to say, in "baby steps"—it's an ambitious project to explode sixty years of myopia.

"There is a huge need for Anglo-Americans to understand the Black Hills before the arrival of the white men," Baker says. "A lot of Indian people all over America look at Mount Rushmore as a symbol of what white people did to this country when they arrived— took the land from the Indians and desecrated it. But I'm not going to concentrate on that. We need to talk about the first 150 years of America and what that means. We need to make sure that our young people don't forget who they are."

That history is not a proud one; indeed, Borglum's "shrine of democracy" was erected on the site of one of America's harshest injustices. The entire Black Hills were—and remain—a sacred landscape to the Lakota people as Paha Sapa, "the heart of everything that is." Natural formations such as Bear Butte and the Devil's Tower (over the border in Wyoming) are the setting for their most important ceremonies, while Wind Cave is thought of as the place where the Lakota ancestors emerged. Under the 1868 Treaty of Fort Laramie, the U.S. Congress confirmed an earlier promise that the area would remain inviolate as the core of the Greater Sioux Reservation. But only six years later, in 1874, rumors of gold in the mountains led to a military "reconnaissance" being sent into the Black Hills commanded by Lieutenant-Colonel George Armstrong Custer. The soldiers found themselves unexpectedly bewitched by the unreal beauty of the Black Hills, whose pine-filled valleys form a verdant oasis in the dry Great Plains. Crusty cavalrymen would lean down from their horses and pluck bouquets of wildflowers; officers enjoyed champagne suppers with wild gooseberries while the enlisted men played baseball.

But for the Lakota families who watched the expedition from the surrounding mountains, the expedition foretold disaster. Custer's prospectors discovered gold in the mountain streams, and within weeks of the news arriving in Cheyenne, a rush to the Black Hills was on, with Deadwood as one of the first illegal settlements. President Grant sent envoys to buy the Black Hills, but the Lakota refused to bargain: Sitting Bull said he would not sell even a pinch of dust. In the war that broke out in 1876, many of the Seventh cavalrymen who had plucked flowers in the Black Hills lost their lives on the Little Bighorn—including Custer and Calhoun. But the Lakota were soon defeated, and Congress in 1877 passed an act obliging them to sell the Hills and move to reservations.

When Gutzon Borglum first came to the Black Hills half a century later, these events were—for white settlers—a distant memory. The Rushmore project faced some opposition from local environmentalists, who felt it defiled the pristine Western landscape, but nobody considered that Native Americans might take it as a pointed insult.

To get a sense of the emotion level, I visited the Defenders of the Black Hills, a Native American group that meets regularly in a Rapid City community center. When I explained to the dozen men and women there—mostly Lakota, but also Ponca and Northern Cheyenne—that I was writing about Mount Rushmore, the room was filled with hoots of laughter that betrayed an underlying bitterness.

"Tell your readers that we'd like to blow it up!"

"Cover those white faces up!"

"They call them the founding fathers? To us, they're the founding terrorists!"

The Coordinator, a bird-like, fiftyish woman named Charmaine Whiteface, of the Oglala Lakota, explained in a matter-of-fact tone: "We all hate Mount Rushmore. It's a sacred mountain that has been desecrated. It's like a slap in the face to us—salt in the wounds—as if a statue of Adolph Hitler was put up in the middle of Jerusalem."

She gave me a badge: The Black Hills Are Not For Sale, a reference to the 1980 court ruling that awarded the Sioux $106 million compensation for the loss of the Hills. The Lakota have refused to touch the money, which has grown to over $500 million in the bank, even though their communities remain desperately poor. Today, the Defenders' main focus is the litany of environmental affronts that are still scarring their sacred lands: there are abandoned uranium mines such as Cave Hills, whose runoff goes into the water supply of Indian communities, and disputes over logging endangered forests, drilling by mining companies, and dumping of waste. Indian petroglyphs are being destroyed by tourists, Whiteface says, off-road 4WDs are savaging the landscape, and there is a proposal for a bar and concert venue for bikers next to the Bear Buttes prayer site.

In this context, Mount Rushmore is reviled as a symbol

of how non-Indians treat the Western landscape, summing up all that has gone wrong for Native Americans in the last 130 years—so much so that Whiteface wrote an editorial in the Rapid City newspaper against Gerard Baker accepting his appointment at the memorial.

"My personal feeling is that when they put a Native American person up there as superintendent, then it appears as if we approve of Mount Rushmore," she said. "His presence implies to the millions of tourists that we agree with that monstrosity!"

Her position is hard-line. "We want the United States to uphold its constitution," she says. "We want Lakota ownership of the Black Hills."

Does that mean that white people would all have to leave? I asked.

Whiteface smiled serenely. "That is up to us."

When I mentioned all this to Baker later, he laughed. "Hell, Indians are always telling me to blow up Mount Rushmore, but they know that's not going to happen." He naturally has to stay above the political fray. "The bottom line is, this place *was* stolen from the Lakota. That's a historical fact. But we're not here at Mount Rushmore just to talk about broken treaties or make people feel guilty. The Defenders have a cause, and it's a good cause. But we're here at Mount Rushmore to educate."

Baker is a towering, gregarious figure, with his hair in braids and a booming laugh that echoes through the National Park office. No stranger to being on the front line of historical debate, he served in the early 1990s as the first Native American superintendent of Little Bighorn Battlefield National Monument in Montana, where he received regular death threats from white pro-Custer fanatics. But when he was offered the position at Mount Rushmore in 2004, Baker admits that he felt torn.

"In my mind, I said yes to the job immediately," he recalls. "But as a Native American, I did take some time to think about it, and the challenges it might involve. I consulted my relatives and elders, and their response was overwhelmingly positive. I'm the first American Indian here; there are only two other Native American superintendents in the whole park system. This is a great opportunity to showcase Indian culture."

The new programs include expanded historical talks, films, interactive exhibits, and cultural events such as Lakota dances. Judy Olson, Chief of Interpretation at Mount Rushmore, said that there had been a strong positive response among Anglo visitors to the approach. "We have four white guys up there. They represent the first century and a half of U.S. history. But there's a larger story to talk about. Who were the people here in the Black Hills before that? To broaden the old themes, to bring in other cultures, to include the good and the bad of American history, is what people want and need."

"Fire in the hole! Fire in the hole! Fire in the hole!"

As the voice rang out, all eyes were fixed on a scarred mountainside, where the enormous head and torso of the Lakota Chief Crazy Horse can be clearly made out. Then a dynamite blast tore the silence, sending a shower of granite boulders thundering to earth: the charge, one of two or three every week in summer, barely made a dent in the neck of the warrior's horse.

Only fifteen miles from Mount Rushmore, a monolithic new image is emerging from the granite of the Black Hills: a 561-foot-high sculpture of the famous

Native American who defeated Custer at the Battle of Little Bighorn in 1876. Today, a visit to the site testifies to the growing interest in Native American themes: even as a work-in-progress, Crazy Horse is a must-see counterpart to Mount Rushmore, luring over 1 million visitors in 2005. (Rushmore lured 3 million).

Its scale is mind-boggling. When finished, the sculpture will be the largest carving in history—dwarfing such monuments as the Great Pyramid of Giza or the Statue of Liberty. In fact, the four presidents of Rushmore will fit inside Crazy Horse's eighty-three-foot-high head. It depicts Crazy Horse responding to a taunt from a white trader before his death in 1877. Asked what had become of his lands, he replied, "My lands lie where my dead lie buried." He was bayoneted in a scuffle with soldiers soon afterwards.

This new monument was conceived in the late 1930s by Chief Henry Standing Bear of the Brulé band of Lakota, who, as Mount Rushmore neared completion, wrote that he wanted to show the world that "the red man has great heroes, too." The chief invited a Boston sculptor, Korczak Ziolkowski, to undertake a sculpture of Crazy Horse. Ziolkowski was a muscular figure with movie star looks, a prizewinner for sculpture in the 1939 World Fair and veteran of Omaha Beach; in 1948, he leased a vast chunk of the Black Hills and started work, declaring "Every man has his mountain—I'm carving mine!" In the late 1970s, Ziolkowski was still carving—and he had become a local fixture with a huge white beard and broad-rimmed hat like a latter-day Walt Whitman, laboring away with his wife Ruth and brood of ten children at his side.

Perhaps mindful of Borglum's years of wrangling with bureaucrats, Ziolkowski refused to let the U.S.

government become involved in the project, twice refusing $10 million grants of federal aid. Instead, he funded the project with private donations and the contributions of visitors. When Ziolkowski died in 1982, the sculpture was only a vague outline; many locals assumed it would be abandoned.

But Ziolkowski's family rallied to continue work on the mountain. In 1998, Crazy Horse's completed face was unveiled, creating the sort of publicity that Borglum had enjoyed in 1930, when his first finished image, of Washington, was revealed: overnight, a chimerical project was given a distinct reality for the public, bringing streams of enthusiastic tourists, all evidently eager to learn more about Indian history. At Crazy Horse, the momentum has led to the opening of a cathedral-like Visitor's Center in 2000, with a museum, Native American cultural center, and cinema. Crazy Horse is now squarely on the Black Hills sightseeing circuit, although it has still maintained its down home, family feel—perhaps because seven of Ziolkowski's ten children still work full-time on the site, and twenty-eight of his grandchildren are seasonal waiters in the restaurant.

Although carving is proceeding on the twenty-two-story high horse's head, nobody in the family will discuss when the monolith might be finished. "There's no way to estimate," smiled Ruth, Korczak Ziolkowski's widow, now in her mid-seventies, when we met over a lunch of Indian tacos. "It would be nothing but a wild guess anyway. We're not trying to be difficult. We just don't know! Korczak always said it wasn't important when it was finished." Today, the Crazy Horse workers are using tools that would have been science fiction to Borglum's men at Mount Rushmore: ground-penetrating radar, electronic detonators, precision explosives, and 3,272-degree Fahrenheit torches to polish the granite.

"Only in America could a man carve a mountain," Ziolkowski once declared—a sentiment that has not won over the Defenders of the Black Hills. In fact, they're not fans of this monument either. To Charmaine Whiteface, the fact that the sculpture involves an image of a revered Lakota leader does not make it less of an environmental or spiritual violation than Mount Rushmore. Work should simply stop on Crazy Horse, she said. "Let nature reclaim the mountain!"

❧ ❧ ❧

The need for perpetual motion has always been Tony Perrottet's most obvious personality disorder and his travel stories have been widely anthologized. He is the author of four books, including Napoleon's Privates: 2500 Years of History Unzipped, Off the Deep End: Travels in Forgotten Frontiers, Pagan Holiday: On the Trail of Ancient Roman Tourists, *and* The Naked Olympics: The True Story of the Greek Games. *He is also a regular television guest on the History Channel, where he has spoken about everything from the Crusades to the birth of disco.*

❧ ❧ ❧

The Tides of Burano

Traditions come and go.

THERE EXISTS AN INHERENT SORROW IN THE ITALIAN culture—the kind that drives you toward theatrical hand motions, delicate flicks of the tongue, and designer fashion instead of prescription drugs. It is grief channeled in its most artistic form. Were it not for Italians' emotional fragility, there would have been no Renaissance, opera, or Versace.

You pick up on these things when you're half-naked and stranded at sea. Somewhere during the forty-minute ferry ride between Venice and Burano our *vaporetto* sputters to a float. Marco, our captain, is busy slashing his hands to conduct an orchestrated overture in Venetian curses, turning to blame any inanimate objects he can find for his luck: the sky, his dead cell phone, the steering wheel, the sky again. He interrupts this opus just long enough to mention that he forgot to add gas before we left. As he peels off his shirt and reclines against the life preservers, he says all we can do now is wait for help, and work on our tans.

Of the thirty-two islands sprinkled throughout the Venetian Lagoon, Burano is one of the few—along with its better-known phonetic twin, Murano—to have distinguished itself from Venice's wake. Its rows of squat, pastel houses reflecting in the island's four canals (actually making it an archipelago) only came to be the subject of poetic rapture centuries after the four-thousand-person fishing enclave established itself as one of the world's leaders in lace production. Yet fate isn't to thank for this unlikely distinction, but a beautiful Italian girl without access to anti-depressants.

The Romans who fled the mainland for fear of the Goths were left with few options. While Burano's location in a pocket of the Adriatic is far-flung enough that no land-flung spear could reach it, the island itself is best measured from end to end in human steps. Because fishing was the island's only sustainable industry, the male Buranelli spent much of the year at sea, leaving the female Buranelle at home to repair their husbands' nets and anxiously await their return.

According to legend, one such sixteenth-century Buranella awoke each morning clutching the only tangible memory her young lover had given her: a piece of algae. He promised he would return before the ephemeral being died, and she passed each day shedding heartbroken tears, waiting for him on the dock. In her grief, she took a needle and began to stitch the algae's design into her father's fishing net to preserve it. Her love eventually did return to the dock, but only months after the algae had died. In this romantic marriage of fact and fable, the lace of Burano was born.

Marco only offers me half of the smile-wink combo he extends to three blond coeds as I descend from the *vaporetto* to Burano's dock. His rectangular mirror, formerly used as a bronzing enhancer, had doubled as an S.O.S. flare to lure another *vaporetto's* attention with a series of well-aimed reflections. He then looped rope around the bows and sterns of the two matching boats close enough together to stand straddling the middle, and we arrived in Burano as tugged, Siamese twins.

I opt for the usual tourist itinerary and load my camera before winding through Burano's rows of vibrant homes, divided by canals and arched bridges. Though humble in size, each house is baked in a coat of warm tones with white trim, following a precise sequence that, when presented together, becomes a testament to civic beauty and a varied palette. The color scheme originated in the sixteenth century and is maintained so closely that any resident who wishes to repaint his home must appeal to the local government which will specify the permitted shades for each lot. In effect, the island is the essence of Italy on a 0.21-square-kilometer scale: seemingly random charm springing from hundreds of years of meticulous detail mixed with bureaucracy.

Despite Burano's proximity to its theme-parked neighbor, the island remains much as it always has: a self-reliant fishing village. Its diminutive size has helped sustain its culture. The island's few thousand residents are so densely packed that it cannot physically accommodate a significant tourist industry, let alone a high school (teenagers have to commute by ferry to Venice). The trickle of day-trippers is relatively new to the Buranelli who haven't learned to treat tourists with the same insolence exhibited in other parts of the Lagoon. There are no gondoliers prepared to bellow opera lyrics for tips. Nor do waiters line canals to reassure those with backpacks or cameras that their *trattorias* offer spaghetti and pizza in fluent English. Instead, I am left alone to absorb the island's serenity and am welcomed in a morphed dialect of Italian and elongated consonants that would leave Dante scratching his head.

As other lonesome Buranelle soon shifted their focus from fishing nets to lace production, a unique style emerged from the Lagoon known as the "Burano Air Stitch." Trademarked by a fine needlepoint pattern embroidered entirely by hand with delicate oval motifs at the base of the design, the lace's international demand soared, extending throughout Europe's most privileged clientele—including Louis XIV who, at his coronation, asked for a "bed of white hair" to conceal his bed of no hair.

But when the Venetian Republic fell in 1797, Burano's lace industry fell with it. Without their reputable ally's sponsorship to facilitate international trade, the elderly Buranelle who continued to practice the craft did so only for pleasure. And as they themselves neared extinction, so did the secret of the Air Stitch.

By 1872 the practice of lace in Burano had vanished, and a frigid winter covered the lagoon in ice, crippling the island's fishing industry and threatening its survival. In a desperate attempt to revive the island's economy, a primary school teacher convinced an eighty-year-old Buranella to disclose the tightly guarded secrets of the Air Stitch. The teacher opened a school of apprenticeship to reintroduce the lost art of lacemaking to the island's young women, eventually training over seven hundred apprentices by the turn of the twentieth century. As international orders revived, the Buranelle not only saved the island's population, but reestablished the quaint fishing settlement as the unlikely benchmark of worldwide lace production—once again stitching beauty from sorrow.

I reach for my camera when I am hit by a wafting draft of lemon and pepper. The aroma lures my nose over a bridge, my feet following. On the far side of the canal I come upon a woman bent over an open coal stove fanning three decapitated fish with the bottom of a broom. Her head is wrapped in a scarf that does its best to keep its long, haphazardly dyed contents from the smoke. She turns, showing a profile that reveals considerable age before shooting a round of vowels and a smile into a violet house a few feet away. Rotating slowly at the neck, she greets me with the same congenial grin. I match her smile, and try to match her vowels.

"*Che tipo di pesce è quello?*" I ask, curious about the type of fish I'm smelling.

"*Cefalo,*" she beams, exposing a set of natural teeth that belie her age.

We're onto each other. My crimson sunburn and Reef sandals advertise my foreign passport well before my accent can. But I understand her perfectly. She's not from Burano either. Curiosity leads her to upturn a washing basin, and offer me a seat.

After a year in Italy, I have found that when you first reveal you are American, many Italians react in one of two

distinct ways: while Italian youth often see America as a
nation of corporations, capitalism, and control, they will
acknowledge the merit of *Scarface*, Michael Jordan, and
rap music, and their interest gives way to interviews. Yet,
many older Italians remember the America from years
past. Americans are not only liberators, but descendants
of Italians themselves—either by way of Ellis Island, or at
least Columbus—and are met with genuine affection.

The broom gains momentum as the woman fans the
cefalo excitedly. She's never been to America, but her
friends Enzo Pisano and Paola Lazzarino have. And,
it's possible her second cousin, Annamaria, has too. She
turns toward the violet house again to announce to the
other side of a striped curtain hanging from the doorway
that they have a visitor from America.

When I ask what brought her to Burano, she proudly
states that she is actually Buranella, born and raised, but
that any lingering traces of the island's dialect have been
left in nearby Maestre, were she has lived for the past
forty-five years. She points the broom toward the violet
house and leans over the stove, speaking from a cloud of
fish and coal. She was born in the kitchen, just like her
mother was. I'm interrupted before I can even respond,
as she follows with something far more unexpected.
"*Mamma, è pronto il cefalo.*"

Mamma?

Just then a woman pushes through the striped curtain
holding a watering jug. She feels for the wall before
emptying the jug evenly onto two batches of potted pe-
rennials hanging from windowsills on opposite sides of
the door. Her thick, hoary hair is coiled with a bobbin
and glows in the June sun, contrasting with a plain blue
dress that hovers around her shins. She is blind.

"*Ecco l'americano, Mamma,*" the daughter calls.

Mamma's response is in dialect and unfamiliar to me. The daughter translates with her standard smile into standard Italian. "Go make a ninety-year-old woman happy."

I meet Mamma's extended hand with delicacy, which she returns with a firm grip. She releases me only to pass her fingers across my forehead, nose, and three-days worth of razor neglect. She again states something in doubled-consonants, and her daughter explains that she finds my face "sweet."

Mamma's five-foot frame stands upright with shoulders back, displaying a silent dignity. Her olive features are preserved in the kind of deep, creased frames that come from living on a wind-swept island for nine centuries. She exudes a certain lucidity, even as she stares at me from behind a cataract glaze. While I need her daughter to decipher much of her dialect, Mamma bridges the gap between us fluently. She instructs her daughter to take the *cefalo* inside as she grabs my arm and leads me toward the house. I suppose I'm staying for lunch.

Without thinking, I ease into the American ritual of "courteous" questioning when presented with an offer of accommodation, which translates into "ungraciousness" in Italian culture: "Are you sure I won't be imposing? Will I disturb you? Do you really think there's enough food for—" I am interrupted at the curtain by Mamma who turns toward the questions, raising her voice and her hand in protest. For the first time, I understand her clearly. "Of course there is! I caught three fish, didn't I?"

The curtain is pushed aside, illuminating a substantial wooden table separating a refinished kitchen from a larger living room. Tiles cover a spotless floor and a hint of potpourri sweeps away any lingering dirt Mamma couldn't find with a broom. A suffering Christ is tacked to the walls in various poses and a black and white television broadcasts Mass from the Vatican in a soothing German accent. Mamma eases her way forward, towing me by the wrist to the back wall where a jigsaw puzzle of white patterns hangs, softening the dark oak. As I approach, the designs seem to expand from their frames, presenting astonishing three-dimensionality and detailed texture. I am drawn to a man stitched from lace who returns my stare from behind an 18x11-inch frame. He is handsomely rendered in his old age, and his downcast eyes and thick moustache weighing down his top lip present a hauntingly pained fatigue. At the base of the oval motif, *"Il Pescatore"* is written—"The Fisherman." Mamma tells me it was her husband.

I press my curiosity and receive translated answers from the daughter who stands a few steps away garnishing the *cefalo* with parsley and butter. Everything I see hung on the wall was stitched, point-by-point, by Mamma's hands. She is one of the last remaining Buranella to have produced the Air Stitch before Burano's lace industry deteriorated. As a child, she attended the local trade school and was chosen to be the personal apprentice of a *Cencia*—one of the great embroiderers—before teaching at the school herself until it closed in 1972. The school has since transformed into the Museum and School of Lacemaking and Burano lace exists today as a mere framed artifact for display.

As I move to inspect another piece, Mamma moves with me. A series of bridges shoot out from behind one another, taking the viewer on a deep, stitched tour of Venetian canals. A gondolier is portrayed in impossibly

tight points under the second bridge, using the wooden
masts that line the canals to moor. Mamma asks me what
I see. I tell her, as best I can. She then asks me if I like it
and presses her fingers to my cheek just in time to feel
me smile.

When the daughter calls us to the table, Mamma
disappears down a flight of steps. She reemerges with
a clear jug of red wine. The daughter explains that her
brother made the wine and had given it to Mamma
when he last visited, and that she had been saving it for
a long time.

Mamma leads me to a single bed in a corner by the
television. An unfinished warping of a woman crouching over stitching a piece of lace lies next to the pillow. I
recognize the design from a finished version hanging on
the wall and ask her who has been working on it. She
responds with a raised voice and furrowed eyebrows,
"*Ma chi altro?*" tapping two fingers to her chest. I look
to the daughter in utter confusion, and ask Mamma,
in so many words, how exactly a ninety-year-old blind
woman stitches lace. The daughter explains that, after
seventy-five years of practice, her mother can reproduce
all the patterns by memory. Mamma's hands are still
as agile as they ever were. Since cancer stole her husband and cataracts stole her sight, she often passes her
days stitching lace as a way to ignore her solitude. The
unfinished image is a self-portrait. The daughter then
reminds us that the *cefalo* are getting cold.

The Mass remains on during grace. Mamma sits close
to me and I ask her why the lace school closed on the
island. She responds by asking me how I like the fish
before wiping my mouth with her napkin. She eventually replies that the younger girls didn't have the same

patience as her generation did. They found lace too time consuming and didn't understand the importance and culture of the Air Stitch. As machines started replacing hands, and competition from third-world markets increased, the Air Stitch has been mass-produced in faux facsimiles. Fewer and fewer Buranelle continued the trade, until it virtually died out. The few embroiderers on the island who still know the Air Stitch create the patterns, like she does, as a hobby, and most of the lace for sale by the docks is either machine-woven or imported.

She dissects the *cefalo* like a surgeon, stripping each piece of smoked, white flesh from the spine cleanly before delegating it neatly to the side of her plate with her knife. She asks me if I'm putting the meat on bread or not. There is a correct answer, but I don't know which it is. I tell her I'm not using the bread. She blames her daughter for this oversight and scoops her *cefalo's* remains onto my plate.

After her daughter clears the plates, Mamma shows me her most cherished pieces. She explains the work behind each Air Stitch's evolution in great detail: from its birth as a drawing on paper, maturing into a warped design, and finishing as an ironed collection of points. Each pattern captures its subject with such dramatic delicacy and detail—be it the Last Supper, a Greek Goddess, or her son—that its soul seems to jump from the lace's points and land on my skin in goose bumps.

The Mass finished hours ago. I'm almost hungry again. I check the kitchen clock and suddenly realize that the last *vaporetto* leaves Burano in five minutes. How do you say goodbye to a ninety-year-old woman who has confided

in you her life's work? I apologize profusely, but confess
I must go. Four minutes. Mamma passes her hand over
my face again, telling me I remind her of her son. Her
misty eyes show a tear before her daughter confesses
that her mother gets very emotional. Three minutes.
I explain that there is no way I could ever repay their
hospitality. I am on the other side of the curtain when
Mamma offers me a piece of lace. She insists that I take it
to remember her and that, when I return, I can give her
something from my home, far, far away. Two minutes.
I am speechless. I can only offer Mamma a final kiss
on the cheek and a whisper of gratitude. I leave for the
docks, unable to accept her offer, or promise a return—
knowing that some things really are ephemeral.

❧ ❧ ❧

*Eliot Stein graduated from Emory University with a dual-degree
in Italian studies and journalism and left for Rome the next
morning. He has studied sociolinguistics at the University of
Siena, hosted an Italian-language radio show, and led tour groups
throughout Italy. He currently lives in Sardinia where he teaches
English and is a contributing editor for* The American *magazine.
His writing has appeared in* Creative Loafing, Budget Travel,
*and in weekly e-mails home to his grandmother. She thought he
should have taken the lace.*

❦ ❦ ❦

The Secret of the World Sleeps in a Calabash

There are still "more things in heaven and earth than are dreamt of in your philosophy."

IN A TAXI SPEEDING WILDLY INTO TAR-BLACK NIGHT, THE car's headlights met the blindness of dust stirred and scattered. The famous wind known as the Harmattan was blowing angrily over the Sahel of Niger, carrying its fury south and leaving a veil of dust over the desert's ever-expanding domain.

Earlier, as I had entered the taxi, the other passengers looked away, quiet in their own pensiveness. As the car began to move, the older, heavier woman beside me crossed herself and murmured a prayer, while the Muslim cattle herder to my right balanced a walking stick on his knee, and let his prayer beads slip purposefully through his fingers. My eyes peered into the darkness looking for signs of the bandits I'd so often been warned about, yet I was unsure if my neighbors prayed in fear of these bandits or...something else.

As night falls in Benin, the dead are said to stir, to walk among us in shadows where they are less visible. The language of the dead moves in circles. They have surprisingly little to say, these entities. Only their attachment to life and our attachment to them move them forward, quietly into the night.

Because night had already fallen, the taxi was not terribly crowded. Rather than the usual four people packed together in the back seat in an assortment of intertwined limbs, shifted hip bones, and baggage, we were only three. This arrangement allowed me just enough room to spread my legs a few inches apart and rest the full width of my back onto the seat, giving a semblance of comfort. I had just fallen asleep only to be awakened by the taxi's sudden loss of inertia—we were stopped at a checkpoint. The driver begrudgingly exited the taxi to pay the customary bribe to local authorities while the other passengers in the car muttered about corruption. When we slipped back onto the narrow strip of concrete which passes as a national highway, the headlights reflected a white wall: fog. *No*, I reminded myself, *dust*.

As we rushed through a landscape we couldn't see, a man suddenly appeared in the middle of the road facing the opposite direction. He was immediately identifiable as what villagers call a *fou*, a crazy person. His hair, unkempt and long, formed makeshift dreadlocks down his back. To my alarm, the driver did not slow down as we hurtled towards the *fou*. Taxis do not slow in the night. It could be a trap. If we stopped, bandits might descend on our vessel in an instant. The driver accelerated in a slow-motion moment that stretched back and forth with the elasticity of a rubber band.

The *fou* turned towards us and the whites of his eyes reflected in the glare of our headlights. Then, just as suddenly as he had appeared, he was gone.

I turned and looked out the back window, but there was nothing. The night, the dust had enclosed the event in its fold. The taxi driver gripped the wheel tightly. The woman next to me crossed herself again, dropped her head, and prayed. The man to my right continued praying, grasping his beads with renewed intensity. I waited for someone to acknowledge the apparition so I could confirm to myself that it was real, but no one said a word.

During my time in Benin, it was this silence in the presence of something that could not be spoken that defined voodoo. True, there were macabre voodoo ceremonies where locals danced, played drums, and invited spirits to possess them. There, they would perform superhuman feats: I saw a man run a screwdriver into his eye socket and move it around the circumference of his eyeball without harming himself in the slightest. Another man swallowed gasoline and blew fire. Another lay on the ground and held a mortar on his chest while others beat cassava into powder with wooden pestles. Despite the enormous pressure on his chest, he never so much as grimaced.

There were also healing ceremonies performed by local traditional doctors. One such ceremony involved exchanging the life of a chicken for the life of a man. I watched as a man suffering from an unknown wasting illness held a chicken while the healer chanted a song in which he asked the chicken to give up its life for the life of the man. And indeed, the chicken slowly went limp in the hands of the condemned right before my eyes.

Yet such outward manifestations of the mystery always seemed premeditated, awkward, and full of unfulfilled expectation. Conversations with voodoo priests and healers were circumlocutions around some central point upon which I could never quite focus. When I asked a voodoo chief of the Adja, an ethnic group who migrated from Nigeria to Benin, whether or not he had ever heard of zombification, he told me, "Of course I have. We invented it and our ancestors took it with them to Haiti." He said that he knew how to raise the dead, make a man a mental slave, and, with a menacing grin, he added, "You aren't the first Westerner to come here looking for a recipe."

Surprised, I replied, "I'm not a scientist," while imagining executives from Eli Lilly rolling through the tiny village waving dollar bills and bohemian Harvard botanists trekking through the surrounding forest with elderly medicine men. "I'm just interested in voodoo," I said as he took a shot of *sodabi*, a local palm wine that hits the palate like a dose of rubbing alcohol.

Unaffected by the drink's momentum, he replied with the same enigmatic smile, "A person like you should be careful with such an interest."

A person like me found it impossible to be careful with such an interest. Long accustomed to the linear tocking of an Enlightenment clock, my mind swam in stories of the living dead and the cursed living. Somehow, issues of life and death, mortality and immortality were jiggled loose as time passed over me like an invisible tidal wave in West Africa. I watched people die only to hear them resurrected in the walking dead folklore of my neighbors. I ignored neighbors' warnings not to leave my house (even for the latrine) in the "spirit hours" between two and three A.M. I would dismiss these warnings as superstition only to find myself frozen in my footsteps by a sudden draft of cold air that mysteriously arrived every time I passed the village cemetery. I heard rumors of an evil sorcerer appearing in the dreams of children only to carry them away to the underworld. While my Western mind initially categorized such reports as traditional explanations for infant mortality, reason squiggled underneath my gaze and the presence of ill intention seemed to hover like the endless midday heat.

In the lush undergrowth of a village in southern Benin, the possibility of malicious unseen forces rustled each time the wind blew. At night in Grand Popo, the darkness was thick and impenetrable. The only light came from the cooking fires of women preparing *pate noir* (a corn-based mush) with gumbo sauce. Between these flickers, the scent of fried fish hung in the heavy air along with salt from the ocean. It was in these primordial forests that voodoo was born centuries ago, alongside man. And it was here that my friend Cimion invited us down a narrow path to his home in the forest, away from the village.

Cimion made his living collecting shells and driftwood from the beach, assembling them into necklaces, and selling them to the wives of French diplomats at a resort that none of the locals could afford. When I first met Cimion, he was living in the remains of an abandoned building near the highway which ran from east to west connecting Benin to Nigeria on one side and Togo

on the other. Cimion sat on the dirt floor in the corner
of the room assembling shells with fishing line. Between
us, tin cans lay in the sand waiting to be used as drinking
cups. A yellowing picture of Bob Marley lay underneath
a rock to keep it from blowing away. When I asked
what he was making, Cimion responded in the vaguest
way, never once referring to the necklace. His narrative
seemed to bob up and down like the fishermen's boats
out on the water of his native village. His voice rose and
fell like someone telling a story, but the words were like
fishing nets with gaping holes; the meaning continually
fell through. I found myself listening to him, unable to
follow the story, but enjoying the cadence of his shy,
stumbling words.

The next time I visited Grand Popo, Cimion invited
me and two friends to come and see the house he had
recently constructed with his bare hands. His friend
Levy, an extroverted and gregarious man from Côte
d'Ivoire, accompanied us and acted as an interpreter
even as we all spoke the same language. Cimion's rolling, nonsensical stories became clear through his friend.
As the five of us began our walk down the narrow dirt
path, we heard drumming and singing coming from a
nearby family compound. The frenzied pitch of their
song seemed to unsettle our friends who hurried us past
the house while looking in the opposite direction. We
had not gone much farther when we encountered the
remains of a village.

"What's this?" I asked Levy.

"Grand Popo," he said.

"But, we left Grand Popo back there."

Through Levy, Cimion explained that this village
was deserted when Benin gained its independence and

the president encouraged his people to move out of the bush and closer to the highway in order to promote commerce. Ever obedient, the people moved to the shore next to the highway artery connecting Benin to the outside world. They left behind a series of huts that quickly disintegrated into walls, sad remnants of former homes. A cemetery lay to the side of the path, stirring with energy in the eerie emptiness of abandonment.

We spent that night next to a fire in front of the home that Cimion had built with parts of the forest. Cimion built the house with the trunks of young, flexible palm trees that were easy to bend and mold into a frame. The roof was then twined together with gigantic fronds from the jungle's limitless foliage. We sipped citronella tea boiled over the fire and chatted in low, muffled voices. The lake just beyond Cimion's house was home to hippos that floated sleepily through the dark. The thick stillness of night surrounded our quiet stronghold of firelight, but when mosquitoes found the only source of life in near proximity, they invaded our refuge in droves. It was time to go back, but everyone hesitated. Cimion was the first to betray his uneasiness about walking back to the village.

"I don't have a flashlight," he stammered quickly, "Why don't you all just stay the night?"

With malaria and a sleepless night looming ahead, we all began to feel trapped by the darkness around us, the edges of which seemed to move inward, towards us, trying to penetrate us, already moving through us.

Sensing our uneasiness about spending the night in the forest, Levy jumped in and said, "Cimion, you know this forest. You lead. I will follow behind to make sure no one gets lost."

Thus, moving through the darkness, we began what felt like a mythological journey led by Hermes into the underworld. I could see nothing, not even my hand a foot away from my face. The air, though empty, was charged with energy. When I tried to focus my attention on my feet moving step by step over the ground, I became distracted by what seemed to be people moving towards us. As I was accustomed to doing on narrow paths in Benin, I moved aside to let the people pass. Though I saw no one, the physical energy of a human being passed by each time I moved aside. I heard their footsteps, imagined their form in the night, but there was no one except our line of five people pushing through the jungle towards town.

Then, as though welcoming us, lightning bugs illuminated the undergrowth in response to the sound of our footsteps. A feeling of warmth and safety rushed over me. The village came into view.

As we exited the forest, the tension of the walk melted away. We hugged and said our goodbyes, all of us with the same question on our lips.

"Did you...?"

We all nodded but were unable to say more. In Benin, there was always something unnamable, unutterable, and this something seemed to be the critical element of every story.

Each year, the *revenant* (the returned) take to the streets of southern Benin. They are said to be the spirits of the dead and their solemn but volatile dispositions seem to epitomize death. Their costumes are elaborate—often appearing to be the robes of royalty. Velvety, shiny fabrics adorn the backs of the *revenant* as they walk slowly through the crowded streets of Cotonou, Benin's largest city. Their boxlike shape and construction make them reminiscent of the king in a deck of cards except darker, more inscrutable. Their faces are veiled and often they have horns stolen from the crown of a dead bull. They are given a wide berth as they walk streets crowded with women carrying fruit for sale, motorcycles zipping around broken-down cars, goats whining their way through smog and dust, and chickens rushing down dirt paths.

Normally, all these people and objects push close together to form a nearly coherent whole out of the chaos, but when the *revenant* walk by, the area around them opens and a strange silence ensues. Cars don't honk and people stop haggling over the price of a pineapple to turn and gaze. Women whisper to their children, "Never touch a *revenant*. If you do, you will die." If an unruly child or drunk approaches the *revenant,* he is likely to be beaten with a whip—or worse.

Friends might whisper to one another, "Go touch him. See what happens." Of course, no one does. That indescribable feeling, that not-quite-knowing falls upon the stunned crowd. Men whisper amongst themselves as someone moves closer to the *revenant* in an attempt to take a photograph. They smack their lips in disapproval and speak of how they've seen people attacked for such an act. A woman from behind chips in that anyone that she's ever known to photograph the *revenant* either breaks their cameras or gets blurred images returned from their film.

As I climb onto the back of a taxi-moto in the middle of the crowd, the driver turns to me and says, "He's a *revenant*."

"I know," I reply.

"Oh, so you know voodoo then?"

"A little," I answer. "And you?"

"A little," he agrees with a smile.

It's that smile again. I've lived in Benin for two years, but his smile comes as a revelation. I used to think it was a smile that hid something, a smile indicating that someone did not want to share his or her secret with an outsider. But, now I realize that it is a smile of complicity. It says, "None of us understands these things." And, I am finally O.K. with that.

At the New Year's celebration, the voodoo chief sits above those who have come for their ancestors' blessings in the New Year. His bright Kente-cloth robe is composed of bright blues and yellows interspersed with golden threads and voodoo symbols. His hat, made of the same fabric, forms a shimmering cube above his head, red and yellow yarns of thread hanging from the hat's center. Completing the attire are the beads: greens, pinks, oranges, whites, blues, long square beads interrupted by circular ones. They are supplemented with shells collected from the ocean, feathers, cowry shells, and sachets of red and white filled with magical curative powers. Around his neck, the powers of the ocean and the air. In his presence, the promise of possibility: to see into the future, to auger human suffering, to reflect and reframe the worries of man.

On this day, practitioners of voodoo dress in white to welcome the winter solstice, which is New Year's Day in their tradition. From this day forward, each twenty-four-hour cycle will bring a little more light, a little more hope. Those long melancholy African sunsets that expand indefinitely in all directions will now be prolonged in space and time, impregnating the evenings with relief after another long day's heat.

The chief speaks to the assembled and they respond, sit and stand in bewildering intervals, chant to the gods of air, earth, and water. The chief asks that everyone present be rid of evil in the coming year—free of illness and accidents. His blessings are answered by priests and priestesses who fall to all fours and pound in rhythm, bang drums, and shake rattles. The practitioners move in jaunting movements that remain somehow graceful, ecstatic. They are moving with the cosmos, with the physics of existence, with the sun opening its light once again for the earth. We, the assembled, wait, believe that our presence is our blessing, that the year ahead is one of promise and light.

When the chief begins to speak again, I notice the calabash at his feet. The man next to me explains that the secret of voodoo is said to reside within that calabash. At important voodoo rites, the calabash sits at the feet of the voodoo chief, never to be opened. Unlike the Western tradition where the contents of a box tempted Pandora to release evil into the world, the voodooists seem content to leave the calabash closed. If opened, it could destroy mystery and the world would implode into a desolate wasteland devoid of human curiosity or faith.

This secret is the essence, that which cannot be spoken but felt in the uncomfortable glances of strangers, the tense behavior of friends hiking through a voodoo forest, the inexplicable silence in a taxi moving through an impossible fog, the ambiguous smile of a taxi-moto driver, and the nebulous ecstasy of ritual. Whatever the secret is, it does not belong to us. It cannot be released into the world. It cannot be written down.

⪜ ⪜ ⪜

In addition to traveling the world with a question mark in hand, Kelley Calvert enjoys the usual joys life has to offer: coffee in the morning, long, leisurely weekends, live music, and intelligent conversation. When not trying to decide which word goes where, she teaches others about deciding which word goes where. She currently resides in the Sunshine State in a town that is usually foggy...but next to the ocean nonetheless.

❧ ❧ ❧

Once That Gun Goes Off

Mob rule can be loads of fun.

THE ONLY REALLY BAD LUCK I EXPERIENCED DURING A solo tromp across the remotely parched, but lovely, continent of Australia, was that one of my running shoes had gone missing. This bummed me out immensely. After sucking dust in the Outback for several months, I planned to be in Sydney for just one day before heading back to the States, and the only thing I craved, believe it or not, was a long coastal run—a soothingly simple means of appreciating what the place had to offer without giving in to the candy-coated tourism that surrounded every large metropolis. Of course, with time running out, I now found myself with other, less exciting, options: I could take a harbor cruise to Manly Beach; play tourist and visit a museum; shop away my last five dollars on cheap Australian souvenirs made in China; get drunk.

After moments of contemplating the thick morning sunshine trickling in slivers through the blinds, I decided to start walking. Sydney is a massive place, with an international smorgasbord of humans, surely I would find something exciting and memorable to do.

In my room at The Big, a trendy hostel in the downtown area, I quickly packed up every item I couldn't afford to have someone borrow indefinitely: my camera, journal, and money. I put these into a moderately sized daypack and then stashed my passport and credit card into a personal safe kept at the front desk. Though it was August in Australia, and the tail end of winter, the sun was already intense. I remember well that first strike of light as I walked out the front door. I was a believer in karma, and fate, and that things always fell into place as they should.

My walk should have been simply that, a walk, but as I neared Hyde Park—the central park complete with large shady areas, flower gardens, a giant chessboard, and a towering, stoic water fountain—I spotted huge red banners splashed across every light post. Almost immediately I felt a shift in the air. Something was about to happen.

Then I saw the people.

Hordes of people. There were hundreds, thousands. Looking at the red banners more closely, my heart nailed an extra beat: THE 25TH ANNUAL CITY TO SURF 14 KM RACE. That was today. A run was taking place today, perhaps the "largest run Sydney ever sees." Stunned, I looked at the amassing crowd. People were coming from everywhere, from behind trees, getting dumped out of slowly moving cars, running down the streets towards some general area which I could only guess was the starting line. Then a voice boomed over a massive speaker system—a low voice, deep, and loaded with enthusiasm.

"RUNNERS! ARE YOU READY?" A loud cheer erupted from the crowd—it sounded like a freight train. Then I heard the opening snap of the gun.

We started to run, or rather, everyone else started moving around me. Astonished and even a bit afraid, I realized that I'd wandered right into the last wave of runners, easily 15,000 people. I was jostled along as old people in tight running outfits pushed at my back. Then children began to pass me. My fierce sense of competition finally kicked in and I began to run-walk faster. "Maybe just until we get away from the park?" I thought.

After all, I couldn't realistically run the entire race. Fourteen kilometers equates to about nine miles. Even though I considered myself fairly fit, I still hadn't run more than two or three miles at a time in the last six weeks. And, had I known I'd be running in public, I would've dressed more appropriately. I was sporting sandals (yes, sandals), heavy brown sweatpants I scavenged from some throwaway bin, and a ratty t-shirt with a hole in the back. Along with this horrible attire I was also carrying at least twenty pounds of crap, albeit valuable crap, on my back.

Less than a kilometer into it the whole horde of us began to head up a huge hill along Williamson Street. The pavement was thick with runners—elbow to elbow a good mile ahead of me and a mile behind. Some were running along the medians or jumping over benches, anything to break away from the suffocating strength of the crowd. Panting, I found myself turning to one of the many runners pushing up against my shoulder.

"Where does this race end up anyway?" I asked an elderly, bearded man (with a body like Popeye). It seemed like a good question. The man gave me a quick once-over and a smirk developed in his eyes as he took in my outfit, but then his look turned to one of pity. Australians feel sorry for Americans anyway. Actually, Australians feel sorry for anyone not born in Australia. The place is hard to beat.

"Bondi Beach," he said easily, as if he wasn't running at all, and then he too left me in his dust. I was starting to get some heat on my left heel. A blister would surely finish any chance of reaching the beach assuming, of course, that I was going to keep running.

But just the utterance of those magic words elicited new energy in me. *Bondi Beach.* One of Australia's most famous sand traps. I'd heard plenty of stories. I knew about the buff surfer dudes with the yellow-and-red striped caps, and the shark siren—sounded when someone sees a fin rip through the surface—and the relentless swell of waves. I'd seen pictures of the famous mural wall stretching the length of the beach and strikingly decorated with graffiti art, the scantily clad bodies, gorgeous water, hot sun, and breathtaking sunsets. If I didn't take advantage of such a random opportunity to see the place I might never have another chance.

Three kilometers later I was barefoot in the grass alongside the main street, and running hard. One sandal had flown off during a series of quick maneuvers around a patch of scattered stones, a slow runner, and someone's loose, and very excited, dog. I grabbed the sandal off the ground, flipped off the other, and hit the grass. I was obviously out of place, and obviously American, but I was also gaining what I gathered to be a few fans. One small boy maybe eleven years old took off both of his shoes and joined me on the grass for a few hundred meters. And I wasn't the only tourist running. There were others in jeans and dress shoes. There were men and women in business suits, their Sunday best, with cameras, briefcases, and small children in their arms. Young adrenaline-charged teenage boys roared along for a kilometer or so trying to impress the ladies before getting winded and disappearing. One man ran with wheeled luggage and sported the biggest grin this side of the sun.

Five kilometers along and people were working overtime, sweating and shining in the sun, shirts unbuttoned all the way, ties wrapped around their heads. An entire men's rugby squad ran by in pink underwear. And in between every obvious "touron" the thousands upon thousands of numbered runners stormed the streets. *Sixty thousand* runners in all and that number only reflected the ones who had registered.

The subtle curves and deep blue of Double Bay suddenly appeared to my left, the impossibly clear water chock full of very large and luxurious sailboats. Then came Rose Bay, even clearer and deeper, and as I ran past admiring some of the distant ships out at sea, music began pumping from the storefronts. The morning was still fresh at 9 A.M. and shop owners stood outside with their arms raised in encouragement. We soaked it up, every one of us. We ran through historic neighborhoods; neighborhoods with cobblestone sidewalks and old money; neighborhoods that opened up late and closed early so that families could still enjoy one another.

The race itself—the fans, the sudden camaraderie— was completely unexpected and while I was thrilled at the spectacle around me, I was beginning to struggle.

I wondered how much farther I'd be able to make it. Failure, of some kind, seemed decidedly imminent as I approached the bottom of what the runners had so appropriately christened "Heartbreak Hill."

"You've got to be shitting me," I whispered under my breath, perhaps too loudly.

"Yyyyep," a large, hard-breathing Aussie gasped behind me, right before he began to walk. I noticed many runners slowing to a walk for the famous hill. I wasn't sure of the length or elevation of it and it didn't much matter. What mattered was that every step hurt and every step seemed to make me appear farther from the top. I put my head down and tried to think about something else as I fought the twinge of lactic acid coursing through my calves. I simply *couldn't* stop, even though at moments I desperately wished I'd never started. There was some kind of inexplicable union created among people that were suffering together, as if I was bonded with every anguished, grimacing face, even though I would never see any of them again.

Halfway up the hill a woman passed out. The heat of the morning was growing and the pace was picking up. Aware that heat exhaustion was a very real occurrence during any endurance event I knew that my heavy sweatpants weren't going to cut it. Though it would have been nice to take them off and throw them to the breeze, I decided to forgo any chance of receiving an indecent exposure ticket (I did get one, once, for trying to spell my name in the snow during Oktoberfest in Lacrosse, Wisconsin) and instead asked around the sidelines for a pair of scissors. A few knife swipes later and I had a very homely pair of shorts excitedly flapping in the breeze.

The running became easier as we continued towards Old South Head Road and people began to spread out. "We all want the simple life," one t-shirt stated in front of me and another declared, "Stop starting." Yet another read, "Blood donations do work." Runners could be heard yelling out encouragement to one another, offering a hand, water, snacks to those stopped or slowed. I tossed my ratty t-shirt into a rubbish bin as I passed the ten-kilometer mark, my hot skin relishing the breeze as I continued on in my sports bra.

For the first time in a long time I felt complete and total liberation. The sun pounded down, the streets roared. Horns were blown, race numbers shouted, high school cheerleaders screamed (much to the delight of middle-aged running men), and the classic—"Eye of the Tiger"—boomed and hit me in the legs like a jackhammer. Waves of energy flushed through the crowd, but we were also beginning to mentally relax, settling into the groove. *This* was why we ran, this mental relaxation, this settling down—not for all of the painful steps that came before or after.

And then, maybe out of sheer pity (but I like to think not), I received invitations to post-race barbeques, beach-side barbeques, next weekend barbeques, two offers to join running groups, and even a job offer. Suddenly I wasn't alone but surrounded by a massive community of almost-friends and fools, discovering the intricacies and the streets of a city the most glorious way imaginable.

To set foot in Australia is to experience a land so biologically backwards and environmentally ruthless that one can't help but be surprised to find the people to be the exact opposite. There are an obscene number of gorgeous people in Australia. They are the ones that go out of their way simply because it is in their nature to do so. They somehow affect you; they somehow change your life. They *are* around us, all of the time, but we cannot see them because we are too busy, or too distracted. They open doors, offer umbrellas, buy you lunch because they know you are just a poor backpacker in a foreign land. I never seem to notice them unless I am on my own and very far from home but they are everywhere, and they were stuffing the city streets that day.

Soon enough, and thankfully so, I sensed the end approaching. The last three kilometers of the race were quite thrilling as the road moved closer to the ocean. The crowd and runners grew thick again, almost morphing into a tangle of people with one indistinguishable from the next. Salsa bands played music on rooftops, drum circles pounded out beats, and the storefronts were still loyally adding their own individuality by blaring whatever tunes were handy out onto the sidewalks. The last kilometer leading up to Bondi, the streets were on fire.

And then, finally, in one dramatic moment, I turned a corner and beheld the huge expanse of the Pacific Ocean swallowing up the edges of the land. Bondi Beach was exactly what I thought it would be. Hundreds, soon to be thousands, of people pushed with a last effort of exhaustion towards the tumbling silver line of the tide. I crossed the finish line and followed the others—the bleeding, the limping—straightaway to the medic tent. It seemed that whoever wasn't behind us stripped to barely naked and raged into the surf.

"How did you go?" a voice asked from above. I was bent over, busily assessing both feet, briefly fearing that I might never walk again. When I looked up I saw an older woman, her face flushed, a grin dancing across her weathered cheeks. I had to laugh at the orange peels stuck in her teeth. She was already busy peeling another.

"Oh, one hour, fifty," I said. And then, as if to justify the time (though it was still faster than half of the runners), I added, "But I ran barefoot and had my camera in my hand the entire time." I wanted to add the distraction of the ocean as a culprit in slowing my pace as well but she was off before I could say another word. A few minutes later I could still faintly hear her, bent over another runner, "How did you go?"

I accepted the invitation to the beachside barbeque. The couple I befriended during the race (we became friendly after one of them snotted into the wind and it landed on my shorts) guided me over to a huge green tent erected in the sand. Most of the people assembled under it looked delirious, sunburned, and happy enough to be still. We passed tales and beers around a circle. They were generous with me, with their time, with their food and laughter and in talking to them and reveling in the sun and downright awe of the moment, I realized that maybe I could be gorgeous, too.

The day had been so unexpected in its beauty and inspiration that I even decided to walk back to the hostel, even though I knew I was at least fourteen kilometers from The Big and downtown (wherever downtown was). Back home I used the mountains in Colorado as an external compass to help me figure out where I was, or in which direction I was facing—mountains to the west, plains to the east. But it wasn't that simple on the beach, gazing out at the ocean and knowing that Sydney was a healthy mess of harbors and crooked streets.

I took off in the direction of my best guess—barefoot, bleeding, in a sports bra and torn shorts. I stopped at the first person I saw (who laughed), and then the second, looking for directions that matched. Everyone told me something different while at the same time agreeing that, "It's a bit of a walk." Then I met an elderly woman who admitted she wished she were "young enough and strong enough to make a walk like that again."

I do *more* when I travel with others. More dinners, more planned itineraries. More. But more doesn't necessarily mean better. If I'd been traveling with someone else we would have had a plan for our only day in Sydney. We probably would have hit the manicured trails of the botanical gardens, went to lunch. *Boring.* But I would have, without a doubt, missed the opportunity to run the streets with the masses, alone but at the same time engulfed by the energy of a community that until that moment was mostly foreign to me. I even would have missed out on personally exploring nearly thirty kilometers of the city on foot. The entire day further confirmed the vast amount of potential that lay in the unexpected, and the paradox of traveling alone—it can be the most lonesome, the most terrifying, and sometimes the most exhilarating.

I stayed awake awhile that night, sore as hell and buzzed off cheap boxed wine that a dorm-mate had offered up. I wondered if I would notice the gorgeous people in America when I went back. I wondered what it would feel like to run the City to Surf with proper shoes and a sprig of preparation. I wondered what it would be like to travel somewhere else, a place where women weren't even allowed to run. Would the wind feel as fresh? As safe?

Sometimes I have to laugh at the wondrous fact that some of the simplest things in this life are still free. I can run in any direction, fast or slow, fighting the ache in my bones or giving in to the wind if I want to. Like life, there are the huge hills that we swear at, our hearts beating hard and thick in our chests. Then we coast, always keeping an eye on the horizon, always wondering about the next steep bit, the next scenic turn, the next easy breath. Nothing matters once that gun goes off, the world changes and so do I, but I continue to move, knowing there will always be something new ahead, something curiously unfamiliar, something, or someone, to keep me going.

꙳ ꙳ ꙳

Laura Katers coexists with three bikes and one cat and lives in Fort Collins, Colorado, where she is a teacher, and an editor and photographer for Matter Journal. *She enjoys writing about, and exploring, the intricate ways in which all of life is connected.*

PAUL B. HERTNEKY

❧ ❧ ❧

The Village *Kazani*

"The secret of Crete is deep. He who sets foot
on the island feels a strange strength penetrating
through his veins and his soul widens."
—Nikos Kazantzakis

GO AHEAD AND THINK OF GREEK ISLANDS AS SUN-
baked bliss in blue and white. I had fallen into
the habit of hopping to Athens and hightailing to Crete,
accustomed to the way the light, the culture, and a
skin-tight friend brightened my year. But from the first
hours I spent there, the mysteries lurking in the shadows
beckoned me in a way the beaches never could. For all
of Crete's sunshine, its heart resides in darkness, in its
starlit nights, its mountain shadows, and chilly caves.
And so, I finally managed to schedule my tenth trip to
coincide with the onset of winter, to join Persephone on
her annual excursion into the nether regions.

162

As the reputed birthplace of Zeus and Western culture, Crete lived up to its standing in a sneaky way for
me. For years, my wife, Robbie, and I had bypassed
Knossos and other common sights, rushing straight into
the arms of Debb Papadinoff, our long-time friend.
Stylish, intriguing, erudite, worldly, and determined,
she sashays past the ordinary, and misses nothing in life.
Following her lead, we entered the island through a
back door, where I felt the people and the landscape of
Crete had thrown a gauntlet at my feet, challenging me
to look deeper.

I found *tsikoudia* (tsick-oo-thee-ah), the Cretan version of grappa, served to me within three hours of first
setting foot there, to embody that gauntlet. Distilled
from must, the skins and stems leftover from winemak-
ing, it flows inexpensively from the mountain villages.
Cretans drink it throughout the night, and some drink
it throughout the day. A clear and assertive brandy,
flavored with ingredients close at hand—herbs, com-
monly thyme, or citrus rinds—my first sip knocked my
head back and goaded me toward a masochistic second,
but from then on, it has given me pure pleasure. Debb
described the ritual of its making, throughout the long
nights in one of the darkest times of year, as a portal into
the Cretan underworld.

She convinced John, an old acquaintance and fellow
American expatriate, to take us to a *kazani*, one of the
legal stills that are licensed for a day or however long
it takes for a villager to distill a supply of wine must.
John balked, uninterested in acting as a tour guide. The
Brooklyn native bolted to Crete in the 1970s, a time when
American kids flocked to the island. He stayed, working
as a carpenter, learning the language and slowly gaining

entry into the culture. Debb must have guaranteed that our behavior wouldn't get him shunned for eternity, because he agreed. But he insisted that we go to a *kazani* in a nearby village, not his own. And he warned us that he would keep the location secret.

We took a bus to Drapanias, not far from Hania, and stepped into the main intersection, dusty and blinding in mid-afternoon. Debb knew the way, up the hill, past the armory, the church, and down a lane hemmed in by ruined walls and rusty chicken wire. We found John's house and he greeted us with a spatula in hand, and then introduced us to his teenage daughters who were giggling and teasing each other at the kitchen table. Giorgina, an electrifying Greek woman who was raised in South Africa, worked to clear the mess John left behind as he commandeered an angry wok full of boiling oil and a pile of sliced potatoes. The half-English, half-American, Crete-residing daughters waited for daddy's chips.

With baking mittens on both hands, John kept loading the table with fortifications for the night ahead, spinach and cheese pies, chips, sausages, pork chops, frittata. By cooking madly, he escaped questions about what we should expect. His own hospitality overtook him as the evening wore on, and his long arms and workman's hands flew as he slowly revealed stories of living more than thirty years in Crete.

Long after dark, John guided his rickety hatchback through labyrinthine olive groves, the headlights sweeping over their pale leaves, a low forest without landmarks. I could have driven forever without finding my way through.

He had wedged his daughter into the boot where she braced herself against a half-barrel of wine must that had been left to ferment for three months. He lashed the barrel to the hatch, giving it some stability, but the skinny kid held it upright through every switchback.

A full moon greeted us as we entered a village along a hillside, and pulled over to a house on the side of the road. Beneath its terrace, halfway down the hill, in a pit big enough to hold twice their number, a dozen Cretans tended the *kazani* fire. An outside corner of the dug-out room accommodated a fireplace with an opening five feet square. All eyes rose to us as John untied the barrel and hoisted his daughter, hollering in Greek, "I brought dancing girls!"

In the middle of the pit, a bare light bulb hung over a plastic dining table, where men and women sat and drank, smoked, and nibbled on the most basic and rustic foods in the Cretan diet. Chestnuts fall at this time of year, and they were roasting in hot coals. The fire consumed vine cuttings and heavy, twisted olive limbs that were at least a century old.

At ground level above us, a copper kettle boiled over the fire, its tapered beak running off to the side. The man in charge, in his fifties, covered with grime and wearing shorts and flip-flops, stood over the kettle, the whites of his bulging eyes and his teeth picking up the moonlight. His left hand, missing two fingers, cleaved to the handle of a pitchfork. He spoke no English, and issued orders to a younger man who had signed on to help him through the night.

When the time came to refill the kettle, the men worked a story above those of us in the pit. After lifting the lid, they used the pitchforks to scoop out steaming, sodden loads of stems, skins, and sheaves of thyme placed in the bottom of the kettle to prevent scorching.

These dark burly men, swaddled in steam against the night, the inferno crackling and blistering in my face, smoke hugging the dirt and rock walls, and the fresh *tsikoudia*, all tugged me toward an underworld.

From the lid of the kettle, a coil of copper tubing spiraled down the length of an oil drum filled with cold water, allowing the brew to cool and condense. At the bottom of the coil, from a crooked spout, dribbled the clear object of our desire. That's where the women took over. Below the spout, they had set a pail with a sheet of muslin stretched over it, and a clean kitchen sponge to serve as a filter. They checked specific gravity, monitoring the alcohol content.

The warm brew cast its spell on the gathering. John picked chestnuts out of the coals with his bare hands, juggling them to the table. Neighbors and relatives showed up with cheese pies, more chestnuts, and freshly gathered snails, abundant as winter settles in. A cousin set a skillet of olive oil and garlic near the fire, and then dropped in handfuls of snails. When they were done, we splashed them with vinegar and set upon them with jackknives and sharp sticks, yanking out and slurping down the mollusks.

Any time I'm raising toasts with greasy fingers, I'm a happy man. Feasts like this seem to erupt right out of the earth in Crete. But this time, we had fallen in, as if the ground had given way under us, fallen into the islanders' legendary generosity and spontaneity.

The *tsikoudia* supply will last a year. They will drink it daily, sometimes judiciously, sometimes not. Home distillation of the last pressing takes place all over the Mediterranean, but it had its roots here, in Minoan life. Archaeologists have scraped residue of *tsikoudia* off pottery that's 3,000 years old. The myth of Hades could well have been spun under its influence. Scholars describe *tsikoudia*-soaked bacchanals that gave rise to *mantinades*, ancient Cretan verses:

> The love I love is one
> My God is one as well
> with others I simply laugh and play
> just to flirt with hell.

We caught the scent of *kazani* fires while driving along the road from Rethymno, on the north coast, to Spili, a mountain village tucked into the island's spine. It was late Sunday afternoon, and Debb's friend, Niko, had invited us to join him at the village *kazani*.

Smiling as he entered the inn, Niko hugged and kissed the mother and son who ran the place. We could tell that he had already been to the *kazani* (in fact, he'd been to two) for several hours. He told us the whole village had been there, but the party had moved to a café just a short walk away.

We followed him to a backstreet where a couple of cafés faced a bluff, along which is a linear fountain, a trough catching spring water that gushes from the mouths of nineteen lion heads, sculpted into the mountainside. The café hummed with young villagers, laughing and flirting, several sheets to the wind. When the waiter finished setting down our ouzo, he crossed the street to the lions' heads, and returned with tumblers filled with frigid water. For all the drinking of spirits and wine, Cretans love their water most. It plunges from the snowy peaks through deep gorges, gushing from subterranean springs and into ubiquitous glass pitchers, always sweating against the heat, as if the transition from dark and cold to bright and warm had been too sudden.

Niko led us out of the village, a half-hour walk along a ridge, to a roadside taverna where another family stood to welcome him. The father and sons set us a table with extra chairs (for themselves, eventually) on the terrace, overlooking a black chasm, miles wide, dotted with lights twinkling from shepherds' cabins. I scoured the valley for *kazani* fires.

The sons brought snails, in heaps, and pitchers of the family's wine, and grilled rabbit, and octopus, more water, more wine, and sliced beets atop their greens anointed with oil and vinegar. Everything on that table had pushed its way through earth or waves, through careful hands and stretches of time. We made a mess of shells and dishes, but we had the taverna and the family to ourselves. Finally stanching the flow of wine, we hit the road, over which a late harvest moon had risen, lighting our way. Niko wove down the ridge, singing and dancing, still determined to take us to the *kazani*.

A quarter mile outside the village, we heard singing and clapping. As we stumbled into town, it grew louder, until there we were, passing an old-style *kafeneion*, flooded with cruel fluorescent light, decorated with fading political posters and Spartan tables, laid open to the street through glass sliders. Usually, places like this buzz quietly with soft voices and the clicking of worry beads or dominoes echoing off the terrazzo floors. But that night, all hell had broken loose. Young men in leather jackets sat at a long table with old men in cardigans and one young village woman, all singing at the top of their lungs, thumping tables, and drinking *tsikoudia*. Seeing Niko, they called to us and leapt up to add another table.

They gave me a chair on the end, with my back against an old sewing machine. The proprietor plunked down carafes of *tsikoudia* and dishes of sliced cucumbers, peanuts, feta, olives, and tomatoes. Debb sat next to me, translating lyrics, and Robbie sat at her other arm, wearing a full blown smile for all to see.

The din of laughter, singing, clapping, and banging shot glasses on tables cut my tethers to past or future, throwing all my senses into the scene before me. Suddenly, I heard Debb say to Robbie: "He wants you to open your hand." One of the men reached a closed hand over the table. The women stretched out their palms, and the man said nothing while he dribbled pomegranate seeds into their hands. The sight of those ruby-red seeds struck me, knowing, as did everyone in the room, that they expressed a profound welcome and a certain kind of claiming that goes back to Persephone. By consuming them, she bound herself to return to Hades every winter. Debb pitched them into her mouth and Robbie ate them one by one, to the applause of the giver and the old man sitting next to her.

One man gathered himself, got up to leave, and was caught by the coat and thrown right back into his chair. He shrugged and put his hat back on the table. A stout guy in his thirties barely entered when a seated friend grabbed him around the middle. Half tackled, he bent over his friend's shoulder, snatched a glass off the table, drank it down, and smashed the glass on the floor, causing an even greater uproar.

He laughed and squeezed in next to me. Throwing money on the table, he poured *tsikoudia* for everyone within reach. At the other end, the young village woman, to the delight of her husband, hopped onto the tables in mid-step of a dance with another man. We dove to clear tottering carafes and glasses, as the man's work boots pounded out the beat and the woman egged him on. Raised hands, a kind of clapping wave, surrounded the dancers, who barely kept their balance. But at our end, the wild man next to me grabbed the corner and shook the tables under them. Somehow, they stayed on their feet until they could get back on the floor, yanking the old men near them into their dance.

Such exuberance often leads to plate-smashing, but in this place, metal ashtrays and a few shot glasses were swept to the feet of the dancers, then a pomegranate went spinning to the center of the circle and they all danced around it. An elderly man lost his balance and fell backwards, into a pile of chairs, but found safety. So the song spontaneously shifted to a cheerful wail about a shepherd who had broken his back. The wild man next to me poured me another drink, and toasted. Cretans never take a sip from a fresh glass without saluting, "*Yamas.*" In broken English, he yelled "What is your name?"

"Pavlos," I said. (It appears I had gone native.)

He straightened his back, narrowed his eyes, touched his sternum with his fingertips and said, "You are Pavlos?" Uh-oh, I thought, as his friends took notice. Then he shouted, "I am Pavlos!" Surprised, we toasted again, drank again, and this time he took my glass and lobbed it onto the floor near the dancers. He beckoned Christos, who once lived in Chicago, and who immediately said, "All his life, living in this village, he has never met another Pavlos." Just when I thought I had reached the limit of camaraderie, I suddenly had eight more comrades.

He asked why I wasn't dancing. And I asked why he wasn't. But before Christos translated that question, he explained that Pavlos had worked for the power company and had lost both legs, below the knees, to a high voltage wire. Insisting on hearing my question, though, Pavlos laughed and supplied an answer: "The last time I danced, it was the ultimate; I danced with lightning."

Anything could happen. Fear was a joke, injury a song, and death a dance partner. Half in the bag and surrounded by madmen and my favorite women, I privately saluted the mysteries remaining in my own life.

I dreamt that night of the Cretan winter sky, blinding sun eclipsed by angry clouds. To the sun, I closed my eyes and sought darkness, and with the clouds overhead, I searched for rays of light. In dark corners of Crete, where the secrets are stashed, Zorba can be found, celebrating "that this life and the next are but one."

On the way out of town in the morning, I spotted Pavlos by his smoke shop, leaning on an ice cream chest. I got out to say goodbye. He hugged me hard. "I love you," he said. A lump clenched in my throat. I avoid empty promises, but blurted, "We'll come back." And, like the king of the underworld himself, he waved and said, "I know you will."

The pomegranate seeds and Persephone prove that we have no choice but to go back and forth, from dark to light. With *tsikoudia* as my ferryman, I found a vibrant spirit in an underworld, one that dispels fear and defines life. Cretan author Nikos Kazantzakis defines enlightenment as "gazing with undimmed eyes upon all darkness."

Crete won't look the same again. Nothing does. Shadows fall on me like mercy. I toast the demons at my table. The unknown cools my quest for answers. And if I go into the darkness, I must be ready to find secrets that defy the light of understanding, that lie there for reasons all their own.

❧ ❧ ❧

Paul B. Hertneky writes about food, culture, travel, the environment, and industry. His stories and essays appear in magazines, newspapers, and anthologies, and can be heard on National Public Radio and Public Radio International. A journeyman cook, most recently at the MacDowell Colony for artists, he lives in Hancock, New Hampshire, teaches writing at Antioch University New England, and travels frequently to Crete.

❧ ❧ ❧

Baguio City Angels

Worlds collide in a Philippine highland town, and the
AMA would not approve.

I SAY YES, I'LL GO WITH YOU TO THE PHILIPPINES. YES.
I'm talking to my best friend. She's been my sister
since she cried in my arms in her garden; since I had to
tell her that her real sister was dead.

When her Filipina sister died, and she lived in a shack
down an island road with no telephone, we were neighbors. I lived in the next valley. And I was sent to tell her.
I drove up my dirt road and followed the ruts and twists
of hers, rehearsing terrible words. It wouldn't be possible to say it right.

Her painted lavender house seemed empty. No children around. The goats were staring. I found her alone
in her garden, her back to me. She was pulling weeds,
humming *Blackbird singin' in the dead of night...* just off

key. I came to her stiffly, stopped, circled her with my useless arms. She turned in them and tensed.

Babe, I whispered as evenly as I could, *I'm supposed to tell you, your sister Christine died this morning.* Her eyes went black. *They called. They just called, they asked me to come get you.* I nodded my head like a toy clock, to let her know it was true. She coiled, like a cobra about to rise in full fury. Then she yowled in my embrace, her waist-length hair whipped in every direction. *My sister, my sister, my baby sister!* Her Filipina ancestors filled her lungs and her wail sang and caterwauled with all of them. *My baby sister, my sister, my baby sister.* We rocked and held in the dirt of her garden, crushing new sprouts and purple vegetables. Suddenly she raised her face and looked fully into mine, wild, agonized, transcendent. Absolutely aware, absolutely tiny, absolutely void.

You be my sister now.

Her gaze was black lava, and golden. The sunrise flared blood behind her. Again, soft as dirt, *You be my sister now.* And then she planted her head in my lap to cry. On the other side of the sky, the moon descended in her own wet garden.

We don't see each other much these years. She's a midwife, and busy, and exhausted. Now I say—*Yes, Babe. We'll go.*

We're flying—with the Baguio City angels—to what end of what world?

Manila might be one room in hell. A television special stood on its hind paws at twilight. Those, the Filipino streets I'd only seen on *60 Minutes*, stagnant rivers through the spine. Those, the begging babies in the traffic, the alleys of homeless, heaven-less, hope turned to tin-rust and rag. Every night some eight-year-old skinny child surely sniffing glue too near our bus window to bear fearing. The Victory Bus Line climbs its well-known unfenced overhang to Baguio City. Different and the same. Colder. Pines. The trees of a sky's conscience. Down there, Satan's streets, perhaps. Here—a little air.

She's a born-again Filipina these days, my best friend from the island, looking for a home. I'm a born-again Catholic, on the road. Maybe it's the roar of the incense, the humility of the crowd, or the silence of the light, in some nearby cathedral. In fact, I like churches. All churches. My father, a Jew, politely gave up converting me once he'd passed away. Before that, it was a fight. He demanded I learn the Old Testament in exchange for my childhood ballet lessons. As soon as I could, I kneeled in churches. Maybe it's a past life sort of a thing.

So we take a journey that might change our lives. Why not, when the world might end and we really need to be prepared spiritually? Why not, when the world might continue forever, and we might need to know a little or a lot more? It will only take a minute, in the grand scheme of things.

So I make a Christmas bargain. I'll invite us to the Philippines, where there are births happening, more strange than baby Jesus'. And faith, the size of bleeding mountains. I'm speaking of us two born-agains of different stripes. My longtime friend the midwife, and me the poet-vagabond. I'll take us to her mother's village for two weeks. She has always wanted to go to Baguio. It's Christmas.

I know the feeling. I had to go to see the Russian birch trees one winter, and to feel my grandmother's pale-eyed ghost kiss my head in the person of a rotund babushka at the feet of an Orthodox icon; she then poured her chill holy water on my head as well. I know the feeling. The midwife wants to touch the back of her hand to the forehead of every old person in Baguio City, the way her cousins do when they say goodnight to their father. We smile conspiratorially at each other's sentimentalities. What are best friends for?

She wants to see her spiritual home in the Philippines, to find her own mother's street, between her not-yet tattooed hands. In the outdoor market, she buys a red woven *tapis* and its matching belt from a very old Igarot. She wants the one the wrinkled woman is wearing! Not the ones in the basket. She insists, demands, cajoles until there's a laughing and a play-act dancing, and a little indecency as the old lady strips to her slip with her busy black tattooed fingers, to please the born-again Filipina who wants roots, who wants to come home. She needs cloth that smells like her grandmother.

What is the end…of what world? How long is a minute, in the grand scheme of things? She's a midwife. Her hands are itching to catch another, and another baby, to make birth gentle and world-safe in a Christmas season when *60 Minutes* has told it all or most of it, and we cannot bear to believe it. I like her idealism. She believes in birth. My own heart is itching for Christmas, I who do not do it very well. I itch for a kiss from God. We want to know more. We stretch the hour to a bubble-gum membrane, and hide in the inner pink, with terror and laughter. What else to do, three days before Christmas, post millennium?

I know, go to a faith healer!

Her mother's sister, Auntie Babe, mentions him. And I seem to have hatched the idea myself somewhere on the way across the Pacific. The *Espiritus* "take" on holy miracles cajoles my heart into a little more faith. The inner chick in me is clucking, wishing to be of great faith. I want to see the mountain.

We agree to explore what is being born here, besides the obvious. The Baguio Auntie drives us to a vaguely run-down hotel painted in shades of pink, and there are two unsmiling Germans in the courtyard, one with a video, one with a green baseball cap, one is a doctor, his wife is there to be healed of breast cancer. There is a chipped, once brightly painted terra-cotta zoo, peopled with more muddy ducks, geese, and three barking deer, all lounging on cement, over the railing below us. Soon after 9:30 in the morning, Ramon Jun Labo, the once mayor of Baguio, now a globally reputed psychic healer, now married to a pencil-eyebrowed Russian blonde named Leeza, arrives in his chauffeured black Mercedes. I remember how to say hello in Russian, and I do. His wife lights up at the sound of her homeland. Then she remembers she's the wife of a famous Filipino healer, and she lowers her gaze.

There are still tin shacks on the hill slopes. There are too many Baguio blind men, crouched on near streets, and markets too dense to breathe in, too poor for tears, still people all over the world who need health and miracles. But we are in the hills and there is some sense of religion here, some sense of peace and waiting in me, in the even-tempered morning air. And how to be closer to Jesus than to offer our blood...to believe?

The scent of the miraculous is in our heartbeats, and roadside sunflowers so yellow they defy the ever-present dust.

The midwife and I wait for Labo. *Are you ready to do this?* she whispers to me as urgently as last rites. What else to do, two days before Christmas, in a post-millennium?

He emerges from a Mercedes, in a blue silk suit tailored for a rock star perhaps. Indeed, the slicked black hair of a Presley, the round face and lips of Liberace. And the eyes of a surprised and wise child. A man of confidence. Too slick, some would say. I ignore the packaging. I am mulling quietly, guided by a minute of truth that will seem to last.

Soon, his hands are at work. Blood spouting from beneath his gnarling fingers, from one of the now prone German's bellies, and the next one's left breast, more, from the leg of a man who has written ten books on the subject. Everyone may watch. I'm allowed to make some photographs. But the light is low.

Soon, he nods at me. *You want to come?* Soon, barefoot and humble as a maiden en route to the proverbial minotaur, I surrender my own belly and uterus and God alone knows what else, to a surge of very quiet faith. I am without question. I am certain as the simple morning. Trance, or truth, I am willingly involved, listening to the canned music, and at peace. What else to do, two days before Christmas, even after a millennium?

What is the problem? he asks as I close my eyes to the red glow of the plastic Jesus which I know is real as a Sistine Chapel at this very moment.

I have an infection which returns and returns, I speak to his boy-eyes, with child's faith. In a moment I am prone and being cleansed of all God wishes out of me, this I know, and God is watching, from not such a distance, this I know. In a long minute, a light tap on my right forearm urges me to rise to sitting and I am shown a mass of matter, gross to any eye, I am glad as hell to have out of me. *What do you do with the waste?* I remember to ask him, later.

Burn and bury, is the reassuring reply.

You should return one more time, he tells me matter of factly. *There was infection. It will all be gone.* I want it gone. I want it done. My ears focus on a tinny tape somewhere, playing a version of Jesus-music.

The midwife assures me as she helps me to dress, *That really did come out! I could see everything! And his hands were really in there! And he closed you up again without a stitch! And I know real blood when I see it, I'm a midwife!* Wordless, a little tired, a little holy, for hours to come, I think I may have been flying with the local angels for their long-breathed minutes.

I palm the little coral rosary I've brought, its skinny crucifix like a silver Giacometti in my tight right hand. I'm about to enter the faith healer's salon for the second time, and I'm more scared than yesterday. The midwife has whispered her doubts to me over breakfast. She doesn't like his Liberace looks. She wonders if he treats the poor for free. She hates the lace and plaster Jesuses with red lights glowing, that constitute his office and his chapel. I concur. The statuary is distinctly not Italian Renaissance but Spanish-influenced kitsch. But there's a hush in my heart that whispers—*Increase my faith, God, that's all I ask.* And if it's here on this bizarre stage set, let it be. Let me be born, and born, and born.

A pause at the open entry to Ramon Jun Labo's salon. Cross myself like a good Catholic child. What else can a woman dressed like all the rest in cotton panties and her black bra still on, do in the circumstances? The protocol says strip. The holy music has started again.

The Germans have already spouted their blood under his experienced fingers, and been healed, they say. The healers are donned in white coats and holy but work-manlike faces. The tape player has its own version of born-again *Espiritus* music and Jun Labo appears to have entered the trance I noted yesterday, his lips are moving, simultaneously praying and singing along with the music, sotto voce: a little theatre, a little inspiration. I rather like the sounds. I like Country Western when I drive my truck, too.

I lie again on his white sheeted table surrounded by the three men in white coats, clasping my little coral beads, and close my eyes, the better to feel, the better to pray—*Increase my faith, sweet Jesus, I'm a little scared this time, You know? Strengthen my faith.* I know that's what I'm doing here, whatever else it looks like.

The rest is silence, so Shakespeare once taught me.

I can feel the warm and liquid of what is surely my blood under his quickly moving hands. They enter my flesh, my psychic flesh, his real hands, my real flesh, his hands…which seem to have more pressure, seem to be digging deeper into my unimaginable innards than yesterday.

I hear a vague click. The photographer in me is still shockingly aware. Someone is making a picture of this. I shall make my own, later…soon. I remain in prayer, still and yet. I remain prone. I begin to wish that the process will be over very soon and that he will close me up very soon, but let me be healed! I believe that God has me in the right place at the right time and these are the right hands to do it, in a rundown pink hotel with it's own mini zoo of maybe attending angels, in Baguio, in the Philippines. It's almost too late in my life for mistakes. What else to believe, a day before Christmas, on the road to a little more purity and the ever present post-millennium?

"O Come All Ye Faithful" still brings a choke of tears to my voice, I never know why and it always does. So I kneel in a Baguio pew, and stand and sing and swallow the wafer with all the rest, forgetting what world I may or should belong to. It's Christmas morning, and my friend and I are in the cathedral where her mother was baptized. The crowded streets outside make me yearn for my poetic hermit-life…but I am a long minute away from that, and I stand out like a marquee. Blonde and wide hips, maneuvering the masses, with a smile for babies and beggars and a sudden obsession for photographing blind people, and healers. I sing, the traditional holiday carol, stuck like a wet cracker to my throat.

If once is good, and filled with un-answerables, why not observe a second, we reason. Besides, the midwife continues to make semi-ribald jokes about my experience with Labo, even as she blesses me for bringing her home. She just didn't like his costume, or his decor, or his fee, geared, I have admitted, for Western wallets. *What about the poor?* she demands. I protest, protect. For the next thirty-six hours, his child-face, I must call it, innocent and clean-eyed, continues to appear to my psychic inner screen, just slightly to the left. It is there as though to reassure me that, in spite of her humored denigration, this is the being who healed me.

She concurs. *He did. I know he did!* But she hates his style.

So, we'll go to another hill slope, this one with a river snaking through the steep gorge below, and banana trees hanging onto the dirt as those who come to be healed cling to their own faith. It's a double bargain…faith plus faith, this, we know.

So to Brother William Nagog, down the steps below the local police outpost. My best friend immediately likes the atmosphere better. The waiting room is jammed at 9 A.M., with all ages and variations of poor and Filipino, clutching their own wads of toilet tissue, to clean up, after.

She whispers that she might have the courage, this time. I nod, remembering my own. Her lungs are scorched from years of island fires; and the tensions of life and death in midwifery have accrued, all along her vertebrae.

The gray cement-walled room huddles beneath beams of a larger frame, under construction. There are open spaces where windows may eventually be made. People perch in them, the space is packed to overflowing. There's a wooden crucifix and pews where we are welcomed by shy smiles, a few giggles at our English. Sit, and move forward a space at a time, as each patient enters the room.

There. Over there. The small door opens and there is a beam-smiling pony-tailed man in a purple shirt and a blue apron. His hands are at work on an old man who is still wearing the old bandaging from a hospital operation for liver cancer, which did not work. He's prone on one of the two tables. Brother William jokes. Talks. Works. He may in fact be having fun this morning. The hands are again entering flesh, there is again the undeniable crimson of splattering blood, a plastic pail of water, and two attendants mopping up. He removes a small piece of matter that looks like a clot, and flips it onto the back of his own hand, and continues to work. He moves to the second table, excises a tumor from the bulged eye of a young woman, her little son, waiting, watching, in the doorway.

Why are you here? He looks up amiably at us newcomers. We admit a desire to observe. I ask if it would be permissible to photograph so others might see, might understand. He looks at me directly. *God sent you today. You are very close to God. Sure.* He returns to his business. Again, we're welcomed, and invited into the inner room: a small statue of Mother Mary, a donation basket, a painting of Jesus in the clouds, a clock, two tables cloaked in faint spatters of blood. A sincere and prayerful looking man dipping his hands into flesh as though it was cake batter with splashes of red. Sometimes he pauses, to concentrate, sometimes he keeps a running chatter.

Massage, the scent of coconut oil, a prevailing good humor as the good brother jokes with the smallest children, and the fearful, and the elderly, and the cancerous, and the twist-limbed, and the goitered, and the belly-ached. Each receives about the same. A few receive only a touch, but no blood. Most bleed. Almost all are first rapidly cloaked with a pale not totally clean sheet, which is just as quickly removed, and the healer's hands set to work. He answers our questions, our looks without words. It helps to see the appearance of what is wrong. I have a momentary thought of an imitation shroud of Turin; soon I'm again fascinated and non-judgmental of the next display of God's presence, the repeated births of faith and healing in a tiny basement room on a hill slope of Baguio.

My friend has finally screwed her courage to the sticking place, and she lies down to be worked upon. Surely, there are angels in the vicinity. I just don't know who is who and what is what. I make sure that my camera is working and there is a good flash, and make the photographs to attest to the un-testable. We are flying so fast, in another small room with the faithful. He pulls matter from her spine, and from her lungs and midriff. He says softly, *It was pre-cancerous.* She tells me later that it feels like warm needles as his hands go "in."

And what do you do with the waste? I remember to ask him, later.

Burn, and bury, is the now familiar reply.

So, what difference?

I had heard of mutterings and beliefs that there were frauds, but these were not. I have known those who follow the fads and crystals. I do not. I had heard of healers who hid tiny blades in their fingernails, but these did not. The man who had written ten books on the subject, called Licauco, bore a scar on his right shoulder from one of the "blade-frauds," yet he lay on Labo's table the day that I did, to be healed by a psychic surgeon. This one. I had heard of the debunkers, and the believers, and the old controversies, yet I was no personal ghost buster, and no ghost tester and haven't a scientific hat to wear, at this time in a life. I'm an aging poetical mystic. What I came to know in its simplicity was: here was a kind of collaborative trance, and a bargain in faith. What I came to know was what I and the camera I carried could see.

One...is showy and proud, sings along with a tape, has glass cases of his precious gifts, Russian eggs, Middle Eastern swords, was videoed by *20/20*, and the tape was verified and then canceled by pressure from the AMA, he says. This, the man of ten books and the German doctor corroborate. He speaks little, he delivers what seem like prepared and well-seasoned stories about himself, a child who didn't want to be a healer. He is neither distant nor friendly. He is experienced and busy, like many surgeons in the practical world. Yet a rarefied and "safe" space surrounds the plain table I lay down upon. He has been doing "this" for thirty years. He seems to be in charge of a going operation. There are usually large tours of foreigners, we are told. He will leave for Mexico, then Moscow, on the twenty-seventh. We have had an opportunity to be among a very few this time. It is easy to look...very closely. In adjacent cubicles there are younger assistants who would offer "psychic massage." I'm less trusting of them. I demur. Despite the presentation, my body is at peace following the healing. The German doctor tells us he was cured of blindness twenty years ago, he has returned with the "incurable" ever since. The rundown hotel with its apparently useless zoo and a healer who dresses in silk suits and designer pullovers, is unquestionably a place of miracles. This I know. Why? I know.

One...is humble and joking, and his basement room dispenses miracles to the poor and donating, but he has also traveled, also been invited to the scrutiny of the world. He will fortune-tell for the superstitious, crack an egg into a water glass to discern the evil that may attend an illness, tease the oldest into giggles, pause for explanations. My friend worries that he will become famous, and the poor will be bereft. I am content to leave the finger of fate to other hands than ours. Both serve God and the ill. Both have hands kissed by something inexplicable but known, dramatic, and holy. Labo says he was his mother's bad boy, and pretended, until he was knocked over by an apparition of Jesus, and a "calling." Brother William asks casually if we believe in reincarnation, then expounds that his grandfather was a healer, and his great grandmother was a healer, and he is the both of them, now, here. A small child, he could close his friends' wounds with a touch. Being a healer is not a peaceful life. This, he warns. He has a little more youth, a little more "man of the people" packaging. One day, massaging an old lady, his hands went "in," did what they needed to do, he pulled them out, and the wound shut. He had a calling he could not, did not want to turn back from.

The midwife still likes but one of the pair. Poet-vagabond-mystic, I find I like both. Baguio beauties, angels, in a short minute in a world with distortions, and darkness that has a hole in its lung...sometimes I believe I can hear it breathing, rattling, nearly dying.

A speaker of many languages, I pride myself on being the linguist, determined to look beyond the cos-tumes, or the languages, or even the miracles. Maybe a minute lasts forever. Maybe we can learn to fly around the birth of God, for Christmas. I do not know what costumes angels certainly wear. I determine to hear the simple equation: human plus a certain longing for God and health equals a journey to strange sides of the mountains. I have climbed a few, for this Christmas, near the end and the start of another century. I've made some photographs to prove to my nervous heart or doubtful eyes that what they know, they know, for a minute. What else to do, on a voyage to the Philippines with my friend the midwife, when so much must still be born, and a minute has no certain calculation, nor does the sound of near wings and wonders, in the smallest scheme of things?

I'm a psychological experiment in polarity...*beware the jub-jub bird...*

I know about faith. I've beheld the holy. The would-be miracles. The needy. What the hell must I find on the seventeenth-century wooden beamed third floor, back in my darling, glorified Paris? I feel a metaphorical psychic drill, turning in me, inside. A reaching through the whole globe, I who miss Parisian lights reflected in carnelian and amber, statues drowning in their Right Bank midnight when I'm somewhere else; a psychological experiment in polarities, I feel stretched by my chosen loci, and then splayed at an epicenter. Roaming and hungry sea turtle, ocean after ocean, I'm a traveler. Morning owls—or some ever present *bandersnatch*—present, as dualities.

(I hear later, of one addendum. I learn that Jun Labo was lured to Russia, to "perform" his faith healings as he had done numbers of times over the years; the Russian public was enamored of so-called faith healing. He was arrested, jailed in Moscow for three months, then released. He had been suddenly accused of fraud and practicing medicine without a license, a contradiction in terms, but so it was. Eventually, as suddenly, he was released and returned to his once brightly painted terra-cotta zoo, peopled with muddy ducks, geese, and three barking deer, waiting patients, all lounging on his pink cement.)

∼ ∼ ∼

Margo Berdeshevsky likes to quote Jean Cocteau: "Poets are liars who tell the truth." She is the author of But a Passage in Wilderness, *a book of poetry. She has been a recipient of the Robert H. Winner Award from the Poetry Society of America (selected by Marie Ponsot), four Pushcart Prize nominations, the Chelsea Poetry Award,* Kalliope's *Sue Saniel Elkind Award, places in the Pablo Neruda and Ann Stanford Awards (selected by Yusef Komunyakaa), and Border's Books/*Honolulu Magazine *Grand Prize for Fiction. Her work has appeared in many publications including* Agni, The Southern Review, New Letters, The Kenyon Review, Poetry International, Runes, Women's Studies Quarterly, *and more. Recent exhibitions of her "visual poems" were in Paris and in Hawaii. She is currently living in Paris.*

~ ~ ~

Why

In the highlands of Mexico's Michoacán state, one
traveler tells his story to another.

I T WAS THE BEGINNING OF THE RAINY SEASON, AND THE
sopping, summer clouds that shrouded the peaks
above the pueblo of Santa Fe de la Laguna vented cool
draughts of air, making the citrus trees in the courtyard
quiver. Sitting stiffly beside me, Mateo, a small, solidly-
built young man with soft brown eyes, a shy white smile,
and a nature enduringly sweet, projected an air of trepidation and resolve. We exchanged pleasantries for several
minutes and then fell silent, the moment for the inter-
view having arrived quite naturally. "¿*Listos?*" I asked,
turning to Mateo, "Are we ready?" Bracing himself, he
placed his elbows on his knees and leaned forward, clasping his hands together. "*Sí*," he assented, looking at the
floor between his feet and nodding his head.

"Mateo," I said, and he nodded his head once more, though he didn't look at me. "Mateo, I want to know your story, about how you crossed to the U.S. I'm interested in everything, everything you want to tell. *¿Esta bien?*"

"*Sí,*" he replied, as if to say, *of course.* "Well, at the beginning of May I left from here in the bus, from here to Sonoyta on the frontier. Then I took a taxi to the desert, that is, to get outside the town. There were fifty of us, and from there, we started to walk. And the coyotes, the ones who were taking us, had told us we were going to walk two hours until we reached 'the Line.' We were walking for an hour and we went up a hill, and then, going down, some thieves came out to us, three thieves with guns."

"Thieves!" I said.

"*Sí.* We were many, but without guns. Four women were with us, too, and well, the thieves scared them. For us, the men, just giving them the money was enough. But they wanted to rape the women. Well, that's what they said they would do if they didn't give the money to them. And that was when a young woman took out her deodorant. She had the money hiding in it. And since they had already roughed her up, she took out her deodorant and gave them the money.

"Then a thief told us to take out everything we had, even the loaves of bread we had brought to eat, to make sure no one was hiding money. I was carrying some money here, in the waistband of my pants, where the belt goes, here behind it. I had cut the waistband and I had put some money in there. But I was also carrying some in my billfold, so I told them that was all I had and they didn't search me. But the others who didn't have any money separated out, the thieves took everything from them, everything."

"They knew what they were doing," I observed.

"*Sí*," Mateo agreed, "My cousin, who has long, shaggy hair all the way down to here..." he moved his hand horizontally, palm up, across his lower chest... "they even took off that thing you tie your hair up with because they thought he had money there."

"What about the guides?" I asked, "Did they rob the guides, too?"

"No, not them. There was a ditch, and they had put us all in there, and the two coyotes were up above. They were not put in the ditch."

"Doesn't that sound suspicious?"

"Yes, yes, we thought they had contact. But, well, we didn't say anything to them."

When the thieves had left, Mateo and his group moved on, arriving at the border in the early evening.

"How did you cross?"

Mateo laughed, as if to say it wasn't hard. "There is a fence, but it's all broken. It doesn't work anymore. There's even a path there."

Having crossed into Arizona, the group walked through the desert until, just after dark, they came upon a track used by "*la Migra*...the Border Patrol," Mateo said. "Since we were all walking in a line, the coyote told us to cross the track stepping in the footsteps of the person in front so we wouldn't leave a trail. So we stepped in the same place, all of us. And the one who was last, he erased the footsteps."

Suddenly, out of the night a patrol vehicle emerged onto a nearby rise. Its headlights were off, but, as Mateo explained, "They carry...what are they called?...those infrared lenses."

"Do you think he saw you?" I asked.

"Yes, I think so. At that point, everybody ran the best way he could." The majority followed one of the coyotes, but Mateo and five of his comrades decided to follow the other one, who turned suddenly and hissed at them to "follow *him*, the other coyote, because he was *el mero mero*, the Boss!" Mateo laughed contemptuously.

The group fled in a bunch, crouching low, until they came to a tall thicket, whose height Mateo described with a hand raised high above his head. While the migrants waited, el Mero Mero said he was going to take a look around. "He left us! The patrol was over there, but the coyote ran the other way!" Mateo said with another laugh.

"What about the patrol?"

"Well, they don't go everywhere, *la Migra*. They stick to their trails, and this thicket was far from their trail."

The coyotes eventually returned together and reprimanded the group for breaking formation and fleeing. "'Why did you run?' they nagged. 'You were supposed to stay in a line. We'll let you know if we want you to run. You only run if *la Migra* turns on the floodlights and starts to chase you.'" Mateo chuckled, shaking his head, and observed that it was the coyotes who had run first. Everyone else had just followed *them*.

At that point, the guides called a twenty-minute break. Everyone was exhausted. "In, like, five minutes," Mateo said, "we started to snore. We didn't see anything then, no *migra*. We were all alone, except for the coyotes that were starting to howl in the distance." He smiled at the joke.

"After that we walked again, always walking. We only rested for five minutes here and there, when we would take the opportunity to eat something. But we never stopped. Just five minutes, and then chop-chop, off we would go again. Finally, at seven in the morning, el Mero Mero said we would rest for an hour. 'We only have five more hours left to walk,' he said. So we slept. But it was cold. Cold! In the *desert*!" Mateo shook his head in wonder, and then, after a thoughtful silence: "Very cold."

As the sun climbed, the coyotes roused the group and divided it into two lines of twenty-five. They were moving quickly through the mounting heat, scuttling from thicket to thicket as the vegetation thinned, when they heard the rap of two *cuatrimotos*, all-terrain quads, in the near distance. Hearts in their throats, the group broke from the brush and rabbited in the opposite direction. "Those who were fat, they couldn't run! They could only run a little bit!" Mateo laughed merrily, patting the small roll around his midriff.

The coyotes gathered the migrants together in a thicket and told them to sit down and be quiet. And then, as the quads moved closer and closer, the coyotes told the migrants to wait while they took a look around. Crouching low, one coyote crept away to the right and the other to the left. And then a loudspeaker shattered the desert silence.

"The Border Patrol, they told us not to move. And then one of the coyotes stood up over here and the other one stood up over there. And they just whistled to each other. And that was it. We never heard from them again."

For several seconds we contemplated the depth of such wickedness in silence. Finally, I asked, "What did you do?"

"We ran! All of us!"

"In different directions?"

"Uh-huh. And there were many of those *huizache*, those plants that have thorns. They scratched me all over."

Mateo took off after four of his comrades, but soon lost sight of them in the scrub. Scrambling among the thorny bushes, he stumbled into a shallow arroyo and threw himself down on his belly in the bottom of it, and as he pressed himself into the sand, a helicopter zoomed low overhead.

"The Border Patrol, they had called the helicopter in?" I asked.

"Yes, I believe so, because it came right away. At that point, everyone hid. In the ditch, I couldn't hide very well, but I stayed there without moving."

As the helicopter passed over a second time, Mateo sprinted from the arroyo and threw himself into a small thicket, pulling thorny branches down to conceal himself. He lay in the thicket for a long time, listening to the two quads working through the scrub and the helicopter as it repeatedly buzzed over. Sometimes, as the helicopter passed, Mateo said, he could see the pilots.

Mateo lay in the thicket until all was quiet, and then for a while longer before emerging.

"It must have been afternoon by then," I observed.

"No, it was just nine o'clock in the morning. Nine or ten. *Y este*, when I came out there was nobody there. Then *I* started whistling. Just like the coyotes!" He laughed nervously. "But there was nobody. I started to look around for footprints. I walked for about twenty minutes, this way and that way, and at last I *did* see footprints, footprints from four different shoes, so I ran to see if I could catch up with them. I realized that they

were running, because the steps were long. They would
go, and then they would hide, and then they would go
again. Later I saw that they were walking, but they
were far and I couldn't catch up. So I followed the footsteps for about an hour and a half, and then I heard the
moto..."

"Again."

"Uh-huh. I ran to hide, and I hid, and the *moto* passed
by with dust, but they didn't see me. It passed by. And
then I continued walking, like this among the thickets,
crouched down. Crouched I went," Mateo's voice rose
an octave, "and suddenly there was a dead body, just the
bones, and it was covered with a burlap sack. Or maybe
he was inside the sack. I don't know, because the burlap
sack was also disintegrating."

Cautiously, he approached the desiccated sack of bones
and flesh, from which a distressing scent emanated as it
melted into the desert soil. "A water bottle lay beside it,"
Mateo said. He glanced at me, seemingly anxious that I
should appreciate the gravity of the circumstances. "And
I only had a little water left, and the sun was beating
down. And I thought that, well, he didn't really need
the water bottle anymore, so I picked it up. But it was
empty. And then I understood why he was dead, the
body, and I panicked and ran."

He ran aimlessly until his alarm had exhausted itself
and his feet began to pain him. Removing his shoes, he
discovered plump blisters on his toes and heels, which
he pricked with a thorn from a nearby *huizache*. The
remoteness of the desert worried him. He didn't know
this land and it didn't know him. He was alone, lost,
torn between fear that the Border Patrol would find him
and that it wouldn't.

Then, in the far distance, he saw a water storage tower perched on steel girders poking up from the desert scrub. "And so I went in that direction because I thought there was a town there. And then I saw a row of electric poles. So I decided I'd better go toward them instead because there might be a road. I had started to hallucinate from heat and thirst. I had started to hallucinate that...I don't know...like, I heard noises. Like somebody spoke to me. I would turn around, but then there was nothing. I was only carrying a little water, and so I would not drink. I would only put a little water in to rinse my mouth. I was still far from the poles, but then I heard a motor, and that I did see. It was another Border Patrol. It was coming through the desert on a small trail. But at this point, *yo me había rajado*, I had already surrendered. So I said to myself, I don't care, pick me up."

Disoriented, dispirited and afraid, Mateo sat down in the meager shade of a small bush and waited for the patrol to rescue him. "But it drove by and they didn't see me. They passed by as close as from here to my house, but they didn't see me."

Heavily, Mateo rose from the shade of the *huizache* and continued to stumble toward the line of telephone poles. And suddenly, as happens in the desert, the monotonous scrub parted and he emerged onto a two-lane highway. Looking left, he saw an Immigration bus parked by the roadside. Then he looked right and saw three men approaching through the quavering heat rising off the tarmac in the narrow distance. He whistled to them, rending the desert air. The three figures raised their arms and shrugged, but otherwise did not respond. Mateo whistled again, and again they shrugged.

Anxiously, he set off in their direction, whistling and signaling, but received no answer other than their repeated shrugs beneath the empty dome of the sky.

As he closed the distance between them, Mateo recognized the three figures as men from his own party of traveling companions. They were on their way to the bus to give themselves up. "They told me they were going to turn themselves in," Mateo said. "'We're going to turn ourselves in, there where the bus is,' they said. So I told them, 'No, let's go, let's go!'"

"You had gathered your courage again," I suggested.

"*Sí*, and yet, I walked back to the bus with them, and we were talking, and they told me that they knew the area more or less, and that the town was far away and they were going to give themselves up. And then I saw that the patrol was coming back again on the highway. And I told them, 'No, I'm not going to turn myself in.' I asked them if they knew which way was Phoenix and which way was Mexico, and they told me, and then I went back into the thicket again."

"Why did you change your mind?" I asked.

"Well, I thought somebody on the road would give me a ride. I was encouraged because I had found the highway. Soon the patrol drove away and the bus followed. And then I went back out to the highway and there were some cars driving by. I signaled to them, but none of them would stop. About thirty cars drove by, and then one stopped."

The vehicle, a Jeep SUV, was occupied by a blond man in his mid-thirties, Mateo said. "He told me to get in. And I got in, and I took my backpack and I put it like this, on the floor, and I looked in the back of the Jeep, and he had a cooler. And there I was, all dry."

Noting the direction of Mateo's gaze, the man told him to open the cooler. Inside, Mateo found a bottle of Gatorade, cold, beaded with condensation. "Take it," the man said in Spanish, and lifting the bottle to his lips, Mateo drank it off in a single draught. "*Y este*, he asked me where I was going. And I told him, 'I'm going to Phoenix.' And he said, 'No, you're going the wrong way.' So, at that point I asked him to take me to Phoenix. And he said, 'I can't.' '*Por favor,*' I said. But he said, 'I can't. I'm in the Air Force.'"

"'Please,' I said again."

The man regarded the young migrant unhappily. "Wait," he said, holding up his hand, and reaching for the cell phone on his belt, touched speed dial with his thumb and called his girlfriend to ask her opinion.

"She was Mexican," Mateo informed me, his voice rising in wonder, "but she said, 'No, you can't do this.' Then he called his *mamá*, but she also said no. 'I just can't do it,' the blond man said, and then he gave me forty dollars. But I said, 'No, I don't need money. I'll pay *you*. Just take me to Phoenix.'"

In my mind's eye I imagined the two sitting at stale-mate in the Jeep by the side of the road as the desert sun turned it into an oven on wheels, and inexplicably my heart broke: not at that moment for the young migrant who had come so far with such resolution, but for my countryman, the American, who in spite of what his conscience so clearly told him was the right thing to do couldn't bring himself to act.

The enlisted man started up his Jeep and drove Mateo to the sun-scoured town of Why, Arizona, nothing more than a couple of gas stations with attached convenience marts a quarter of an hour away at the remote junction of State Highways 85 and 86. Instructing Mateo to wait in the car, the man entered one of the convenience stores. Returning after a few minutes, he told Mateo he had asked the clerks their opinions, but they, too, had told him he shouldn't take the migrant to Phoenix. He had done all he could, he said, and wishing Mateo well, left him in the parking lot.

Weighing his options, which at that moment seemed meager, Mateo stood by the side of the highway in the sun. He was still thirsty. His head felt light and he saw spots in front of his eyes. Shouldering his backpack, he entered the convenience store to buy a soda. At the counter, he paid the woman attending the cash register and returned to the highway.

"There was another man there, *un...un indio*," he said. Mateo didn't know the names of the indigenous people of this desert, and so in Spanish he simply referred to the man as "an Indian." "He told me he would drive me to Phoenix if I gave him money. So I reached into my pocket to take out the money, but it was gone."

Dazed by heat stroke, Mateo discovered that in the convenience market, instead of giving the clerk two one-dollar bills, he had inadvertently given her a one and a hundred, nearly everything he had. He asked *"el indio"* to wait and went back into the store, where he informed the woman of his mistake. "She spoke Spanish," he said, "and she told me that I was wrong. She said I could look in the drawer, and she showed me, and so I showed her all the money I had. But still she said no."

"She took the money from you?" I asked.

"*Sí*," Mateo replied sadly.

"And so what did you do?"

Mateo shrugged his shoulders. "I said to her, 'For one hundred dollars you won't be rich, and for one hundred dollars I won't be poor, but it will stain your conscience for the rest of your life,' and then I went back outside to the highway."

"And then what happened?"

"Then she followed me. I thought she wanted to say something, but she said nothing, and then she went back inside."

"And *el indio*?"

"I told him I didn't have enough money, but I would pay him when we arrived in Phoenix. I told him I had friends who would pay. But he said no." A look of incomprehension crossed Mateo's face. "And then he left."

"And then?"

"I remembered I had a telephone number, and so I went to the telephone and I called a coyote. 'I need you to pick me up,' I said. But he refused."

The coyote told Mateo that shuttle buses to Phoenix passed through Why regularly and that he should catch one. Mateo stood by the side of the highway and waited. He waited for an hour, then two, but no shuttle passed by. The sun was going down.

And then, finally, in the withered heart of Why, he gave up.

He crossed to the other side of the road, and almost immediately a shuttle to Lukeville arrived. In twenty minutes it deposited him at the border. With what little money he had left, Mateo took a bus from Sonoyta to Guadalajara, in the state of Jalisco. He told me that many of the other passengers were returning from *el Norte* and spoke happily about the money they had made and what they were going to do with it. Some intended to open small businesses; others were going to repair their houses; most would use the money to help their families. The man sitting next to him kindly fed him during the two-day journey. In Guadalajara he told the bus driver he needed to get home but didn't have any money. The driver considered the weary young man for a moment and then quietly told him to get back on the bus, which he rode as far as Zamora, in Michoacán, where by chance he met a man from his village who lent him enough money to return to Santa Fe. When I spoke to him, Mateo had been back a month. I asked him what his plans were now. He replied that he was saving to try for *el Norte* again.

◦≈ ≈ ≈◦

Dustin W. Leavitt contributes articles and essays on subjects including travel, social commentary, and art criticism to books and periodicals. Much of his travel writing visits Asia and the Pacific, where he has lived, worked, and wandered at various times in his life. He teaches at the University of Redlands, near Los Angeles.

Gods Who Smell Like Goats

She joins the river of souls
that is the Way of St. James.

ULRICH, A ROBUST FIFTY-TWO-YEAR-OLD PILGRIM dressed in a red flannel shirt, told me, "I want to walk through the world without leaving footprints. It's hard work to be silent."

Sitting alone inside the walls of the convent of Santa Clara in Carrion de los Condes, Spain, I stretch out my legs under the early summer sun, relax my back into the warmth of the bricks, and listen through the silence to the twelve chimes. A fresh-faced nun in full black habit pokes her head out the door. I lean my head against the wall, close my eyes, sigh.

Ulrich the pilgrim started walking to Spain from his home in Austria. Paul started out from France. Others came from Scotland, Holland, Brazil, North Carolina, and the Czech Republic to walk the Camino de Santiago de Compostella (the Way of St. James). The Camino, which became known in the twelfth century, is a key Christian pilgrimage to the alleged burial place of the apostle Saint James (Santiago) on the Iberian Peninsula. His bones were happened upon centuries earlier by a shepherd following a field (*campo*) of stars (*estrellas*).

The Camino is actually several pilgrimages running across Europe, starting in Holland, France, Germany, Poland, Austria, and Portugal with all paths leading to Santiago. The most popular and developed route starts in the Pyrenees (at St. John Pied de Port in France or Roncesvalles in Spain) and cuts across the North of Spain. This 500-mile route is marked with bright yellow arrows and provides *refugios,* municipal- and church-sponsored places to stay for only a few coins a night.

I set off on the thirty-day pilgrimage from Roncesvalles last May with my friend Paige. Both of us had recently stumbled through a life portal (master's degree for her, academic tenure for me). I wanted to escape for a while from the world of the mind and was attracted to the Camino because it was a physical challenge (a month of walking fifteen to twenty miles a day) made comfortable by the promise of a nightly shower and a bed in a beautiful old convent or monastery.

I did not walk the Camino for religious renewal, I did not go to fall in love all over again with my Catholicism, my spiritual birthright, my doctrinal heritage. I did not go planning to spend my days dwelling on the hospitality of Mary Magdalene, smiling into the gentle faces of Benedictine nuns, eating cheese on the warm cement of the convent of Santa Clara, learning to say a slow-paced rosary with imaginary beads. I did not go to hear the Our

Father spoken in seven languages nor to have long afternoon conversations about the importance of *fe* (faith). I
did not go to return to a childlike trust in Jesus Christ that
I had last felt in third grade with the curly, black-haired
Sister Kathleen Marie at Holy Name School.

I went to walk and to clear my head. I went because
of the wretched monkey of yearning that never lets me
know what exactly it is I am yearning for. Along the
way, the innocent faith of an eight-year-old came back
to me as I walked without a map or knowledge of the
language across the foggy mountains, blue asparagus
fields, and enigmatic silent villages of Spain.

*Day 5: Leaving Estella, we pass tall clay cliffs—vertical
shadows long in the morning sun—tromp through fishnets
of spider webs bejeweled by water. The May morning air
chills my bare knees and licks the top of my ears. A cool
constant rush of wind sifts and shakes the heads of silver
and green poplars. Midday, the peaks of the blue and purple
mountains lined up in the distance are hazed flat in the hot
sun; lunch on the side of the road with a million ants, my
body balanced by opposites—warm sun-dipped skin with
cold-wind goose bumps.*

Both young and old people walk the Camino. I met
comfortable sixty-year-old pilgrims, wise and satisfied
with their lives, walking for solitude and sensual pleasure (walking fifteen miles gave even the most penitent
pilgrim reason to enjoy a glass of Rioja wine), and uncomfortable old gerophobes anxious and scared of their
age, walking to accumulate Catholic merit points as a
way to escape hell (and perhaps strengthen their hearts
and muscles to give them more years to do so).

Some pilgrims walked the Camino expecting Santiago to give them something—forgiveness for their sins, determination to stop smoking, or something more concrete, such as a limited edition 1982 Alfa Romeo that one pilgrim said he found in his driveway after his first pilgrimage (this time he was asking for a wife). Many of us were at a turning point in our lives and walked for courage and guidance. Some were deciding about relationships—to have them, to leave them, to change them; others were deciding about jobs—to have them, to leave them, to change them. Rare was the person simply walking to walk. Yet that is what we all did. Walk.

Throughout the day, I followed the etchings of slugs and the footprints of pilgrims—people whose names and stories I learned over the miles and meals, others whose names I never learned because of both language barriers and our common desire to practice solitude and learn silence. Still, we shared nods, bits of chocolate, palm swigs of water from the town fountains, and the ritual of praying the Our Father and the excitement of watching the World Cup. I felt a connection to the past, to the centuries of others who stumbled over these same stones, to the tribe of slugs and pilgrims. They made me grin.

Day 10: I feel the Camino through my feet—luscious and extravagant is the earth. I feel the thick red clay that clings to my boots in clumps, gobs of dirt that I carry with me from one village to the next. I feel the hard black tar that bruises my soles as I pound along the highway. I feel the hot sun that tans and then burns my skin. I feel my backpack blistering my back. I feel my hands thicken and my fingers swell with blood. And then one morning, all morning, I feel the brush of flowers crowding my legs.

I am present to my mortality—my muscles, my soles, my ligaments. The hot June sun fatigues me, like a strong wind it slows my steps. Pain slithers through my body up the shin of my right leg, over to my left shoulder, down into the ball of my feet. I am alive. I lighten my pack, throwing out everything that is not necessary.

At night in each village we celebrated together at the Pilgrim's Mass. I looked out over the heads in the cold stone churches but did not find the dark curly hair of Paige. She does not go to Mass. She is not Catholic; even more, she is anti-Christian. Having had a dismal, unfulfilling, even abusive experience with Christianity, she has not simply fallen away from Christianity but has run away from, in her view, a misogynistic and Eurocentric religion that defines God as a mean and cruel superego and a church full of people chanting shall-nots. Tales told by other people I know suggest that her experiences are not unique. Perhaps this is more typical of my friend's Southern Baptist version of Christianity, but I have met too many people who define themselves as "recovering Catholics" to dismiss the reality that Catholicism also makes people anti-Christian, anti-religion.

Religion is a nasty word among my peers, tail-end baby boomers, New-Agers, twelve-step program followers who explore exotic Vietnamese Buddhism but reject the Christian religion of their youth. Religion, they say, is for people who fear hell; it is institutionalized, exploitative, and, in fact, un-Christian. I understand. I agree. When I show movies in my college classrooms of the horrors inflicted on the indigenous peoples of the Americas by Christian missionaries, I cringe and want to deny my religious heritage. It is easy for me to explore religion from a distance as a sociologist, through the works of Max Weber or Jacques Ellul, for example, but up close with my leftist academic peers I keep silent and downplay the fact that I like to go to church and observe the religious holy days. A colleague asks me to take her daughter to church on Easter Sunday and compares the experience to a Grateful Dead concert. I wince, yet understand how she conflates the two events—rituals, motion, incense, followings, ecstasy. Religion is something I submerge even in front of my therapist, who defines my weepiness in church (which I attribute to the presence of the Holy Spirit) as an inability to master my emotions.

In my modern day professional life I am Peter-like in my denial of Christianity, but on the Camino, on my Camino, I fell in love, unashamedly in love, with my religion, Roman Catholicism. I fell in love with the Mass, the rituals, the dogma, the rosary, the Word, the beauty on the faces of the statues expressing pain, joy, sorrow, peace. I sang hymns to the new flowers, clumps of brilliant golden yellow splashed about the mountainside, and kissed the base of crucifixes in the fields to express my gratitude.

Halfway along the route, I left my friend in order to walk my own pace inside my own head. I walked fast and hard for a week, walking long days over the high flat mesa in the middle of Northern Spain—twenty-five to thirty miles a day with few stops and little conversation with others. The discipline of walking returned me to the heart. The flatness awakened my mind. The mesa, expansive miles of green, new-growth grain fields, reminded me of my grandpa's farm in Michigan.

My days took on a soothing uncomplicated rhythm—pack, walk, eat, shower, sleep. Through the monotony of routine, in the space of silence, the demons appeared (fears, frailty, the flawed nature of our very being, our humanness—the barren desolate ground of private hags). They developed a body and form that could be addressed, dealt with and then put away. I had a long conversation with my father.

I walked on alone, long, long hours alone every day, every day, every day, thinking about my life, my loves, my work, my God. And then the thinking and self-dialogue riffed into non-thinking as the rhythm of monotony pulled my soul into the moment. I spent the long hours of slow-motion movement absorbing the blue of the sky and the green of the grass. Days passed in this blue-green mode. Past and future lives funneled into the fulcrum of the horizon and returned as the present with the thought that everything I will ever need has already been given to me. God is within. Out on the open mesa of tall green grass and below the endless skies of cloudless blue, there is no space for past regrets or time for future worries—there is simply the blue and the green.

The Buddhist monk Thich Nhat Hanh teaches me to live in the moment, an easy thing to do when days are simplified by the repetitious tasks of walking, eating, sleeping, praying. Hours and miles expand when covered by foot, day after day after week after week. The minutes open to the face of God in the green wheat fields against the blue skies.

The Catholic Church is not God, and therefore the church is flawed. The church is the map, and on the Camino I fell in love with the terrain. The church was made by man. I do not deny nor dismiss the misogyny, the imperialism, the stupidity of past and present church leaders—but they were men, simply men, and the church an institution created by men. The beauty of the church should not be denied me because of the sins of men. Roman Catholicism is my language, it was given to me to help my search for the face of God.

Catholicism gives me something that Buddhism, Hinduism, animism does not. Not because it is right. I have no idea if it is or not. Catholicism is the religion of my innocence, my childhood. It bypasses my cerebrum and enters my nostrils, floats into my eyes, resounds in my ears. The smell of burning incense, the delicacy of Madonna statues and the gruesome horror of Santiago Matamoros (Saint James the Moor Killer), the deep resonance of Angelus bells at noon, the hymns of eating the body and drinking the blood, the brass cylinders of the organ, and the chorus of novitiate faces framed in the whiteness of the wimple: I fall to my knees and cry. Cry because it touches something deep inside of me, it touches my child, my soul, the nipples of my breasts.

On the Camino, time reached back and pulled me forward. The bricks of the old churches were the color of earth—slate, yellow-grey, copper—the color of age, and stood in contrast to the bright newness of poppy orange and spring green. The churches and my religion were old, old like the earth, softened and settled in their dull colors, comfortable in their stability. Yet, I loved the bunches of orange poppies and the fleeting chalky-purple butterflies. I found delight in the brilliance of their colors, the urgency of their temporariness. The church grounded me in the past and prepared my future; the poppies and butterflies centered me in the day and I remembered to give thanks to the Creator.

The sun slipped out from behind a cloud and the heat released me. I thought of being here now, and all the nows that created this moment, and how this now would add to future nows, a string of life beads, each as precious as the next. My worries about what to do with my life receded—but stayed with me. So what? They would always be there, like the ants every day when I stopped for lunch. I know too little to have big worries.

Day 25: Shrouded in the early morning mist, I climb straight up to the small mountain village of O Cebreiro. The higher I climb the thicker becomes the shroud. My legs are drenched in the dew of outstretched ferns; my neck and hair damp from the wetness of sagging branches. I climb through sleeping hamlets spackled with cow dung, pass regal black stallions munching in yellow-sun pastures. I listen to the wind talking, jabbering through the branches of the poplars; I drink in the little purple heather and the fields of flowing wheat. I wander into ancient churches and stare at the statues; waiting, listening for one to talk to me. I search the rivers of rushing water. I forgive my feet for hurting. I forgive myself for being human, for smelling like a goat.

❧ ❧ ❧

Mary Patrice Erdmans is a professor of Sociology at Central Connecticut State University. The first mountain she ever climbed was in the Himalayas and it has been downhill ever since. She is the author of The Grasinski Girls: The Choices They Had and the Choices They Made *which won the Oskar Halecki Prize in 2005. Her articles and essays have appeared in* North American Review, The Sociological Quarterly, Notre Dame Magazine, Polish American Studies, Journal of American Ethnic History, *and* 2B Quarterly.

❧ ❧ ❧

Tortola

Paradise, you say?

THE SUNSET HOTEL AND BEACH CLUB IS LOCATED ON the western coast of Tortola, isolated from Road Town, the island's capital, and miles from anything of consequence except a few houses along the ancient one-lane road that passes by. It's a frugally-priced, thirty-person resort, "Tortola's Best Hidden Secret," a thin, bleached brochure declares. It's the only resort, the only anything, on Sugar Cane Bay, a wide, calm, idyllic cove. I went there from New York for a much-anticipated vacation. I felt that the remoteness and standardness of the place was more than made up for by the low price, and by the long, scythe-shaped beach I had to share with hardly a soul.

Seated on one of the Club's frayed reclining chairs, I could read my magazines and the three or four books I hauled with me from New York, let my toes trail in the sand, and imbibe the sun. Which is practically all I wanted out of my week in the Caribbean. Periodically, I would look up from my reading and gaze at the expanse of beach, pristine as freshly smoothed cake icing and slowly curving into a quarter moon to a point in the distance. The city where I worked and lived, with its dark harsh winter days, didn't exist. Tortola, Tortola—a fine choice, I thought. I'd never heard of it before a few months ago, had no idea where, or what, it was. Friends had just returned from a week at the Sunset Club, eyes wide with pleasure and peaceful speech, and urged me to go. So, I did.

At any given time, there were never more than ten or twelve people on the beach. It was a typical sprinkling one encounters at a small Caribbean resort—a few young families, a few childless couples, two pairs of single women, a gay couple, and two or three couples vacationing together. Most were Americans, with a few Canadians and the odd European. I was forty-two, had just emerged from a ruptured three-year relationship, and was burned out from my job in advertising. I was so depleted, I hardly noticed I was by myself. When I did notice, I didn't care.

My room, which was at the back of the resort, was austere: a bed, two chairs, small table, chest of drawers. The floor was cement with a few braided rugs. The bathroom was aircraft-small. The sink fixtures were flecked with rust, and the water tasted of something strong. None of this bothered me. My room faced a steep hill. I noticed that to one side there was a garbage heap a few hundred yards from my window, rising up from the fronded greenery. It was a misshapen hill of empty Tide detergent containers, old tins of cooking oil, withered boxes, car batteries, various depleted bottles, lots of undetermined refuse, and all crowned by a blazing-white, split porcelain toilet. Why was this heap there, I wondered, and not thirty feet to one side or another? I kept my windows open and my shutters closed.

The owner of the Sunset Club was named Derek. I never learned his last name. Derek was a large-faced, profoundly-voiced black man who reminded me of the singer Lou Rawls. Derek was usually dressed in a pair of fresh khakis with a loose, brightly-colored short-sleeved shirt, two buttons opened at the neck. He wore sunglasses and a fat gold watch that shone like a sun against his inky skin. He was friendly enough, but I had trouble understanding his island English. I had trouble understanding almost everyone I talked to on the island. It was like trying to decipher an English distorted in a verbal house of mirrors. I frequently found myself saying, "What? What did you say?"

Every day, after about 2 P.M., Derek could be found stationed at the Club's little outside bar. It faced the beach. He sat on one of the barstools smoking a cigarette and drinking a Coke and talking to whichever of his four employees happened to be near. He had a bartender and grill man, Wilson Gray, a slim dark man one of whose front teeth was brilliant silver. He had a handyman named Dyer who could usually be found hacking away at the vegetation with a machete next to the resort. And he had two island women who came in about mid-morning to clean and make up the rooms, Sandra and Cleo.

Sandra, the more talkative of the two, was a tall, brown-skinned woman who always wore strapless dresses made of thin, nappy terrycloth. They revealed her broad shoulders and collarbones, which were so pronounced they looked as if they had been chiseled. Her whorled hair was cut short, and she always wore oversized earrings. I noticed she had a short fat scar on her cheek. She was brash and sarcastic. When she found out soon enough that I was by myself, unattached, she challenged me to conversation whenever we met. She liked to provoke, and she was good at it. I learned Sandra had two children, four and six, and was not married. She had a boyfriend who I gathered she had left a few weeks earlier. She looked to be about thirty, but it was hard to tell. Sometimes an expression passed over her face that made her look older.

Cleo, her workmate, was almost six inches shorter than Sandra, and much darker. Her skin was the color of tar, and seemed, in certain light, as if it were polished. She had sly eyes and a witty cynicism. I enjoyed that. When Cleo laughed, she covered her mouth with a hand, a habit I found intriguing. I wondered if she were hiding some defect. She wore dresses I thought might have cost fifty cents, and, like Sandra, the cheapest flip-flops for shoes. She had one child, a boy, and a boyfriend with whom she did not live. These two women liked to flirt with me. I wasn't interested, though. Too soon after my breakup. Still, I enjoyed the banter.

Derek didn't pay the women any mind, but when he did speak to them, it was usually to give a curt order.

I quickly got into a simple routine at the Sunset Club. I liked to rise early. This was easy, due to the incessant shrieks of roosters that began even before dawn. I would lie in bed and read for a few hours. As the sun crept up into the sky, I could sense the room getting brighter and hotter—I refused to use air conditioning. Then I would begin to hear the muffled voices of the couple in the next room and, a little while later, the sound of Dyer's machete. I would slip on a pair of bathing trunks and shirt and walk out to the beach. Then I'd go for a swim. The water in Sugar Cane Bay was pacific and balmy. It was saltier than the salt water I was used to. I liked that. It refreshed all parts of me. When I finished, I would go back to my room and take a shower and then get dressed. When I returned, Wilson Gray was usually at the bar cleaning up. Then I could get a cup of coffee. I made no effort to get to know the other guests. I liked my routine, liked the spareness of it, liked the non-commitment of it.

On the fourth day of my vacation, I wandered out to the bar about mid-morning. I asked Wilson Gray for a club soda with lime and edged myself onto one of the bar stools. Near the bar, many of the white plastic chairs were still stacked overturned. The couples with children had already staked their claim to swaths of beach. The water was still, with an occasional wavelet flopping onto the wet sand. Morning in Tortola. How strange it seemed sometimes. It came not so much with a sense of possibility as mornings did up north, but with the sense that nothing would ever change. Maybe, I thought, that was because the weather was always the same. The morning air had an eerie lightness to it. There was a sense of forever.

The door to a guest room near the bar opened, and Sandra and Cleo came out. They had just finished cleaning. Sandra had a bucket, and Cleo carried a small basket stocked with cleaning spray and old rags. They were giggling. They saw me.

"Here come pretty man," Cleo said, tilting her head toward me.

"*Scrump*tious," Sandra said. She moved her tongue across her lower lip. Then she put down her bucket and walked over to the bar. She faced me.

"Good morning, ladies," I said, acknowledging them. "Another day in paradise." It sounded idiotic.

Cleo snorted. "Come take this basket and go clean rooms in my place, and then tell me your stories about paradise," she said.

Sandra, who was by far the bolder of the two, moved closer to me. Wilson Gray, who had been following this, gave her a look.

"What are you doin' later, sir?" she said. She put a hand on her hip. "Come party wit' us."

"You two bitches shut your mouth," Wilson Gray said.

A wave of shock and fear swept through me at the fierce ugliness of Wilson Gray's words.

Sandra turned to Wilson Gray. "You think 'cause you Derek's cousin you *big man?*" she said defiantly. "You *little* man! *Tiny* man!"

Wilson Gray picked up a cutting knife from the bar and made as if to lunge at Sandra. She shrieked and turned to run. Wilson Gray laughed and waved the knife at her theatrically. His silver tooth flashed from the bar. Even Cleo laughed.

"It's O.K.," I said. "I don't mind."

Wilson Gray seemed not to hear me. He moved back to his station at the bar and began cutting limes. He paused and cast an eye at the two women. Cleo went around the corner of the Club, and Sandra followed her. Cleo poked her head back out and beckoned to me to come. I shrugged, got off my seat, and went toward them. I went out of curiosity, but also out of guilt for not having spoken up more forcefully to Wilson Gray. When I turned the corner, both women were there.

"Ladies," I said, "I don't want to get you into trouble. Or for you to lose your jobs." I glanced backward to make sure Wilson Gray couldn't see them.

"I don't give fuckin' care about this fuckin' job!" Cleo said.

"Derek can take his club and place it where the sun don't shine," Sandra said. Then she looked closely at me, her eyes moving up and down my body. "You like horseracing, sir?"

Cleo laughed.

"Horseracing?" I didn't know where this was going. "Not particularly. I've gone to the track a few times. It's O.K."

"Because," Sandra said, "we lookin' for a jockey."

"Are you a *good* jockey?" Cleo said.

"We need a *good* jockey," Sandra said, taking one step toward me.

I could see the dark naps in Sandra's cheap terrycloth dress and some greasy stains from cleaning. When she lifted her arm to bat away a fly, I saw small coils of damp underarm hair.

"I don't know what you mean," I said in mock inno-cence. "Jockey? I've never ridden a horse professionally in my life." I thought pretending not to understand was the best course.

"We teach you how to ride," Cleo said. I had to admit, she had a wonderful deadpan delivery.

"It never too late to learn," Sandra said.

"Ladies, I don't think I'm the man you want," I said. I wanted out. "And with that, I bid you adieu."

"Come party wit' us tonight!" Sandra said as I turned

the corner. She walked after me, turning the corner. "Party wit' us! We come back for you later!"

When he saw Sandra, Wilson Gray slapped his knife hard on the bar. "Move on away from there, you black bitch!" he said.

Sandra looked hard at him. She spat in his direction. Then she went back around the corner and disappeared.

I started to say something to Wilson Gray, but I let the moment pass. After all, I was a guest here, not a policeman. Anyway, no matter what I said, things would stay the same. Wilson Gray wasn't going to stop the way he treated Sandra and Cleo because of something *I* said to him. This was the way it was here, deplorable as it might seem. Pity.

I decided to take a walk. I hadn't been outside the confines of the Sunset Club yet, and I wanted to see what was nearby on the island. Besides, I wanted to get away from those ugly words of Wilson Gray's. I walked to the rear of the Club and climbed some crumbly concrete stairs to the old road that ran along the northern fringes of the island and past the Club's entrance. The day was beginning to seethe. I wore a baseball cap against the sun.

There was no traffic. The road was empty, the kind of empty you only find in a place that is sparsely populated by people who can't afford cars. I could walk in the middle of the road, without concern. The day was silent, too. What a sense of freedom! Of abandonment! On the other side of the road—the non-Club side—the land rose up some two hundred feet on a slant. It was covered with untamed tropical greenery. I started walking. I walked away from the direction of the refuse heap. A sudden sense of liberation swept over me. Here I was, on Tortola! Here I was, unknown to anybody, without an identity. I was just a person. I had no past, carried no baggage from my life in New York. I was just *here*. How often can you start anew, I thought, with an absolutely smooth slate, just *you*? I was a stranger to everyone— even, in a sense, to myself. There was an oddness of being in a place with no emotional reference points. That came with the liberation.

I walked down the road, looking this way and that. I loved this sort of adventure, walking alone, free to go at any pace I wanted. Everything I saw was absorbing, because it was new to me, even the weeds and the jagged stones on the side of the road. Then I saw a house. It was a small, one-story dwelling just barely off the edge of the road. It was painted white, with fiercely yellow shutters. The windows were open; they had no glass. Two fat-tired bicycles and an old motor scooter were propped against a side wall. There was no car. The front door was open. I walked up to the house, looked in, and saw someone seated on the floor playing a guitar. I could see he was a young man, white, with curly hair, wearing shorts and no shirt.

The sight of a young white male in this small house in the middle of nowhere surprised me. I poked my head in.

"Hello!" I said. "Hi!"

The man stopped playing, looked over, and saw me.

"Hey, hello!" I said to him.

"Hey," the young man said. He put down his guitar, got up, and walked outside to meet me. He was indeed young, maybe twenty-three, handsome, with a Caravaggio-like body and curly hair in abundance. He was tanned and his lips were whitened with zinc.

I introduced myself. "I'm staying at the Sunset Club," I said. "Just down the road."

"I'm Billy Robin," the young man said.

We shook hands.

He was American, that was clear.

"You live here?" I asked.

Billy laughed. "No. I'm just staying here for a while."

"But—how did you end up in such a remote place? This isn't a hotel, is it?"

"No. Weird, isn't it? I'm a mate on the *Wellfleet*. It's a sloop. We cruise the Virgins. We got here a week ago. The last time I was here I met Daria in Road Town. She owns the house. She said the next time I come to Tortola I could stay with her. So—I am. I give her some money to help out, she won't take much. It's a lot cheaper than staying in town."

"Can't you just stay on the boat?"

"Naw. It's up for repairs for three weeks in dry dock."

"Where're you from?"

"Maryland. Baltimore. What about you?"

"New York."

"Never been." He paused. "Want a beer?"

"Uh, no, thanks. A little early."

"I think I'll have one. Have a seat."

Billy pointed to an empty plastic crate on the ground. I sat while Billy fetched a beer. I heard a rooster in back make its incredibly loud and penetrating call. I had grown to despise roosters after just a few days on Tortola. I would happily have wrung the neck of any I found.

When Billy came back with his beer, the two of us talked. Billy was just doing this as a lark for a while.

What he really wanted to be was a songwriter. He didn't have a great voice, he said, but he thought he had a way with words. He took his guitar with him wherever he went. He never knew when a song might come to him. He was pretty good at melody, too, he thought.

Even though there was a twenty-year age difference between us, we were completely relaxed with one another. We soon got to talking about most everything— our families, our aspirations, our romances, work, books we liked, life itself. The oddness of the encounter seemed to free us. It was a nourishing two hours we spent together. I thought we could talk all day.

"You know," I said at one point to Billy, "coming here and meeting you—I don't know how to say this, maybe you'll think I'm nuts—but it seems like something that was fated."

"It does seem pretty bizarre."

"Yeah, it's like I'm walking around in a fairy tale."

We talked for a while longer, and then Billy got up.

"I've got to paint the bedroom. I promised Daria I'd do it today."

"Can I help?" I asked.

"No, I'm good. I get into a zone when I paint. I like it."

"Hey," I said, an idea suddenly coming to me, "you wanna get together tonight? Have a beer?"

"Sure. Why don't you come by later. Have dinner with Daria and me."

"Really?"

"Sure. She won't mind. She always makes me dinner. She's an unbelievable cook."

"You sure it's O.K.?"

"Positive. Come on by about seven."

We shook hands, and then I walked back to the Sunset Club. I felt lucky—that was the word for it—to have met Billy. Just by chance. Just by taking a walk. Life was full of promise, I thought, something new around every corner. The sun was high and very potent now. When I got to the Club, the beach was crowded—if you could even use the word "crowded." Calypso music was playing over the tinny loudspeaker system. I was hungry. I asked Wilson Gray to please make me a conch salad. Then I went for a short swim. The water felt delicious. The extra saltiness of the Caribbean felt wonderful to me, a balm for all the shocks my flesh was heir to in my profession and personal life. I hadn't thought about my ex-girlfriend much at all. Tortola was just the ticket.

I walked out of the water and back up to the bar. Wilson Gray had the salad prepared. It looked beautiful. I began to eat.

"Wilson Gray," I said, my eyes closed in ecstasy, "this is *great*. You are an artist, my friend."

Wilson Gray shrugged his shoulders. "It no more than a conch salad. That's all."

"*Just* a conch salad? Oh, no. It's ambrosia."

"You say so."

"Say, let me ask you something. Tell me, what have you got against Sandra and Cleo?"

"Got nothin' against them two."

"You sure seem to."

"They lazy. Lazy bitches."

Wilson Gray's words seemed like a slap across the face. "Well, I don't know. They seem to work pretty hard."

Wilson Gray shrugged. "You done asked me what I thought."

I decided to let it drop. I finished my salad. Then I went up to my room, took a shower and lay down on my bed. I read for an hour, then fell asleep.

When I awoke, it was six o'clock. I remembered the dinner with Billy. I was usually groggy after a nap, but in this case the knowledge that I was going to have a bit of an adventure and spend some time with Billy swept away all the cobwebs in my brain. I was alert, and eager. I got dressed and went down to the bar. There were a few couples having a drink. Three or four people were still down at the beach. I went down to the water's edge. I looked out at the vista before me. I could see various small islands dotting the distance, like someone had heaved them out there. The air was still. I stood there on the wet sand, looking out. I passed about thirty minutes that way, just being there, in the twilight of a Caribbean day. I was beyond content.

I glanced at my watch and saw that it was time to make my way up to Billy's. I began walking, slightly smug in the knowledge that I had someplace exotic to go to, someplace the other guests didn't have access to, someplace completely authentic. I walked along the bare still road for ten minutes until I arrived at the house. Billy was sitting there, on the crate, strumming his guitar.

"Hey, dude," Billy said.

"Hey. Great evening, eh?"

"Sure is. Glad you could make it."

I smelled something cooking, some sort of stew, probably, and it smelled good. A black woman emerged from the house. She was about fifty. She had on a long cotton skirt and a yellow t-shirt. Her head was swathed in an African-like bandanna, azure and crimson, wonderful to look at. She was smiling.

"Welcome, welcome to my home," she said.

"Hi. Thanks for having me," I said as I introduced myself.

"I'm Daria," she said, shaking my hand. I looked at our two hands intermingled, the white and black of them. Her hand felt caressive, a bit rough, but pleasant. What strange thoughts filled my head in that instant! How curious that her hand should be black, I thought.

Daria worked in the post office in Road Town. She got a ride there every day with a friend who had a car. She was an ebullient woman who had obviously taken a shine to Billy. I wondered if they were lovers. If they were, neither of them gave it away. Soon, the three of us went inside and sat down to a meal of guinea fowl stew with okra and rice. I ate with abandon. I learned that Daria was going to have a cataract operation later that week. "I'm getting' old," she said. "Pretty soon I'll be hobblin' around with a cane."

I was enjoying myself immensely. There I was, eating a delicious meal in a house on Tortola, windows and door thrown open to the soft night, with two people I had met just that day. I told them about my job in New York and even about my breakup with my girlfriend. We were drinking beer, all of us, laughing and chatting away. Once again, the idea that life was marvelously unpredictable and rife with adventure came to me. All it took was a bit of courage and gumption and—*shaz-aam*—you would find yourself eating a savory stew in a stranger's home on a Caribbean island.

After the food was eaten, we lingered at the table and talked until about ten-thirty or eleven. It was then that we heard the first scream. It was a woman's scream, and it was coming from nearby. It was more a shout-scream, loud and sharp, half in anger, half in fear. It was a *scream*, though. There was desperation. Billy and I looked at each other in confusion and got up and quickly went outside to see what was happening. Daria followed. As we walked out, we heard two more screams, each short and each sounding like reactions to pain. The voice was coming from the direction opposite the Sunset Club, down the road, perhaps two hundred feet away.

Outside, it was hard to see. There were no streetlights. There was another house down the way, and some low lights were emanating from its front and illuminating parts of the road. Now there seemed to be several voices screaming, perhaps a man and another woman, too. They were threatening voices. Sometimes the screams were one incomprehensible mass, and, then, one voice would break out of the maelstrom to an even higher pitch. I saw shadows and parts of figures moving in and out of the demi-light. Daria listened carefully for a moment, then snorted, and turned and walked back inside. Billy and I didn't notice she had departed.

"Come on, let's go see," Billy urged. "Someone might be in trouble."

"Sure. O.K.," I said. The prospect did not appeal to me. The screaming unsettled me, it was so raw and so close. My whole body and mind told me: Danger. But when Billy walked forward, I found myself following. I stayed a step or two behind.

As we came closer, we could see that it was three people who were screaming at each other in the road, a man and two women. They were screaming and shouting, their voices filled with hate. The figures moved in and out of the limelight. They gestured at each other, thrust and parried, walked dramatically away, then returned with increased anger. I could see the two women were Sandra and Cleo. I couldn't see the man distinctly. He was farther down the road. Both the women were screeching at the man. I couldn't tell what they were saying.

Billy and I walked closer. We came within twenty feet of the two women, but they didn't seem to notice us.

"I know those two girls," I said into Billy's ear.

"You do?"

"Yes! They work at the Sunset Club! I know them!"

The screaming ebbed and flowed, with Sandra and Cleo yelling at the male shadowy figure, then the figure shouting something ominous back at them. It became clear, though, that this was really between Sandra and the man. Cleo's role was to support her friend. Suddenly, Billy and I got a good look at the man. He lunged forward out of the darkness, staggering. He looked like he was drunk. He was dressed in pants with no shirt and no shoes. We didn't know him. He weaved toward the two women. He had a knife. I could hear bits and pieces of what he said.

"I'll cut you! I'll *cut* you!" the man shouted.

"Go ahead and cut me! I *dare* you!" Sandra screamed back at him. Cleo screamed something at the man I couldn't understand.

The scene ran out in starts and fits, with the man sometimes stopping, bending one knee to the road and waving his knife. He was obviously very drunk. Then Sandra and Cleo would approach him and taunt him, pointing at him and screaming. Then, suddenly, he would rise and lunge toward them, brandishing his knife. The two women would then turn and run, screaming, just out of his reach.

"Do you need help?" Billy said to them when they ran toward him and me.

"Come this way!" Billy said to the women. "Why don't you run away?"

Cleo looked at Billy and then at me briefly. She dismissed us with an absent wave of her hand. Sandra stopped in the middle of the road. She put her head in her hands and began crying. Cleo went to her. I was scared that the man might actually stab and kill Sandra. Then I became scared for myself. I wondered if the man might try and stab me, too. He was drunk. Crazy! I stepped over to Billy. I turned Billy around so we could talk.

"Come on, man, this isn't our fight. This is island shit. It's not our business!"

"Damn, I wish I had a knife," Billy said.

"What? Are you crazy? That guy would kill you!" I pleaded.

Then Cleo screamed in surprise. While she had been consoling Sandra, the man managed to crawl forward stealthily and grab Sandra's wrist. Sandra screamed in shock and tried to claw the drunk man's hand. The man dropped his knife and got up. He retained his grip. He slapped Sandra hard across the face. The sound echoed through the night like a gunshot. Sandra didn't scream, didn't say anything. The man still had her in his grip. Then he hit her with his fist in the stomach, like a boxer. Sandra collapsed forward and groaned. Cleo ran behind the man and hit him hard against the back with her fist, screaming at him all the time. When he turned to hit her, Sandra rose up and yanked her hand free. Then she ran. Cleo dodged the man's swerving hand. She ran after Sandra.

Billy and I stood there. We did nothing.

The man spat. "You fuckin' bitch! I kill you! I kill you!" He stood there weaving for a minute. Then he turned and staggered backward, pausing to stop and pick up his knife. He disappeared into the blackness.

Billy and I found Sandra and Cleo by the side of the road about fifty feet away. Sandra was sobbing. Her teeth were bloodied. Blood had streamed down the bottom of her mouth and onto her neck. I could see the snot trailing from her nose mixed with blood. She was sobbing, in rage and in pain. She stood straight up and shook her fist defiantly in the darkness toward her attacker, wherever he was.

"I will kill him! I will cut his balls off! I will *kill* him!"

I saw that her dress was splattered with blood and that one of her knees was bleeding.

"Are you all right?" I said to her, approaching.

She didn't answer me.

"He a *mother*fucker!" Cleo said. "You stay away from him!"

Sandra wailed and wept.

"Do you have a place to stay tonight?" Billy asked her. "A safe place?"

"You should see a doctor," I said.

The two women hardly acknowledged Billy and me. Billy pulled a bandana out of his pocket and handed it to Cleo. She took it without reacting and started wiping the blood off Sandra's face. Sandra brushed her hand away. Then she and Cleo began walking back toward the scene of the fight and, I guessed, to their homes.

I turned to Billy. "See, man, I told you, they don't even *want* our help!"

Cleo and Sandra began walking away. Billy and I watched them as they moved slowly down the middle of the road, Cleo comforting the crying Sandra. Suddenly, out of the darkness from the side of the road, the man sprung. He had a piece of wood in his hand that looked like a section of a two-by-four. He ran over and hit Sandra across the back with the wood, hard, near the shoulder. There was a sickening crunch. Sandra sank to her knees on the road.

I froze. I couldn't move. "Oh my God!" Billy said, and started down the road toward Sandra and the man. The man dropped the wood, then spat on the road toward Sandra. Then he staggered once again into the darkness. Cleo screamed something at the figure. Sandra was bent, holding her knees, moaning. I approached the scene slowly. Sandra shocked me by rising up. How could she, after that blow? She put her head in her hands and began sobbing disconsolately, in the deepest despair, from somewhere at the deepest part of her heart. It was pitiable.

"Oh God," she said. "Oh Jesus." She sobbed as if she were completely broken. It was a long, deep protracted wail of helplessness. I had never heard anything like it. "Oh my Jesus," she cried. "Oh Lord Jesus."

"Why don't you come with us," Billy said to Cleo. "We'll help you."

Cleo shook her head. She began to guide Sandra away.

"Do you have somewhere safe to stay?" Billy asked.

Cleo nodded. Then she began to lead the crying Sandra away.

"But how do you know he won't be waiting for you?" I asked her.

For the first time Cleo spoke, "He no waitin'."

"But how do you know?"

She didn't answer, just turned and led Sandra away. The two women walked slowly down the road. I could see Sandra's back pulsing as she continued to weep, weeping like a lost child, no longer a woman, it seemed, no longer a mother, no longer an adult, but a child.

And then they were gone. Vanished into the night. We heard the sound of Sandra's crying for a moment longer, and, then, even that vanished.

Billy and I stood there on the road, in the still night, by ourselves. It became remarkably quiet.

"God damn," I said. "Jesus. I hope he doesn't kill her."

"Do you think he will?" Billy said.

"I don't know. He sure seemed like he wanted to, didn't he? Maybe we should call the police," I suggested.

"Daria doesn't have a phone."

"I have a phone in my room at the Club."

"Wow," said Billy, ignoring what I said. "What a scene. What a nightmare."

The two of us stood there in silence for a few minutes, simply reacting, in shock.

"Jesus. Out of nowhere," I said. Then something struck me. "Where's Daria?"

"I don't know," Billy said.

We both turned and reflexively started walking back toward Daria's house. I discovered, in the now-quiet night, that my heart was thumping fast and that my throat felt constricted and dry.

We reached the house. Daria was in the kitchen.

"Daria!" Billy said breathlessly. "Jesus, that guy almost killed that girl!"

"They fight like that all the time," she said.

"You know them?" Billy asked.

"They fight like *that*?" I asked.

"Like that. Just like that."

"But...how come nobody's been killed?" I asked.

"He too drunk to kill nobody," Daria said. "He cut her once or twice, though."

"Oh man," Billy said.

I remembered the scar on Sandra's cheek.

"Why doesn't she leave him?" I asked.

"She *done* leave him. But she always go back. He like a drug to her. Like *cocaine*."

"What a life," I said.

"Are you sure she'll be O.K., Daria?" Billy asked.

"She O.K. She go with Cleo. He don't bother her there. Anyhow, he pass out soon."

Billy and I sat down at the dinner table, which was clear now. I heaved a deep sigh. I looked at Billy. Billy shook his head in wonder and disbelief.

"Love in Tortola," I said.

"God, I really hope she's O.K.," Billy said.

"Sandra O.K.," Daria said.

I suddenly felt completely exhausted. It was as if every bit of energy I had was depleted. I was withered emotionally.

"I think I'm going to go back to the hotel," I said.

"I need a beer," Billy said.

I thanked Daria for dinner and said goodnight to Billy. I went out onto that road that had only a few minutes earlier been a bloody battlefield. It was still. I walked back to the Sunset Club. The walk frightened me somewhat. I wondered if the man might be lurking near the side of the road with a knife. I picked up the pace and was glad to see the small lights over the door of the Club's entrance. When I reached my room, I made sure I locked the door.

I didn't sleep well at all.

The next morning I woke feeling some trepidation. What about Sandra? Cleo? I felt very awkward and uncomfortable. But what could I do? This is where I was. I had two days left on my vacation. I was stuck. I had a plane reservation I couldn't change without paying a lot of money.

I got dressed and went outside. It was still early, and there was no one at the bar yet. I walked down to the beach, unenthusiastic about taking a swim. Unenthusiastic about being there. Then I started thinking about the previous evening. Maybe I should have stepped in between the man and Sandra. Maybe I should have at least said something. Maybe saying something would have stopped him. Maybe not, but at least I might have tried. But remember that both Sandra and Cleo had completely ignored Billy and my offer of help. No, I couldn't have stopped it. This was some kind of ritual, some kind of weird sick island dance these people did. Two or three words from me would never stop or change it. But deep inside me, I knew. I knew, and I felt a cold shiver of truth about myself shoot down my spine.

I trailed my foot in the water. Damn. What a vacation.

I went back to my room. I made a decision. I gathered my clothes and packed my bag. Then I went back outside. I had heard Dyer's machete whacking against something near the side of the hotel. I went over and found him, an older grizzled black man who wore a ragged straw hat and faded bandana around his neck.

"Dyer," I said. "Dyer, I need some help."

Dyer paused in his work and looked up at me.

"Dyer, can you get me a taxi? A taxi to Road Town?"

"Why you need a taxi at this hour?"

"I just do. Can you help? I'll give you a tip."

Dyer wiped his hand on the side of his pants. "How much tip you give me?"

I paused and thought. "Ten dollars."

"O.K.," Dyer said. Then he started to resume his work.

"I mean now."

"Now? This minute?"

"Now."

Dyer put down his machete. "You wait here." He started to walk off down the beach.

"Hey, where are you going?" I asked.

"I going to get a taxi."

"Don't you call? On the telephone?"

"I going to get you a taxi. You wait here."

I shrugged. I went back to my room and got my bag. I brought it back and waited by the bar. I was worried that in the meantime Sandra might show up. I wasn't worried about Derek. I'd paid in advance for my room, and had paid for all my drinks and meals as I went along.

About ten minutes later, I heard a car's horn. I walked to the front of the Club and there was a man in a Toyota pickup gesturing to me. I walked over.

"Taxi?" I asked dubiously.

"Yeah. Get in." The driver, a young black man, wore one of those sleeveless undershirts that seemed so popular with men on the island.

"How much to Road Town?"

"Twenty-five dollars."

"Wow," I said. "O.K." I thought it seemed excessive, but, truthfully, I would have paid almost anything.

I put my bag in the back and got in. The man gunned the truck, and we were off.

I heaved a sigh of relief as the truck pulled away from the Sunset Club. I was glad to be gone from that place. The truck picked up speed. As usual, the road was empty. I saw Daria's house approaching. I wondered if she was there and if Billy was, too. I wondered what Billy thought about last night. Should I ask the taxi driver to stop so I could say goodbye? When we passed the house, I turned my head away.

The truck made good time. I had decided to go to find a cheap guesthouse in Road Town and spend the last two days of my vacation there, just hanging out. I was actually interested in seeing the place. I hadn't spent any time there. I'd heard there were some interesting little shops. And a museum of some kind—sailing, maybe. Well, I'd go see. I wouldn't have any trouble killing two days. Then I'd catch my plane home.

The driver lit a cigarette, took a deep drag, and turned on his radio. The music was very loud.

Tortola, I thought, I'd never come back to Tortola.

~≥ ~≥ ~≥

Richard Goodman is a writer who lives in New York. He is the author of French Dirt: The Story of a Garden in the South of France *and* The Soul of Creative Writing.

～ʰᵉ ～ʰᵉ ～ʰᵉ

Breadstick Hydra

Where baking is an act of divinity and ecstacy.

THE FRONT ROOM IS FILLED WITH FRESH PASTAS AND truffle emulsions, meter-long *grissini* (breadsticks), and *baci di dama* (Lady's kiss cookies). I am in Barolo, Italy, in the local bakery, and am enjoying its silence, its farmland smells, the sight of three shadowed heads work-bobbing behind the kitchen's glass door. They don't see me yet and I'm glad for this. I'm tempted even to hide between the shelves of olive oil and vinegar, becoming the bridge that brings the two ingredients together into a nebulous vinaigrette.

I squat to examine the pastries in their glass cases— hazelnut buns, chocolate-fruit truffles, and again, those stretched, cat-after-a-nap breadsticks: the *grissini* dusted in what appears to be flakes of semolina. My eyes stray upward over the lip of the counter and I hold them open with my fingers, water them into focus.

The three-headed kitchen monster whirls about in obvious oven-heat, sputtering with rolling-pin effort, palms surely greased with butter, egg, oil, flour, salt, dough. Two of the heads boast long, grassy, tied-up hair. I can see the loose strand shadows bursting from their rubber bands and dancing airily about the heads as electrons. The third head is what frightens me most, slides me back under my bedroom covers, flashlight tight in hand. It is the squarest head I've ever seen, made even more angular by the fact that it sits featureless in heat-shadow. The square-headed figure—male in shape alone—carries a continuous army of trays first into, then out of a smoke-spewing hole in the wall.

With each added tray, I can hear this brick animal inhaling, then exhaling, doing its job of cooking, rising, browning, melting, toasting, crisping, finishing, each removed tray wearing the label of *DONE*. I breathe with it, trying to inflame my own coals into a large enough glow to summon one of these frantic heads from its lair. I want a stick of *grissini* as long as my arm and two sweet *baci di dama* to kiss it down.

My eyes turn back to the front door. Silver bells lie dormant at its top frame. I inhale again, the wheat-field air rinsing me, taking me, car windows down, at peak speed through western Nebraska, then eastern Colorado—the breadbasket before the mountains. But there is something different here: not just the smell of flour, but the smell of floured mushrooms.

I spin to face the kitchen again and see that the Hydra has lost two heads. Only the square remains. Before I can tear my eyes from the kitchen door, I hear, in angelic choral unison, in an identical-twin hum straight from a microphoned womb, a luscious, lady-kiss of a *"Ciao."*

Each voice extends the vowel at the end for just a second too long, then cuts out all at once as if some hidden conductor had waved a rod of *grissini* in a downward swipe through this fresh-baked air. I swear I see granules of yeast sputter all around me. They are standing side-by-side behind the glass-case counter in matching white aprons, greased in all the same places. Smiles threatening to burst the confines of their faces, they are shoulder-to-shoulder, wayward blond hairs maning their forty-something faces, strands locking them together as if Siamese twins. Mouths equally abundant, they are obviously sisters, richly identical, each defining the other as not one, but two warm slaps across my face.

So, not to deny either one of them, I say *"Ciao,"* exactly twice.

In a ridiculous sideshow feat, they break apart, as if the air itself were a scalpel, and each walks to an opposing end of the counter for balance. They look like weights on the ends of a straight-from-the-oven barbell. My tongue rings in my mouth as I ask about the *grissini*.

"Oh, *grissini*," the woman on the left says.

"Grissini," the woman on the right overlaps.

It's now that I notice that the woman on the left (as opposed to the woman on the right) is wearing eyeliner. This tiny difference settles my heart. They go on to tell me, each interrupting the other mid-sentence, that the *grissini* dough is made simply from flour, yeast, egg, milk, water, olive oil, and salt. It is rolled by hand into meter-long narrow sticks, painted with a coat of egg wash, then baked in the hearth. It is not semolina, but cornmeal that gold-dusts the sticks after their removal from the oven to prevent sticking together while they cool.

The eyelinerless sister bends behind the counter and I'm stunned to see just the one standing there. I've never seen a more solitary sight. She looks like an amputee. Soon, the sister rises from behind the counter with a stick of *grissini* in hand. I spread my arms to accept its length. The cornmeal sloughs from the crust, pushes beneath my fingernails and falls to the floor. I look down and see that the floor is covered in it. Instinctively, like the desire to crush a beer can after the last sip, I break the *grissini* in half and am surprised to find its interior still soft, pliable, and barely warm. The simple smell of pure bread rushes at my nose, captures me like a cold stone plucked exhilarated from a river bottom. I moan even before I taste.

And the taste…my teeth break through the outside crust like a dessert spoon through caramelized *crème brûlée* sugar, the brown shards dissolving on my tongue and bragging the cornmeal coarseness that so arouses the roof of my mouth. The interior of the *grissini*, still warm with oven-memory, goes porous and gummy as I chew, its saltiness, as earthy as soil, as oceanic as brain coral, brings all hemispheres of my mouth together into one smooth swallow. I remember Henry Miller's manifesto on bread—"The Staff of Life"—and wonder if he ever experienced *grissini* like this. I can eat this stuff until I die.

"Mama mia," I quake, already embarking on my second, third, ninth bite.

The sisters laugh as one. In the kitchen, Square-Head evicts a spray of sweat from his brow with both hands. The entire meter goes down as easy as an inch.

"Dove resta?" Eyeliner asks.

"Si, dove resta?" Eyelinerless echoes.

The kitchen breathes hard behind them as if stifling a laugh.

"*A Il Gioco dell'Oca,*" I say, "*per uno mese, due mese, tre mese...*" I shrug and smile. They laugh.

"*Una camera,*" Eyeliner says, forehead wrinkling, fingers rubbing together to indicate the expensiveness of a bed-and-breakfast room for one or two or three months.

"*No, no,*" I say, "*Io resta in una tenda.*"

"*In una tenda?*" they bellow in unison, smiles cracking their cheeks into fault lines.

Together, they descend into laughter. I laugh, too, picturing the dark greens of my tent: my home, my bed, my wine cellar. They speak to each other so rapidly; their mouths career as unmuffled cars around a tight curve. They crash beautifully again into laughter.

Disintegrating into coughs, the sisters notice me staring through the kitchen door's window at Square-Head.

"*Nostre fratello,*" Eyelinerless hacks.

"*Si, nostre fratello,*" Eyeliner hacks back.

He is their brother. The Hydra is a family.

Before I can ask for a bunch of *grissini*, before I can point to the *baci di dama*, the two sisters turn for the kitchen and their square-headed brother, and disappear behind the door. I am alone again in the front room and confused. Was it something I said? Was it the way I chewed? Have they decided not to associate with this unshaven American—beard sprouting as wheat—who lives in a tent? I touch the glass case of pastries, my fingerprints staying there to do my begging for me. As I prepare to leave, the kitchen door swings open; a plume of warmth and grain billows into the room.

It is Square-Head. He is shorter than he looked in the kitchen, in his fifties, and topped with gray hair. His white undershirt is drenched in sweat and his arms burst willow-wise with salt-and-pepper hair. His glasses, each lens as wide as a wine coaster, match the shape of his head. He is holding a cluster of *grissini* in one hand like a nuclear family of magic wands. Without a word, with only a rhinoceros grunt, he waves me toward the open kitchen door with his *grissini*-less hand.

It's cruel what bread can do sometimes: the smell, the taste taking you someplace deceptively familiar, deceptively simple; not the womb, but the conception of the womb in middle-age; a lovely false implanted memory; the soil you only think you're from; the home you always wish you had.

Belted by the warm kitchen air, the smell of a farm breathing, I return to central Illinois, to my college years, to my get-rich-quick schemes conjuring "back to the basics" advertising for the Ford Motor Company. I sat at an outside iron table with two of my childhood friends—a warm spring Champaign day at the Kopi Café, riddled with coffee and idea. The air was dense with cow and flower. Jeff, Keiter, and I, all with hair down to the middles of our backs, spoke of the Everyman-Middle America ad campaign into our collective dictaphone before we ever met the Everyman, before we knew what Middle America might be about. We envisioned a Ford truck parked at the edge of a farm at sunset, flashers on, the flannel-clad driver down on hands and knees in orange or rose or blue light, face in the soil. Then: a black screen with the slogan, *Smell the dirt...Ford*. We saluted one another and our obvious genius with another round of Ethiopian Harrars.

Bread and coffee: that's what I smell, an elixir so intoxicating I feel I am breathing not underwater, but under-liqueur. The circus of Eyeliner, Eyelinerless, and Square-Head call me into a silent barbershop trio of sweat and flour and a better life.

My body, as if possessing a brain outside my brain, answers the call, pushes its dimes of sweat from beneath my skin for their first breaths of air since my waking. My hands, like a mouth, water. And as Square-Head, with a hairy right-angled wink, calls me *"Viene, viene qua,"* to a stainless steel surface coated in a flour-and-egg sheen, I know my hands will not leave unsatisfied.

Heart beats, forehead sweats, hands touch. And I touch a voluptuous mound of dough, yellow as lemon, big as a cantaloupe. I swear I am grasping the culinary world's spirit animal, its orb, its crystal ball, and if I can somehow squint right, I can tell the future; I am only on the *antipasto*, sure, but with this circular soft immortal in my hands, I have the power to see the *dolce*.

Square-Head plucks at his apron strings and I expect to hear a symphony in C. He pulls the white oiled cloth over his head and holds it to me: the uniform, the armor, the *grissini*-baton. Hands absorbing the dough's clairvoyant energy, I know he's going to say *prego* before he does. And before he does, I wink at the dough and wonder if it knows where it is going; if it knows it is only in its adolescence—from flour to dough to oven to mouth. I breathe hard, yeasty air sweetening me like syrup all the way down.

"Prego," he says and unfurls the white apron like a shroud.

I loop the straps over my neck, lace the ties around my waist and feel as a knight: impermeable, sword-

wielding, shining like a Champaign soil. Square-Head
pinches a section of dough and pulls it from its whole
with a thumb and three fingers. His pinky, it seems,
wants to remain innocent. The twins coo at the smaller
bit of dough as if at a chick stepping freshly from the
hen. I picture the larger dough ball running maniacally
over the work surface with its head cut off. Yes: this
dough is ripe for the slaughter. I want its blood.

Square-Head, shaking his head in ecstasy or show-
manship, lets loose a cirrus cloud of flour from his hair
and teaches me the art of *grissini*. It is in the hands. He
rolls the smaller dough piece between both palms—
there is no escape now—until a forearm length snake
dangles just millimeters above the floor. It is sheepish,
a hesitant toe reaching to test cold, cold water. It knows
it will eventually recoil. As Square-Head then takes the
other end, looping the snake into a chest-high oval, and
shakes the dough into full extension, demonstrating its
impossible elasticity, I wonder if I'm trapped in a Bible
story. Surely, there is a first moral to be found in this
kitchen and this dough. Surely, the twins mean something, don't they?

"Prego, prego," Square-Head says, rolling the raw *grissini* in cornmeal and setting it on an oiled baking sheet.

Like the toe, I reach in and pinch a piece of dough
between my fingers. When I don't recoil, I expect the
ball to scream like a boiling lobster, but…nothing—no
sound at all—just a soft easy give like a biscuited hand
to a toothless old dog's mouth. The dough and my fingers come together all gums and jowl and liver snack.
Rolling the dough between my hands, palms going the
way of oatmeal, Eyeliner sings, *"Si,"* Eyelinerless echoes,
"Si," and Square-Head undertones it all with an I'll-be-

damned *"Si"* of his own. Today, I am making *grissini*. Tomorrow, the world.

Behind me the hearth hushes us all with its awaiting whisper. I am lulled into a rhythm: pluck, roll, breathe, pluck, roll, breathe, wipe the forehead, smile at the siblings, pluck, roll, breathe. Soon, I have made an entire tray of *grissini*, dusting the dozing dough-strings with a grainy blanket of cornmeal. *Go to sleep, go to sleep, close your big egg-yolk eyes.*

Square-Head, knowing obviously when to take matters into his own hands, slides a wooden paddle under the baking sheet and carries it to the oven. When it goes in, the fire leaps to embrace it, and gives up, at the same time, a sheet of finished *grissini* to Square-Head's reaching paddle. The hot *grissini* (don't you dare call them breadsticks) lie cooling like coppered armbands unrolled, waiting patiently for the proper ceremony. I am drenched in sweat, covered in cornmeal, gritty as a swimmer going straight from ocean to sand. And I do smell a slight sea-saltiness rising from the hot, hardening *grissini*. For what must be the ten-thousandth time since I've been in Italy, I kiss my fingertips.

"Sale del terra," I say to them all, the twins now unwrapping brand new dough balls—the *grissini* mothers—from their plastic wraps, Square-Head nodding with his hands on his hips, admiring his craft and his student.

Salt of the earth. When the twins lead me back to the front of the store, my hands full of *grissini*—some mine, some theirs—I feel as if I'm not only stepping into a meat-locker, but into the nineteenth century. Time and temperature unspool around me. I am shocked to see that three hours have passed since I entered the bakery.

I wonder if the crystal dough ball somehow transported me, somehow anticipated the synchronous *"Ciaos"* from the twins, the vicious wave goodbye from Square-Head in the kitchen.

The front door's silver bells throw their light at my feet like refugees. Somehow, they too have slipped through space, found their way back to me. I am F.D.R., Margaret Thatcher, Joan of Arc, Tarzan. I have made *grissini*. I am going to the street. When I open the door, those crazy, fantastic bells ring above me. The cobblestone is new and old all at once. The spell is breaking, but it's not broken. When I turn back into the store, before I allow the door to close, I am somehow not surprised to see that the twins' goodbye-waves are not identical at all.

≈≈ ≈≈ ≈≈

After tasting the world over, chef-apprenticing all over the U.S. and Italy, and launching his own successful catering business, Matthew Gavin Frank has settled down in the Chicago area. His love of food has inspired his writing and his work has appeared in numerous publications including Literary Review, The New Republic, *and* The Best Food Writing 2006.

ERIKA CONNOR

Ride to Karakorum

Under the huge sky of Mongolia,
the wheel of life turns.

W E FEEL IT SO CLOSE. SOMETHING IS GOING TO
happen. The wind strengthens. We come to
the highest summit and there it is far below, a space so
wide, a sea dappled with light, something glinting. Did
Chinggis Khaan see this? When he chose this monu-
mental place as capital of the empire? Did his sons ride
from here, where the grass sea meets the sky, like mirror
images, on a 5,000-kilometer journey to the Caspian Sea?
Nothing left of Karakorum. I imagine I can see the white
stupas of the Erdene Zuu temple walls. The wind lives
down there. Ariun gives a war cry. We made it. I reach
for him from my horse and he finds my mouth, a herdsman's kiss, something raw and real and strong. Chinggis
turns his horse on a dime and gallops off into oblivion.

I remember thinking on the first night of our journey: *But this is the modern world. Are there any cowboys left?* I could see him smiling in the dark. What was he thinking, taking a tourist hundreds of kilometers across the land to Karakorum? How was he going to live like this? With a foreign woman? And he had never really done it before, besides the four-day trip in the Gobi last year with the Japanese men drinking and talking dirty and falling off their horses.

And here I am riding the open steppes, with a Mongolian man who is no longer a guide, on a white horse that is not really a Mongolian horse, but a reincarnation of my African horse from so many years ago.

On the Orkhon River. Our place of rest. There is always wind in this land, blowing across the flatness like a sea, blowing grit in your hair and on your skin. When I look at those beige hills so far on the horizon I can't believe we came down them, and crossed this great scorched valley, the rusted combines sitting like memorials, the earth burnt up, a memory of the Russians and their dream of golden wheat. Three, four hours across the heat, with this line of poplars forever on the horizon and out of reach.

The horses are grazing down the line of trees. Earlier a mule came to drink. The white horse wanted to follow him away. He managed to climb down to the river in his hobbles, then inched his way back up the bank. I thought he would tip over. He watched the mule wander away a little sadly. We washed our clothes, our hair, our skin in the swift water, each in our own spot on the riverbank. Once in a while we would look up or down at each other and laugh, humming, happy. Now our clothes are laid across the grass stalks. Now we sleep with the rustling aspen leaves.

In the early evening we ride along the river that becomes a narrow canal, and cross a little plank bridge. Here, on the edge of a town that seems to have no real center, we find a tourist *ger* camp. I had said we should live in style and celebrate. But when we come to the little painted gate a caretaker wandering across the grounds gives us a listless look and tells us to keep the horses out. We tie the horses to the fence and hop over and walk into the giant restaurant *ger*. It is high and spacious white, with no stove in the center. We walk up the middle on a red carpet. There are ten tables, all laid with white cloth, and set with plastic flowers in vases. A great woven yellow and black rug of Chinggis Khaan hangs over the back door that leads outside to the kitchen *ger*. We choose a table on the eastern wall. A group of Americans sit on the other side. There is no one else.

A well-dressed young woman speaks English and gives us two menus, then disappears under the great Khaan and out the back door. We are left looking at our hands, the black earth under our nails and embedded into the skin, and our clothes layered with dust. I see our trail of dirt down the carpet. We leave our prints on the tablecloth. Coffee comes in little white cups, with hot milk in metal pots, sugar cubes in a bowl. Ariun is looking at the prices. I don't know what to order, something with meat, and also a salad for me. I am craving green. The waitress speaks to me in an English I don't quite understand. Ariun speaks to her in Mongolian and she answers me in English. We finish our coffee, light cigarettes.

Ariun gets up to check on the horses. We wait. I go to the door to see the horses standing at the fence, looking lost without us. Across another canal, in a field is a blue Naadam tent. Thundering music comes from there, and across the land four black yaks are pulling a decorated *ger* on wheels, the chariot of Chinggis Khaan. It is a traditional theater being prepared for tourists in celebration of the Naadam Festival, three days of horse racing, wrestling, archery, and a lot of drinking. I walk back across the carpet and notice again our traces of earth.

We are brought two large plates, each with a little round of steak sitting beside a dab of red coleslaw and two small potatoes, a thoughtful display on the clean white porcelain. Ariun and I look at each other. The Americans are laughing at something from the other side. How can you explain the hunger, when you have been wind-worn and sun-beaten? Ariun must wonder how luxury can be so meager. I am thinking about *guanzes*, those blessed canteens and teashops with their hearty thick mutton stews.

We are not tourists, but we can pretend. After dinner we steal into the bathrooms to use the toilets and look into the mirror, and wash our faces and hands in the sink, watching the grime flow down the drain.

We ride back the way we have come, along the walls of the canal that flow on and become a river. At a place where the banks are soft we get off the horses, loosen the girths and let them drink until they lift their heads, water dripping from their muzzles.

We thought we would spend the night in a luxurious *ger*, but this is better. They didn't want our horses. We find a place by the line of aspens and give the horses the grass—that is all they ever need—and we lie in our tent with the door open, each in our own thoughts. Our small words of Mongolian and English have blown off to somewhere. There is just sky, crickets leaping in the grass and onto the thin fabric of our tent, and the horses swishing their tails, eating. What would you say anyway, if you could say everything? We have lived together every day, riding to our destination, looking for water, grass for the horses, food for ourselves, shelter. This is what happens after the day is done.

Ariun sets his alarm clock and stands it in the corner. We stuff clothes under our heads, and my little red pillow from my saddle, and lift the sleeping bag over us. Then Ariun lays his *del,* his heavy red wool coat over us as a final protection and tucks it in around us.

"Ughh!" He makes a face in the last light and lifts the *del* again, sniffing at it.

"Brown horse pee."

He wants me to smell it, as if I don't believe him, but I am laughing. Brown Horse has given him back his own medicine, after all of Ariun's pee-soaked cloths—one of the many Mongolian cures—that were laid across the horse's saddle sores. Ariun must have put his coat out in the sun. It is dry now.

The wind comes in the night, rampaging. It blows in circles, then strikes the side of the tent full force, as if it was a sail. I can feel the cold currents at my back. It pushes against us over and over, as if it is urging us, trying to convince us that it is better to fly across the waves of grass, forget the horses. The noise woke us. The alarm hadn't gone off. Ariun sits up, ruffling his hands in the clothes around us. The flashlight clicks on. I see him shake his clock, then look at it and toss it aside. He shines the light out into the night.

"White horse where?"

I kneel beside him, looking out into the darkness, following the beam of light across the streaming grasses, slowly, slowly, and the brown horse appears not far off, looking back at us into the light. His eyes gleam. Ariun shines the beam around him and into the blowing aspens all the way down, and back again, then to each side of our tent. He leans out the doorway and half stands to see behind us. He comes in again and puts on his boots.

"White horse, no."

I watch him go, walking into the night until he disappears and the little light flickers like some spirit. Even then, it is engulfed by darkness. I find my boots and get them on and step out. The air is as taut as a drum, rippling with tension, walls of pressure, blasts. My hair flies, along with leaves, strings of grass, particles of dirt, sprays of sand. I lose my balance, wavering, walking across the grasses.

Not a drop of rain. This is a stage only for the wind. I stop to listen.

In my long ago journey through the villages of northern Senegal I slept out in the cool winds where I was able to see the luminous hide of my horse in moonlight or dark skies. If he exists, I told myself, then so do I, and I was able to sleep.

My white horse, Léo Lawal, ran away only once, in the large town of Kayes, where the Senegal River forked and became many tributaries. I had taken him to graze on the outskirts, and dropped the rope only for a moment, letting it lie on the earth. The horse turned his head, walked a little farther and lifted his head. Before I could reach the rope he was kicking up his heels and running for the hills, galloping like I had never seen him do. And then I closed my mouth to his little joke. All the places he had dragged his feet, stumbled, stammered, stuttering at the distance of some obscure journey, giving me his solemn eye. Now he was a stallion again, shaking his head, snaking the rope loose in the wind. The little boys I met on the road told me he was up on the hill, and of course he was there, my white horse grazing. He let me take him back again. My African horse was a trickster and a dreamer, just like my Mongolian horse now being led back at Ariun's side, having learned how to hop in his hobbles.

Kharhorin town. Scattered debris of different ages: historic Erdene Zuu walled in by 108 white stupas, and outside the walls, far out on the grass, two stone turtles marking the boundaries of ancient Karakorum, and the factory complex nearby with its towering orange chimney, spewing coal smoke into blue sky, blowing across and staining the white stupas. The Orkhon River has been siphoned off into a series of canals where cows lounge and children swim, and plank bridges are the only way to cross. Dirt roads and telephone poles crisscross the green common laced with broken glass, vodka bottles, and garbage. The settlements of little square wooden cabins behind plank fences under the hills, lace and flower curtains at broken windows, wild plants and grasses left to grow under faded dirty walls. Not one idea of a garden.

We go to find a phone, passing among the scuffed Russian facades, ochre yellow and old pink. I hold the horses in the parking lot outside the post office while Ariun goes to call his father. Noise of motors and music. People are wandering in their daily lives, a man in a suit on a bicycle, navigating the ruts in the road, a woman with flowered kerchief and a plastic bag on her arm, a drunk herdsman without his horse, trying to walk, bumbling along. I pray he won't notice me. No one seems to. A family waits by their car. The brown horse reaches around me and leans his head over the fence for the weeds and when I pull him back he rests his white nose on my arm. The white horse grinds his teeth softly on the bit. Ariun is phoning home. What will he tell them? The trouble at Mongol Els is far behind us, the time we got lost in the swamp grass and fought, and almost turned back. We made it. They will be pleased.

When I crossed the border and rode into town that time in Africa, after 700 kilometers, there was no one to meet me but the officer at the police station who stamped my visa and gave me a form to fill. He looked out the door at the white horse in the parking lot among all the mopeds and asked me his name.

"Léo Lawal." Moonlight, in the Fulani language.

"Write that down where it says mode of transport," he said and laughed.

Three days is maybe too long in Kharhorin, back and forth from the cool rustling aspens of our river place to the dust, heat, and whirling devils of town. We are accompanied by swallows, flitting around us like a school of fish, purple-blue iridescence, swimming at the horses' feet, skimming the earth. The people know us now: "those two strangers who park their horses outside, and that tourist girl who knows how to put on a hobble." Our little restaurant with the lace at the windows. The women in the kitchen welcome us and we sit always at the same table so we can watch our horses.

A British woman comes in to order take-out. I have seen her before walking through town, in that way that foreigners recognize each other, something other-worldly. She looks thin and worn, shy, does not smile. She has lived here for five years, at Erdene Zuu, operating an NGO to help restore the temples and way of life. Had she married a Mongolian? She says she loves it here, but I do not quite believe her. Is it her face that seems so worn? Or is it something in me that fights against staying in one place? Would I choose to live here? She does not seem to see Ariun, or maybe that is because she is looking only at me. I think it must be auspicious. It is time I go to pay my respects.

Ariun takes me to the gates of Erdene Zuu, and stays behind with the horses. He doesn't want to go, not even when I promise to hold the horses on my return. Maybe he is losing his traditional ways. This morning as we lifted the tent he stamped on the little crawling insects that had kept us awake all night, whispering, burrowing under our warm bodies.

"Don't kill them!" I cried. "Aren't you Buddhist?"

Or maybe the ways are no longer useful in a world of tour buses in parking lots, distracted tourists, souvenirs and plastic blowing out of their hands.

I pay my 1,500 tögrögs and go in through the giant wooden doors on iron hinges no human could ever have moved alone, into a vast open space with just the sky above. Tourists walk across the white dust, eating ice cream and taking pictures. Some are pilgrims at the prayer stations, turning each prayer spool as they walk in slow meditative steps. The sounds of the stuttering wheels, the chimes. So hard to see where it all begins. All of this was built up from the ashes and ruins of Karakorum, first abandoned by the sons of Chinggis Khaan, then laid to waste by Manchurian soldiers, and then again by Stalinists. The temples are like the children of the giant temples I have seen in the Forbidden City of Beijing, ancient wooden sky ships, vast terracotta tiled roofs, sweeping prows, casting deep shadows underneath the awnings, paintings of sea greens, of dragons and sea serpents, and pillars of red oxide. They are also in the process of restoration, hung with green nets and plastic. At the end of the great open court is a gateway open to the land. Where is Karakorum? Is it out there in the grass with the stone turtles, or here in the transformed stones? Is it of the sea or the earth?

The last white temple, Lavrin Süm is like a ghost, a dream of Tibet. It is more about the sun, square white cliff walls studded with sun disks and bordered with a pattern of gold and red, clay tiles, wooden timbers, a blood-red door.

The temple is a place of humming and smoke, salt smell and silk darkness, where colors come out like stains of ink, veins of gold. When your eyes adjust to the darkness you are played upon by an elaboration of decoration and pattern, like cells that keep multiplying, from microcosm to macrocosm, in the banners, tapestries, mandalas, tassels, fragments of ancient script, in the faces and forms of countless gods and goddesses. It seems there are no walls. This multitude takes over your mind.

I wonder how this works, after coming in from the land, the openness and distance where everything is earth and wind, weighted with a silence that goes beyond human capacity. Aren't the gods in the grasses and particles? Didn't Chinggis Khaan pray to the great blue sky? All of this color and design seems artificial to me, a little frightening. The monks are drinking bowls of tea at their low benches on the floor, and the tourists move around them, careful not to step on their hands, careful not to brush all the layers of things, like too much storage in a cave. The tourists come to a stop, having made only a few steps in, and stand like lost children, or sit on the benches as if it is a museum. I am also one of them. I sit and watch the smoke rise up into nothingness. There is no ceiling either. All of this color comes from nature: blue silk for sky, yellow for sun, red for blood and earth, and white for purity of snow that leaves no traces when it has melted.

The young monks are reading their scripts, with the steam rising from the tea at their elbows. They are whispering among themselves, sometimes laughing soundlessly. They are dressed in red robes in the old way and their heads gleam, but they live in the modern world. The elders have cell phones. The tourists come in and watch them.

I am sleepy among so many prayers, but I came to say one myself, so I get to my feet and inch my way around to the altars. So many glass cases of shelves that hold hundreds of figurines on pale blue cloth, and open-tiered shelves with incense sticks and more gods. Coins and folded bills have been stuck into crevices and into the folds of cloth.

The words do not come. My mind is a blur of grass. Isn't everything known anyway? Isn't everything seen from the great blue sky? A prayer for my search for home, something to hold me in one place in this land of nomads.

A prayer for the troubles at home. My brother's baby almost died, and his wife, so far on the other side of the earth, so many kilometers behind me. Did I just drop everything and ride away? I travel to get home the long way. Is it some kind of rite of sympathetic magic? If I ride the length of the land, feel thirst with parched lips and the stirrings of hunger, pass in and out of storms, lessen my loads, lay my bed on the earth, and return again on my steps, then surely I will have become familiar with the pathways inside of me.

A prayer for the white horse that carries me faithfully through time, from the cattle trails of Senegal to the open steppes of Mongolia. The wheel of life.

A prayer for my journey with Ariun. Wherever he intends to go after the trails fork off, I don't suppose I will follow in the long long afternoon. I will wonder about him and what it means. I leave a tögrög bill at the feet of a golden Buddha.

I walk out of the temple into blinding sun and can't remember what I have seen, where I have been. I go into a little white tent outside where the British woman has her displays and sells artifacts to raise money for her NGO, but she isn't there. There is a photo display of all the monks who died at the hands of the Russians, tens of thousands. The disappeared.

I buy a long blue silk scarf, a prayer for the eternal blue sky, and hurry away with it across the hot white dust, wondering how long I have been away. I see Ariun and the horses as I come out, so small in the grass beyond the towering tour buses. Ariun is reclining in the shade of his horse. I felt strange without them. It is like I have been in another country.

❧ ❧ ❧

Erika Connor is a painter, writer, and art teacher from rural Quebec, Canada. She has a BFA in studio art and creative writing from Concordia University, in Montreal, where she also won The Irving Layton Award for Fiction in 1991. She has traveled extensively in West Africa, and recently returned from Mongolia where she first worked as an eco-volunteer on a wild horse reserve.

ADRIAN COLE

❧ ❧ ❧

Night, the Desert, and a Car

The hospitality of mother Egypt takes a strange turn.

I
T WAS RAMADAN, AND THERE WAS A QUIET LISTLESSNESS
among the general population, probably because
everyone was hungry all day, and thirsty in the heat.
There were few people on the street of Cairo in the
pounding temperature of the early morning. My brother,
Martin, had arrived the night before, and late the next
day we set off for the Nile Sheraton to rent a car. All they
had in stock was an uninspiring Fiat of some vintage, but
we took it and coaxed it out of the Sheraton's parking lot.
Our first stop was a music store just off Maidan Tahrir.
Here we found all of the recent Egyptian hits, garishly
displayed. Being badly versed in contemporary Egyptian
music, we made a couple of blind guesses, and just for
luck took their entire offerings of the Beatles, which,
apart from Madonna and some Michael Jackson, and

a series entitled "Late Night Sax," was about all of the recognizable Western music the store offered.

Cairo traffic, even in Ramadan, is not the easiest traffic in the world to navigate. It has an organic quality in which the cars truly "flow," somewhat like water, except more damaging when you come into contact with it. We battled our way out of town on the tail end of the rush hour, amidst decrepit trucks laden with camels tied a hundred ways, sheep, chicken, and goats. These jostled side by side with black Mercedes, and other smooth luxury automobiles of the elite, public buses with people hanging off the sides, and the incessant whining of mopeds with frantic, two-cylinder engines.

Under a railway bridge we noticed a long string of railway cars, out of whose windows poked the heads of camels, all expressing the same resigned bewilderment at what was happening to them. These were probably being transported from Upper Egypt—Aswan and the Sudan. The big camel market at Imbaba is a terminal for many of the camel traders from the Sudan who walk their herds sometimes hundreds of miles across the desert to bring them, emaciated and bone-dry, to the northern markets. Camels end up being distributed all over Egypt's Nile delta, and to the oases and the farming communities along the Nile.

In the thickening night we passed the naked gas lamps of local markets selling pomegranates, figs, dates, pigeons; small cafés in nondescript concrete buildings, doors open to reveal a few elderly men in grubby galabiyas, sucking on *shishas* and playing backgammon. Ragged, flickering Coca-Cola or 7Up signs added a splash of color to the darkness. Outside young boys in rags chewed on unidentifiable foodstuffs. Mangy stray

dogs lumbered across the streets. At a traffic light, suspended above the road on a wire swinging in the night
breeze, we heard the evening call to prayer howling
from a nearby minaret. Some drivers pulled over and,
hazard lights flashing in the twilight, unrolled their
prayer mats on the side of the road, and stood facing southeast towards Mecca, the city where, fourteen
hundred-odd years ago, a merchant named Muhammad
started receiving messages from God.

We drove on through scrubby desert in the darkness,
passing the occasional gas station or roadside convenience store. There was not much to see. We could dimly
make out the shadows of some sandy hills away to the
south. We were heading across a relatively empty stretch
of desert towards Isma'iliyya, and the Suez Canal, to
cross over onto the Sinai Peninsula. Then we were to
drive across the peninsula and through the mountainous
interior, and arrive in Dhabab, a fast-growing seaside
community on the eastern coast of the Sinai. We drove
monotonously along a straight two-lane road, the White
Album issuing from the two tinny speakers under the
dashboard. Soon we spotted the flicker of oil wells burning off gas on the horizon: strangely eerie torches rising
from the sand and disgorging heat and light. There
were no towns around here, just a few works buildings,
and little traffic. From time to time one of the ubiquitous Peugeot station wagons that are used as shared taxis
flew by. As they approached they not only dipped their
headlights, but turned them off altogether, presumably
to avoid dazzling the oncoming traffic. For several seconds they would careen towards us in darkness and then
they were gone, their lights diminishing into the night
behind us.

As we approached Isma'iliyya our Fiat suddenly died, without warning and without melodrama, just a loss of power and an end to all electrical activity—the Liverpudlian musical commentary brutally silenced. It was 11:30 P.M., and there was no traffic whatsoever on the road. About ten miles away we could see a few glittering lights, what probably amounted to an oil company out-station, and beyond it some more illumination on the horizon, probably Isma'iliyya itself. We tried to turn the car over again, but there was no juice whatsoever. The car had coasted to a standstill on a sandy island in the middle of the road. We smoked while we wondered what to do, and discussed, while surveying the considerably empty desert, whether the Sheraton had a roadside emergency unit in the neighborhood. Even if they did, we had no way to alert them to our problem.

Twenty minutes passed, and then we saw a figure walking towards us out of the desert. He was a small man dressed in a dark galabiya and tattered running shoes. He looked at the car and then at us, and said, with a twist of the wrist, "Broken down?" We nodded and asked him absurdly where the nearest phone might be, looking hopelessly around us at the emptiness. He turned and looked back into the desert from where he had just appeared, and pointed at the nothingness. "Not far. Just there." Peering into the gloom, we could see nothing, no lights, no buildings, no suggestion that there might have been a telephone for tens of miles. Maybe he had a cell phone in the saddlebag of his mule somewhere. "Follow me," he said with another hand gesture. Seeing as there was precious little else to do, we dutifully stubbed out our cigarettes and, shouldering the bag that held our money and passports, fell in line behind our guide.

For a good fifteen minutes we walked over what seemed to be a huge field of sand. As our eyes grew accustomed to the darkness we began to make out some mountains ahead of us. Certainly there would be no phone there, in those inhospitable, barren hills. In fact the only lights visible seemed to be in the opposite direction, the other side of the road. Martin came up behind me.

"Do you think we should be following him?" he asked. "There's nothing here. Maybe he has some friends waiting behind a rock somewhere...." His caution hit a nerve and I ran up to our guide and asked him, with some anxiety, where, exactly, this supposed phone was. He gestured ahead of us, apparently to the mountains, and said, "No problem, no problem, a little more..." Martin, still at my shoulder, looked ahead.

"What did he say?"

"He said it's just up there," mimicking the man's flick of the wrist. We walked some more in silence, and Martin repeated, urgently, "Look. There's nothing there, for Christ's sake! It obvious this is not about a telephone. I think we should turn around." We stopped as the man disappeared into lightlessness, and we looked at each other, and looked around for the fiftieth time, and I could not put my finger on why, but I didn't feel anxious. I knew that I should have—all the evidence suggested that Martin was right. I had a vision of us from 500 feet up in the sky: two bemused Europeans standing in the desert, fifty miles from the nearest settlement, a dead car behind us and a live guide ahead and a dilemma all around. I looked to see if any brigands were hot on our heels. Then I looked for any outcrops of rocks, behind which death in the form of a blade-wielding Bedouin might have been lurking.

"Look at us," Martin said. "We're easy prey for any-one who cares to attack us." I thought about how, in the Third World, you can easily slip under the thin net of security into a place from which there is no escape, and disappear without a trace.

"I dunno," I said, and I made to keep walking. "You think we should just turn around? I guess it might be wise." Both of us were racking our brains to figure out what our guide could have been up to, in the light of the apparent reality that there was no phone in sight. Were we in for a ten-mile walk? Or was there some other explanation that we simply could not imagine? This situation seemed vaguely familiar. We were suffering from a lack of information, and my experience in Egypt so far had told me that there were many things that I had simply failed to imagine, ways that the story might be resolved that had entirely escaped me. So part of me was not too concerned, happy to keep trudging after the guide and see what materialized, mirage-like from the sands. But part of me was in rational agreement with Martin; I could not see where the guide was going. Should we risk making fools of ourselves by bolting and leaving him bewildered, standing by some unimagined pay phone in the middle of the desert?

I ran to catch up with him again, wanting to quiz him further before abandoning him.

"Hey, wait a minute," I said to him. "Look, there is no telephone here, these are mountains.... Please tell us where you are going!" He muttered something I didn't fully understand, something to do with a "base, with telephones," and urged us to keep following him. For another couple of minutes we kept walking, Martin muttering behind me and looking around vigilantly.

As we were preparing to ditch our guide, however, we noticed a faint light coming out of the ground a little way ahead of us. Around the light was a simple square of concrete with a bulkhead on top of it. It looked as if someone had dropped it here from the back of a flatbed truck. On closer inspection, it proved to be the entrance of a stairway. Our guide stood at the top of it holding the bulkhead door open and smiling broadly, as if he'd just taken us to the Sheraton Hotel, and gestured into the bowels of the earth. We both stood at the top of the stairway and looked down. There was some bright light at the bottom of the stairs, and it seemed to have a concrete floor. Was this some little known Pharaoh's tomb? As we stood there I could hear voices, the scrape of a chair, someone laughing.

"Maybe it's an illegal gambling den," Martin offered. The guide, impatient with these two sheepish foreigners, descended the stairway. We had one final look around at the dusty dim landscape with the mountains towering above us, and went down after him.

Inside we found a huge room, one wall of which was a solid telephone exchange with wires going in and coming out, lights of all different colors blinking and flashing. In the center of the room was a large table around which sat five or six soldiers in the usual ill-fitting uniforms, with trouser legs coming up to their calves and sleeves up to their elbows. These were clearly not the elite guard. The table was covered with half-empty glasses of tea, paper bags with the remains of falafel and *foule* sandwiches, bottles of 7Up, the remains of a Ramadan feast. One or two soldiers were sitting at their stations at the wall, with headphones on, chatting away.

Our guide made a sweeping gesture of the room, as if

he was introducing us to Aladdin's cave itself, and fixed us with a cheeky told-you-so kind of stare. Some of the soldiers looked up, and a couple come over and asked us what we wanted. The old man mediated for us, and after they had listened to him, one turned to us and said in English, "Would you like to use the telephone?" They politely offered us some tea as they asked us our story. We gave them the details of the car, our plan to get to Dhahab, and they had no problem with this. It occurred to me that this must be a fairly important communications post, near the sensitive Suez Canal, and not far from the Israeli border. Finally we gave them the name of the Sheraton Hotel, and sat down to drink a cup of sweet black tea, as their telecommunications experts placed a call to Cairo.

"Looks like we've come to the right place," Martin observed, all dark fantasies of death and brigandry dissipated, as he found himself back in the lap of the authorities who were on his side.

"Right," I agreed. "If there's one place to find a telephone that would be here." We made small talk to some of the soldiers for a while and then the soldier who had gone off to contact the Sheraton Hotel returned.

"Sorry. All lines busy. Too busy to get through tonight. Sorry. No good." We looked at him in astonishment, speechless.

"You mean you can't make a phone call to Cairo from here? In the middle of the night?" Martin asked.

"No. No lines working. All too busy. Maybe tomorrow."

"My God," Martin looked at me, the fantasy that we were in good hands vanished, and the knowledge that we would have to return to the car and find an alternative way out of our dilemma, growing. We picked up our bags and bid goodbye to the soldiers who waved cheerily, and returned to whatever it was they were doing before we came in, and realized that if this was a remote listening post, waiting for the Israeli invasion, then mother Egypt was in deep trouble.

Our guide walked out with us, and escorted us back toward the road. We asked him what his fallback plan was and he offered up the idea of a taxi.

"At this time of night? Are there taxis here?" I asked. He was not perturbed, and on reaching our dead Fiat he motioned up and down the asphalt, and said, "Just wait, a taxi will come by, soon." Then he was gone, back into the darkness, and we were left sitting in the Fiat again.

We waited for an age. Every so often a car came by at breakneck speed. Eventually a taxi showed up and we both jumped up and down, determined not to let it pass without stopping. It duly slowed to a standstill and we ran up to it with our bags. I poked my head through the window and ascertained that the driver was, in fact, going to Cairo, and he was happy to take us there. But as Martin got in the front seat and I made for the back door, I noticed that there *was* no back seat. In fact there was one, but it was occupied by an enormous lump of cargo that appeared to be a coffin. I asked the driver where I should sit and he said I should feel free to sit on top of it. I was torn between asking him if there was a cadaver inside, and not wanting to know, but before I could ask it, the driver answered the question for me.

"Here is my friend," he said. "I am taking home." He grinned into his rearview mirror as I squatted awkwardly on the coffin's lid. "I am taking him home to his family in Cairo. No problem, you can sit there." To the raucous yet melodic strains of *Farid Al Atrash,* we sped through the night, leaving our dead Fiat behind, sitting on top of a dead man and headed for Cairo to demand recompense from the Sheraton Hotel.

❧ ❧ ❧

Adrian Cole moved to the United States from the U.K. for graduate work in Middle Eastern Studies. After working for several years in Middle East-related fields, and living, variously, in Washington, Texas, and France, he recently moved to Maine where he lives with his wife and three children. His story "Night, the Desert, and a Car" comes from a memoir about living in Alexandria, Egypt, as a student of Arabic. His writing can be found at www.adrianvcole.com.

MICHAEL McCARTHY

❧ ❧ ❧

Above Crystal Mountain

Arriving, he found he was already there.

W E ARE AT ABOUT 17,500 FEET, CLIMBING SLOWLY and fading badly when three tiny dots appear like ants on the lunar landscape, far below, moving fast, emerging out of the shadows of the eastern valleys where there are no trails and there should be no people. Half an hour more of excruciating effort and we can make the top of Gandala Pass, then it's down to Upper Dolpo on the Tibetan plateau in this remote corner of northwestern Nepal.

In his classic work *The Snow Leopard* some thirty years ago, Peter Matthiessen described how he had ventured to this hidden corner of the world, late in the bitter cold of the Nepalese autumn, when deep snow had arrived early in the high western Himalayas, on a spiritual odyssey in search of himself. Today, after the passage of so many seasons, it seems that nothing has changed in Dolpo, except today a blazing sun hammers down from a dazzling diamond sky in the sweltering, pre-monsoon heat of a brief Dolpo summer.

After ten hours of steady vertical climbing up from our overnight camp in Black Canyon at 12,500 feet, we are now staggering more than walking, sitting longer than staggering, gasping more than breathing. Somehow we have to cross this pass and get down from this deathly height before dark, when either the altitude or the overnight cold will kill us. Lama Tenzin is still leading our party of six, but Tinle and our Tibetan horsemen have already arrived at the top of the pass with all our gear. High above, himself a tiny dot in the distance, Tinle is waving his arms impatiently, signaling us to hurry.

Shuwang is very ill again, nearly blind from the excruciating pain of oxygen deprivation. It doesn't seem that he can walk much farther. Samchoe has been sitting down for ages, and even Purpa, the teenage jumping mountain goat, has come down with a severe case of altitude sickness that leaves him moaning as he climbs. I sit on a rock, the lone Westerner, struggling with my thoughts, wondering how and when I will ever get on my feet again.

Looking down and to my left, I note the three tiny dots have grown larger and closer and have sprouted legs. Through the zoom lens of my camera I see that they have no horses, and carry no packs. They are bent over and moving fast. I try to think who these creatures may be, but thinking is even harder than breathing. Perhaps they are villagers from Do Tarap, come to pick magic cordycep worms on the highest alpine meadows? But who could be coming from the east, and why so fast?

We squat amid the stones listlessly, trying to summon some last burst of energy to continue our trek, the reasons for which have drifted away into the endless void like wisps of fog. Far above, lost in the roar of the constant wind, we can hear Tinle's urgent cries: "*Alloo! Alay!*" But we sit there like condemned men awaiting the executioner, too exhausted to think, let alone move.

The first Maoist arrives. He appears to be the leader, a wicked-looking kukri swinging from his side and a pistol poking from his shoulder bag. Bizarre in this vast wilderness, he is toting a ghetto blaster on his shoulder and whistling to the atonal Tibetan cowboy music blaring from the box. Looking up from my boot, which I have been studying with vague wonder for a long time, I nod and offer the usual salutation between complete strangers passing each other on the path of life, "*Tashi delek.*"

Good day to you, too, he nods, then murmurs something else in the ancient Sanskrit-like tongue spoken here in the Land of Dolpo, and continues his march to the summit. Right behind him two cadres doggedly follow, ignoring my pitiful existence and my mumbled greetings. After they pass, I dig feebly into the breast pocket of my parka, pulling out my digital voice recorder.

"Day six. We've dodged the Maoists for nearly a week, and now they finally show up, just below the summit. With luck, maybe they will keep going. Looks like they have automatic pistols."

"Pssst, no. Put away," whispers Lama urgently, staggering to his feet. "They think you journalist, maybe CIA. Keep camera hide, too. Come. We go."

We have discussed the chances of a robbery and are

prepared to hand over all our money, but losing the cameras and voice recorder is a different story. Right atop the ridge at nearly 18,000 feet, sitting in the howling fury, we can see the Maoists arguing with Tinle. In the addled mess of my brain I dumbly muse whether there could be any worse place on the planet for a robbery or kidnapping. The money means nothing to me, simply a fee to pay to the cadres of the self-appointed "people's government" that wander the trails of this poverty stricken nation, robbing whomever they meet. Even the gaunt porters who carry immense loads among the highest mountains on earth, for what is nothing more than a pauper's pay, are not immune from Maoist dogma and thievery. But I don't want to be kidnapped.

At Lama's insistent commands we finally stagger up the ridge ourselves. Black clouds race across the darkening sky. Despite the day's blazing heat, at this altitude small pockets of snow cling to dark shadows. Bits of stone and dust flung by the relentless wind sting our faces. Lama says something to me, but his voice is as lost in this grievous wilderness as our battered souls. Arriving at the top, I lie on the ground like a dead man, a silent witness to my own hopeless fate, and say nothing.

Here on the ridge top, the wild tableau of the Tibetan plateau to the north finally appears. It's a panorama I have trudged so far to see, but the Maoists are staring at me closely; I raise my head to look for no more than a second. A blasted landscape of torn and jagged peaks marches off toward a distant gray horizon. As one of the few Westerners ever to see it, Matthiessen wrote: "At 17,800 feet this pass is higher than any mountain peak in the entire United States aside from Alaska, but on all sides even mightier peaks reach for the heavens." It's an astounding sight, and it is not hard to imagine that somewhere down there among the endless valleys lies the invisible land of Shambala, the center of the universe of which ancient Tibetan scriptures speak. But I fear to look; my heart's desire is denied. I sit and ruminate on my upcoming fate.

When I first read *The Snow Leopard* over twenty years ago it never occurred to me that I would ever have an opportunity to travel to such an incredible place. When I met Lama Tenzin in San Francisco, and he first spoke of our trekking together to the almost mythical Land of Dolpo to study the last vestiges of pure Tibetan culture left on earth, it still didn't occur to me—until the last moment in Kathmandu when we studied the actual trekking route—that I would follow exactly in Matthiessen's footsteps. But now that I have finally arrived at the very moment, my mind is blank and self-preservation is my only goal.

Throughout the trek Lama has endeavored to teach me the way, not by words but through example. How to stay "in the moment," to focus on the goal, to understand that happiness comes from clarity of mind and serenity of soul. That desire is the root of all unhappiness, that kindness and giving to others is the only true path to Nirvana. Yet here I am, at the exact moment of reaching my long-awaited goal, and any sort of peace and happiness are denied me. In my befuddled mental state the irony is lost, but subconsciously my soul understands. All desire is illusion. Truly the journey itself is the goal and not the destination.

Tinle, who has been drinking home-brewed *chang* all day, is having heated words with the Maoists. I learn later, through translation, that these bandits want money from every member of our expedition, they want our cameras and camping equipment. But Tinle is the chieftain of Upper Dolpo, and he will have none of such blatant greed. He knows the Maoist leader, a turncoat from the village of Namdung. The Maoists are thieves, he says, no better than vermin. They should be content with simple highway robbery; how will these visitors to our land survive without their gear? No Tibetan acts in this despicable way. The Maoists cower and say nothing under Tinle's bluster, but they do not leave.

"Go get the money," Lama whispers to me. Slowly, without raising my head, I rise to my feet and stumble over to the horses and our gear. The horsemen stand awkwardly, heads down, too, saying nothing. They hate the Maoists as well, and look away during this embarrassing transaction. Every man, woman, and child in Dolpo believes fervently in reincarnation; robbing guests to your home is the path to hell.

Originally I had hidden the money in several envelopes at the bottom of the pack, but constant sifting through my gear brought exasperation; yesterday I had put all the money together in an outside pocket. Slowly I pull out the envelope and walk back to the group, where I hand the money to Lama. In the screaming wind he somehow counts the rupees, slowly, making a big show of it, and then again. He hands the money to Tinle, who counts the hundred note bills over again, also making a show of it. After several countings, he finally hands the money over to the Maoist captain, who grabs the bills eagerly. In this land of utter destitution, there is more cash in his hand than any honest man might earn in a year.

"Get up and walk back over to the horses again," whispers Lama to me, with a nod. "Say nothing. Keep going."

Casually, I get up and stagger slowly back to where the horsemen patiently wait, stoic statues in their tattered clothes and old boots and long hair blowing in the wind. I hear Lama demanding a receipt. Did you count the money? Who has a pen? We will show this receipt to the next Maoists we meet and they must see that we have paid. I turn and look. There is a searching of pockets, and the captain looks for his receipt book. I keep walking, slowly.

Reaching where our horsemen patiently wait, I finally raise my head and cast a long look at the enormous vista lying in front of me. Peak after jagged peak stretches along the horizon toward infinity. Far below, beyond the snow pack guarding the cold northern reaches of this high pass, somewhere lies our destination. Suddenly, two of the horsemen grab me, one by each arm, and we fly over the ridge like wild birds in flight, leaving the horses behind. With whoops and cries we descend like madmen in gigantic swoops, our boots leaving wild skid marks in the snow, dropping like stones thrown down a deep well.

In what seems only seconds we descend a thousand feet. Turning, I see Lama and Schuwang and Purpa and Samchoe also flying down the slope, whooping and yelling, and Tinle following with the horses. I peer through wisps of mist down into the gathering gloom far below. There is Matthiessen's magical valley of Shey, and yes, there is the Crystal Mountain itself, and there are the green meadows he described, and the black river running through it, and the hat-like shape of Shey gompa looming in the twilight. Closer, I make out tiny white tents of nomads from the north glistening in the last rays of the setting sun like the teepees of American plains Indians of a few centuries ago.

Matthiessen's words, long since memorized, come back to mind.

"I am bewitched. The blinding snow peaks and the clarion air, the sound of earth and heaven in the silence, the requiem birds, the mythic beasts, the flags, great horns, and old carved stones, the rough-hewn Tartars in their braids and homespun boots, the silver ice in the black river, the Crystal Mountain."

I put my head down again, and start to walk. I am already in heaven.

᪥ ᪥ ᪥

Michael McCarthy is the author of two biographies and several outdoors books. He has been a radio news reporter and editor, a freelance features writer for many newspapers and magazines, and a writer of travel literature. When not taking his "travels with purpose and meaning" to weird places, he lives in Vancouver, Canada with his wife and son. Much of his recent travel writing can be found at www.intentional-traveler.com.

JANN HUIZENGA

❧ ❧ ❧

Shoes Like Gondolas

She plies the seas of Italian fashion.

THE BEST THING ABOUT MY SHORT-TERM RENTAL IN
Ragusa, Sicily is that it comes with a cleaning
woman. Lucia arrives every Monday morning sporting
a strand of pearls, heels, and a pencil skirt. She doesn't
shed any of them, neither while mopping the stone floors
nor scouring the bidet. I work at the kitchen table in old
sweats and listen to her click-clacking through the rooms
like some sort of busy bar hostess.

Fare bella figura, which roughly translates to "cutting a fine figure," endures as one of the highest Italian
virtues, on a par with making a pilgrimage to the Pope.
As the Sicilians say, *L'onuri è fattu a li robbi*, Honor is
measured by your dress.

I am less honorable than my cleaning woman. Judged
by the Sicilian proverb, dishonor dogs my entire nation.

For it's no secret that we Americans—who revere the gods of Comfort and Convenience and traipse through life looking as if we've just rolled off the La-Z-Boy to fetch another bag of Doritos—are fashion disasters. Everyone knows it, even the swarthy *contadino* at the Thursday Ecce Homo market who hawks socks and lacy black things I assume are funereal veils. "*Beh, signora,*" the disappointed man says when I settle on some socks after pawing through his bargain table, "*Sono passate di moda,*" he tells me, those are out of fashion. He holds aloft some pumpkin-and-acid-green numbers. "These here are *fighe*, cool!" How pathetic is it that I slavishly follow this old peasant's fashion tip and buy a bagful?

While I'm shopping one day at Sma, my local supermarket—which also carries cheap clothes—a matron emerging from the dressing room collars me. "*Mi scusi, signora!*" she brays. "Does this skirt fit me right?"

"*Sì, signora,*" I reply. "It looks good to me. But I'm American."

"*Ihh, mi sbaglio.* Oops, I'm mistaken," she stammers, and hotfoots it away from me toward a battleaxe with a fistful of salami. The attitude in a nutshell.

The topic of fashion comes up one day in the English class I'm teaching at the university. My student Davide posits that belts are political in Italy. "We cannot wear pants or even jeans in Italy without a belt," he says. "Without one, you are a rebel against society." Francesca adds that an increasing number of Italians make political statements with fashion. "If you're right-wing, you put on Dior, Fendi, Gucci, or Pucci; if you're left-leaning, you dress in Dolce & Gabbana."

Well, either way you've spent a frickin' fortune, I want to say, *so what's the diff?*

"I've noticed," Francesca goes on, "that Americans don't care about fashion like we do. My Sicilian relatives who went to the States in the sixties send me a package of clothes every year at Christmas. But I stuff everything in the back of my closet. It's always so ugly—and twenty years out of date!"

What interests me most about this conversation is not the fact that New World Sicilians cling to the image of Sicily as a backwater, or that going beltless here is tantamount to treason, but that these students enjoy discussing haute couture and fashion designers. Not exactly hot topics on American campuses.

The idea of comfort in clothing is as alien in Sicily as the notions of privacy and punctuality—I'm constantly combing the shops for stuff that's actually wearable. All the street's a stage, and she who shows up for a performance had better be decked out for the part. What this means in practice is that Italians dress in spectacularly chic garments that are utterly unwearable. Consider, if you will, the clothing in boutiques right now (all winter collections, though fall is piping hot). You find loads of straight skirts so constricting they allow only baby steps, unyielding leather pants, and strangling all-wool turtlenecks. The blouses *look* gorgeous but are made of fabrics so stiff and prickly that even their names itch— organza, chiffon, pointelle, piqué. It makes one crave the yummy cottons, terries, fleeces, and flannels of hang-loose America.

Everything that's not all stiff and ruffly is metallic. Studded. Distressed to the max. The tag on one raggedy, hemless shirt I buy says, in English, "This garment have soul." It seems nihilistic to pay top euro for threadbare duds that are just a wash cycle away from total disintegration. But then, much of the apparel here strikes me as pointless. I fondle a funnel-neck chenille sweater on a shop shelf, but when I go to try it on, I see the huge hole, like a vent, that has been cut from the back. For what? So you can warm your neck while air-conditioning your back? Most garments, in fact, contain some sort of peek-a-boo surprise—either a sleeve has gone missing, or both shoulders are absent, or the décolletage nose-dives to your navel, or the skirt is so itty-bitty that your bum droops below the hem. Nowhere, absolutely nowhere, can you find a plain old t-shirt. *Non c'è!* They either drip with gaudy sequins or bear some unwearable English phrase like *Party Monster* or *Ride Me*.

Have you ever flicked through the pages of *Vogue* or watched a haute couture show on Fashion TV and thought, "Amusing, but who in their right mind would actually *wear* that getup?" Italians would. Living in Italy feels, unnervingly, like walking through a gigantic theatrical production. Flamboyance and *fantasia* rule: faces painted like Mommy Dearest, dark hair garishly frosted and hennaed, frippery baroque and showy. There's none of that American concern with looking "naturally" beautiful. I mull this over and develop a theory: Americans primp for close encounters, while Italians preen for spectators—fellow paraders in the evening *passeggiata* or distant admirers in a sidewalk café.

It's almost impossible to find apparel without animal skin, feathers, or fur. Glamour and dead critters seem intertwined in the Italian imagination. Shops overflow with crocodilian belts, kangaroo-skin skirts, pony-skin pants, python pumps, bags with deer-antler handles.

A friend once told me she regretted the short Sicilian winter because it allowed only a few months to enjoy her rabbit-fur coat. As I admire Pinocchio pants (what we call *capris*) trimmed with gray fuzz—caterpillar?— at my local Stefanel shop, I ask the clerk if it's real fur. "Well, of course, *signora!*" comes the reply. When I inform her I can't buy the pants then, that Americans don't much like real fur, she recoils in disbelief, as if I'd told her Americans run naked in the streets.

But I wax shrill. It would be wrong to give the impression I have no stomach for Italian fashion. *Al contrario.* I'm gradually replacing my dowdy Puritan wardrobe— hauled here in two heavy suitcases—with more sexational items. Not that I'm aiming for a sexpot look, mind you, but when you buy Italian threads, that's just what you get. Midriff and cleavage and thighs are suddenly bared, you're fettered in strings-lace-studs-chains—and *Presto!* You're a southern Italian tart. It's like playing dolls into adulthood—with yourself as Barbie.

Lest you wonder what a professional woman does with a sluttish wardrobe, well, she slips into it for work. A weatherwoman on Italy's Channel 4 turned up on a recent show busting out of her blouse, looking more qualified to lap dance than read the weather. The louche cameraman—who must have been lying on the floor— slithered up her oily legs, then zoomed in and lingered wistfully on her ripe melons as the sober-suited anchorman raised his eyebrows and opined, "Nice dishabille." In a sudden fit of modesty, she blushed and screened her upper body with her notes. On Channel 2, the news anchor wore a serious look and a black turtleneck sweater buttoned all the way to her chin one night as she delivered news of the disappearance of a little Sicilian girl and atrocities in Iraq. But what riveted me (though I tried to avert my eyes) was the hole in her sweater—big as a picture window—that showcased her ample cleavage. Maybe it's just me, but eroticized news loses its gravitas.

During his year in Washington D.C., Milanese journalist Beppe Severgnini noted, in *Ciao, America!*, that working women there "go from their two-piece suit... straight into their husbands' sweatshirts," and concluded that the Eastern U.S. was "a strangely sexless land" where "feminine fascination is a no-no." *Scusi*, Signor Severgnini; while you may be right about all that, can't we find a happy medium between the sexless and the supersexed?

It wouldn't be fair to *gli italiani* to say their obsession with clothing springs from narcissism. Elegance in Italy shows civic altruism: you are prettifying the landscape for the delight of your fellow citizens. As the old Sicilian saying goes, *Mancia a gustu tò, càusa e vesti a gustu d'àutru*, "Eat to please thyself, but dress to please others."

In Sicily, even I take seriously my civic responsibility. I'm an idealized version of myself. I fuss over clothes and makeup, suck in my gut, walk taller. I have to get all glammed up even for a trash run because reaching the dumpster involves swimming through a sea of Sicilian eyes outside the Caffè Puglisi. Some days, I prefer to let the trash bags full of smelly fish bones and espresso grounds pile up in the apartment. It's just too wearisome maintaining the façade.

The cowboy look is all the rage. Sicilian women attire themselves in pseudo concha belts, faux turquoise jew-

elry, and suede-fringed jackets with whipstitching that
would look phony even in Santa Fe, my hometown.
Cowboy boots, called *texani*, sell like hotcakes. The shop
windows show them in all heights, from little booties to
thigh-high shit-kickers. I curse my luck. I left several
pairs back home, never having considered including
them in my luggage. Of course, my dusty boots are the
real McCoy, which wouldn't work here anyway. The
wildly overpriced Italian versions are long—*lunghissimo*
is the word that comes to mind—with toes that bow
upward to resemble the prows of those Venetian gondolas that nearly capsize each summer from the weight of
sneaker-shod *americani*.

I try on a pair. They're distressed, fabricated to look
like they've already put in years of hard labor out on
the ranch. The box says, "Special feature! Damaged by
hand." The scimitar toes form angles so acute that all I
can imagine as I hobble about is what great tools of self-
defense they'd be if they didn't kill me. "*Molto sexy*," says
the shop girl with no trace of irony. Her own tootsies
have been squeezed into a pink shoe so narrow that foot
fat pours over the edges like yeasty dough.

When my Sicilian-American colleague, Mary, turns
up one day shod in gondolas, I ask, "How can you walk
in those things?"

"It's actually easier than it looks," she says, inching
painfully down the street with me, arms akimbo. You
have to have the balance of a circus performer to wear
these things.

Sometime later, at a *cannolo* festival on the steep
cobbled streets of Mary's hometown, Modica, the prow
of her shoe wedges itself between two cobbles. She
lurches, her chocolate *cannolo* scudding through the air

like a missile. I prop her up as she limps back down the hill. Despite all this, Mary deems my own footwear too sensible and insists I buy a pair of gondolas.

I cave. The cappuccino-colored shoes cost an eye from my head, as they say here, and have killer toes as long as skis. "Looks like they'll take you on a magic carpet ride," says Husband when I get them home a month later.

Lest you conclude that women are the only fashionistas in Sicily, let me clarify: The real prima donnas are the men. On weekends, the *passeggiata* is all about black spandex t-shirts accentuating pecs and abs, starched white disco shirts, diamond studs in ears or noses. Chiseled jaws bristle with manicured stubble, heads are styled and gelled. Picture a pageant of white-hot young John Travoltas on the make. "Each thinks he is as handsome as Adonis," writes D. H. Lawrence of Sicilian men in *Sea and Sardinia*, "and as 'fetching' as Don Juan." They sashay like pimped-up poodles in a Mr. Sicily dog show. *Megghiu moriri ca campari mali,* goes another old Sicilian proverb: "'Tis better to die than to live badly." These glamour-boys are just doing their part to make our lives worth living.

At midnight last week, after my British colleagues and I had had dinner out and were waiting for a cab, young men in their full Sicilian splendor were parading on the *passeggiata*. Bony Brendan sat hunched on the curb in a rumpled shirt, smoking a cigarette and eyeing the catwalk. "God, I hate these bloody Italian blokes," he said.

I understand the sentiment, born of envy and an outsider's sense of otherness. After six months in Palermo, I had jotted the following in my diary: *These stunners* are impeccably barbered, perfectly polished wax figures, the most self-conscious people I've ever seen. I've developed a passion for naturalness. For folks in dirty blue jeans and faces stripped of harlequin makeup. For people who do not daily turn themselves into works of art. For a cleansing hike through Peoria.

Since reading Luigi Barzini's *The Italians*, I better understand the theatricality of Italian life, the importance of spectacle. In Italy, he writes,

> Ugly things must be hidden.... Everything
> must be made to sparkle, a simple meal, an
> ordinary transaction...must be embellished
> and ennobled with euphemisms, adornments,
> and pathos. These practices were not
> developed by people who find life rewarding
> and exhilarating, but by a pessimistic, realistic,
> resigned and frightened people. They believe
> man's ills cannot be cured but only assuaged,
> catastrophes cannot be averted but only
> mitigated. They prefer to glide elegantly
> over the surface of life and leave the depths
> unplumbed.

More than other Italians, Sicilians know sorrow and fear. For millennia they've endured tyranny. Plague. War. Famine. Earthquakes. Burning at the stake. Dictators. Volcanic eruptions. Abject poverty. Gangland-style murders. Excellent cadavers. So what if they want to caramelize life, gussy up and play-act? More power to them, I say. Still, McDonald's has opened its doors in Ragusa. With Convenience moved into town, can Comfort be far behind?

As I reflect on this now, back home in the States, my gondola shoes gather dust in the dark recesses of my closet, along with most of my other Italian costumes—some have already gone to Goodwill. But I *do* have a new Italian look: I always, *always*, wear a belt.

≈ ≈ ≈

Jann Huizenga has lived in Sicily on and off since 2002 and is at work on Kissing Sicilians: My Life in Ragusa, Sicily.

TODD PITOCK

❧ ❧ ❧

As Wind Moves,
So Does Memory

A journey to Niger, in search of jewelry.

I N 1992, JEAN-YVES BRIZOT, NOT YET THIRTY, WENT TO
Niger to create a guild of blacksmiths. He had spent
most of his twenties guiding young adventurers in rugged
environments all over the planet, but the place that captured
his imagination was the Sahara. There, he'd encountered
Tuareg blacksmiths creating exquisite silver jewelry using
a trembling hand technique. The work was not merely
beautiful, it also was an archive of Tuareg values, beliefs,
and culture. No piece could be replicated.

For the Tuaregs, numbering 1.2 million in Niger and
Mali and thousands more in Algeria, Libya, and Burkina
Faso, modernization was creeping like desert sands into
cities on the fringe of the Sahara, and these ferociously

self-reliant people known for their shimmering indigo veils and long swords in leather scabbards were in transition. After a string of devastating droughts in the 1960s, 1970s, and 1980s, and growing influence from outside, including aid groups, missionaries, and even tourists, they now faced the reality—humdrum yet difficult—of making a living. The blacksmiths, among the custodians of Tuareg culture, had difficulty getting their wares to market. Exploitive merchants were paying terrible prices for them to knock out cheap pieces for quick sales to tourists.

Brizot, the grandson of blacksmiths on both sides, wanted to help and got a sympathetic hearing at Hermès, the French company that began in 1837 as a harness and saddle workshop in Paris's Grand Boulevard quarter and has remained committed to preserving handcraft know-how. The arrangement was an autonomous partnership. Hermès helped get things started; the guild then supplied silver pieces called "The Tuareg Collection."

Fourteen years hence, the collaboration between a global company and traditional smiths continues, moving between 6,000 and 8,000 pieces most years, with a high of 13,000—a good living for those associated with the guild, economically insignificant for Hermès. The endeavor has had its challenges, especially after September 11, when orders slowed to a wheeze, leading Brizot to increase his guiding to earn money. That's what he was doing when I met him last year in Libya, where he told me about the guild.

"If you want to see something true and authentic," he said, "come to Agadez."

So it is that on a balmy January evening, accompanied by Jean Jonot, a seventy-one-year-old retired alpine guide from Brizot's hometown of Grenoble, I spend an eternal day hopscotching across continents aboard charter planes, and arrive ahead of my luggage.

"It will come on the next plane," an airline representative says.

"When is that?"

"Next week."

Brizot greets me with a man-hug. "It's only clothing," he says. "We'll get you what you need. Every challenge is also an opportunity."

Ah, Niger, land of opportunity. In any case, the country, a land almost twice the size of Texas, is a fascinating prospect. Landlocked south of Algeria, north of Nigeria, it last made international news for its bread (lack of, see also famine) and cake (so-called, of uranium; see Iraq War; also, Plame Affair).

Getting oriented doesn't take long.

Agadez is an ancient city along the Trans-Sahara Trade Route, an area where merchants and wayfarers have carried salt and slaves since the advent of camel caravans. Its mud architecture gives the entire city a reddish hue that, when the sun slants, radiates an orange glow against the intense blue sky. The Grand Mosque, marked by its eighty-nine-foot-high pyramidal minaret, has stood since 1844; the previous mud minaret had been there since 1515. There is some electricity; but at night, unlit chambers fade into a dark oblivion. Two internet cafés, a fast one and a slow one, opened last year. In one, I look over the shoulder of a Tuareg in a violet *tagelmoust* reading a story on Yahoo: "10 Best Places to Live!" Taxis are low-octane motorbikes; you get on and hold on, and all rides, whatever the distance, cost about forty cents.

The population is a mix of Tuaregs, Hausas, Tubus, and mixed-race "Agadezians." A small population of mostly French expats—Niger was a French colony until its 1960 independence—greet one another with stiff courtesies at places such as Le Pilier, the town's best European restaurant, whose Tuareg chef was trained well by its Italian owner. Rich Saudis come to Agadez to hunt gazelle and other wild game.

Brizot's place is a two-story affair near the Grand Mosque containing warriors' spears, mats, tablets covered in Arabic script, a giant bowl, drums, and books stacked on a black table with elephantine legs. His bedroom opens onto the roof, where he prefers to sleep in the open air.

At forty-two, Brizot's classic Roman features bring to mind busts of Caesar, which is not a bad comparison: adventurer, intellectual, romantic, merchant. He has a facility for intimate conversation and relationships, and also for disputes and rivalries. His healthy ego is additionally nourished by the rafts of children who hail him leaving or entering his house, "Brizot! Brizot! Brizot!"

"You're like a rock star around here," I say.

"Yes," he says, "I am."

What he's most proud of is the guild. The name in French, *A L'Atelier*, means "to the studio"; in Arabic, *A'Allah te leir* means "to get linked to God." The space includes a garden with citrus, quinine, and neem trees; an office; and the artisans' workspace, where eighteen or so blacksmiths each sit on the ground on a clearly defined rectangle, beating, cutting, scratching, and polishing silver that was smelted just across the compound.

Over the following days, the blacksmiths greet me warmly, though communication is no simple matter, requiring translation from English to French, then French to Tamashek. On the traditional ladder of their society, they're above domestics and slaves, below the nobles and teachers at the top. They are born and marry into smith families—marriage to a non-smith is regarded as intermarriage—and go through years-long apprenticeships. They take on many roles: creators, salesmen, entertainers, magicians, intercessors with jinn—a type of spirit in Islam. In the modern world, the hierarchy has often been turned on its head. Nobles whose livestock were killed by the famines are poor, while the smiths, who have learned to earn, are better off.

Tuareg Islam incorporates animist beliefs and mysticism: The universe is inhabited by jinn, and the blacksmiths are imbued with mystery even while polluting themselves by their dealings with the spirits. The blacksmiths encourage the mystique. One man, I'm told, lifts molten objects with his bare hands but is never burned.

"They are alchemists," says Brizot. "What you have to understand, though, is that the object is only the physical, visible aspect of alchemy. For the blacksmiths, the object represents a process of personal, spiritual transformation."

Pieces include twenty-one designs of Tuareg crosses—cruciform pieces, though not crucifixes, that can identify the wearer's place of origin. *Tcherots*, or amulets, are a traditional form; they contain verses of the Koran inscribed by clerics, not unlike Jewish mezuzahs. The imagery is geometric, compositions of lines arranged at angles to give the pieces movement. In recent years, the smiths have started working with gold, a mineral that was traditionally believed to have negative powers—the price and quality of silver became volatile, gold was stable, and there was a predictable market for gold jewelry.

Hermès's "Tuareg Collection," which is all silver, includes bangles, necklaces, buckles, and locks that incorporate tradition with other motifs. The objects' shape and weight and the quality of silver meet certain Hermès-set parameters. Their engravings, though, are drawn from the Tuareg lexicon. "They have Hermès shapes, but they have Tuareg meanings," says Atobeul N'Gatan, the guild's production manager. "For the blacksmith, the underlying purpose is still aesthetic," he adds. "You need to think about what a piece is meant to represent and it should be expressing something. When you give a piece of jewelry to someone, it should represent an emotion."

My own emotional state gets knocked somewhat off-balance the next day, the holiday of Tabaske, which commemorates Abraham's willingness to sacrifice his son for God. After gathering in the cemetery, the community whets knives and appetites for a mass slaughter of lambs, who bleat, bleed, and expire all over town, which clouds with cooking fires and the smells of barbecue.

The sultan, an important political figure in the city, invites us to visit. Brizot has attained a noble's status, and as his visitors, we share that lofty perch. Thanks to a friend, donated clothes arrived in a World Food Program duffel bag. I might have worn a tie instead of this vow-of-poverty look, but Brizot assures me the Sultan won't be offended.

The palace compound is a large house in a big square of dirt enclosed by mud walls with covered bays for the Sultan's various vehicles. His bodyguard is turned out in a brilliant red *tagelmoust* and a luminous red, green, and white robe.

"Is there anything I need to know before we go in?" I ask Brizot.

"Call him 'Excellency' and don't look into his eyes."

We're shown through a side entrance to an anteroom, where we sit on chairs backed against a wall—Brizot, Jean Jonot, myself, and another fellow who is dressed like a goatherd and who is, I have no doubt, using the opportunity of the holiday to solicit charity. Beggary is not unknown in Agadez, and on a holy day like Tabaske, one is expected to give, so an industrious mendicant can really clean up. After we sit for a few minutes, we're invited back out the door we entered. The bodyguard shakes our hands and gives a hale *salaam aleikum* as a send-off.

"What about the Sultan?" I ask. Had I inadvertently done something wrong that canceled our meeting? "Aren't we going to meet him?"

"You just did."

"The goatherd? The goatherd was the sultan?"

Brizot is troubled. Apparently I missed the point. "Normally the Sultan would greet someone very formally," he says. "It was a sign of great deference and even affection that he greeted us humbly, in a small room. He was saying, 'We are equals.' You should feel honored!"

Jean Jonot shrugs. "I also thought he was a goatherd," he says.

There is still, Brizot figures, a big gap in our understanding. "If you want to really get some understanding of everything here," he says, "we have to go into the bush."

The next day, we pile into his modified 1988 Toyota Land Cruiser. Brizot puts on a pair of beaten-up 1970s-style shades he bought from the Sultan, and we set off on a 600-mile loop through the Aïr Massif, a mountain range that slopes into the Ténéré, the expanse of dunes rolling into Niger's northeastern flank.

The landscape starts to change about thirty miles out of Agadez as we rumble on a rutted road. Like the jewelry, the scenery is all about shapes, textures, reflections, and angles of light, with alternations of color—pale yellow brush, burnished orange sand, rows of pale green foliage on desert trees. Brown mountains fade to black, all of it framed by a deep blue sky that loses its intensity as it dissolves into a pale haze. After this fertile area the vista opens up onto fields of black rock, with boulders and craters and formations of rock. Deep shadows and haze form over the massif.

There are signs of life: wells, trees, donkeys, and arrangements of rocks that indicate burial sites or mosques. Most Tuaregs we see are on motorcycles, up to three on a ride; deeper into the dunes and soft sands of the Ténéré, camels are, I'm told, still preferred. People materialize in the most unlikely places, as if suddenly formed out of dust and sand.

Now and again we arrive in a village or a farm where groups of Tuareg men pull their *tagelmousts* below their chins to talk about the challenges of getting their sweet, pink onions to markets in Europe.

We drop our pads and sleeping bags on the sand near an ancient rock painting by a Muslim holy place. The wind in the trees incongruously sounds like the ocean.

The next day we go to Tîmia, an oasis with a hilltop auberge of mud cottages above the sandy valley floor, a green orchard of date palms and a village with a *boulangerie* that sells fresh rolls. Women and girls turn big wheels to draw water from the wells.

From there, we cross the remnants of prehistoric forest, now acres of petrified wood, and follow the seam stitching the massif to the dunes of the Ténéré. Scalloped waves of sand extend just short of forever. It's an extraordinary place that delights the soul with awe and elation—feelings we get to indulge longer than planned after a mechanical breakdown.

A couple of days later we roll at the speed of donkeys into a village called Iferouâne. The blacksmiths descend to peddle their wares. Their single-mindedness brings to mind the word "pushy." "Tell them I'm not buying!" I say.

A blacksmith named Tonka appears in a billowing black robe and *tagelmoust* laden with silver bangles, talismans, hoops, and loops. He clangs and jingles when he walks, and has made his stylized presence heard even in France and Germany.

"In those clothes?" I ask.

"Of course!" he says. "They love it." He sings. He dances. He sells. *Veni, vidi, vici.*

"Do you prefer the French or the Germans?"

"The French are nicer but the Germans buy more. They like the big pieces."

I want to know about the meanings in Tonka's work, but conversation with him is like making small talk in a bordello. He hints at deeper mysteries he can't reveal, then mumbles something in French.

"He says you ask too many questions," Brizot says. "I think there's another reason he doesn't want to talk."

"What's that?"

"He may not know."

Tonka's magic, though, is his salesmanship; somehow we're in a negotiation, and before he goes I have acquired another Tuareg cross.

Back in Agadez, I return to the guild, where Abda Ahmoudou, the quality control manager, takes out some of his own pieces and shows the lines that draw an analogy between wind and memory. "One symbolizes a natural force, the other an emotion. They're related to each other. As wind moves, so does memory." Against that a thicker line symbolizes a home, a physical defense against natural force but the place of love. Yet it's not merely a random expression of feeling, as in abstract art, but a discipline that holds to established motifs, a language of the hands. As Abda explains his work, images come into focus and ideas enter the atmosphere. "Everything is linked to the emotion you experience at the moment of creating."

I ask if he feels intruded upon by my questions.

"Oh, no!" he says. "I'm very, very happy. There are no secrets. You're the first person who has asked since a German fifteen years ago! I say, *merci, merci, merci*."

Two days later, just before I leave, he presents me with a heavy swatch of shimmering silver. Its detailed imagery recalls the earlier conversation about wind and metaphor. Mountains and wells refer to our desert journey. A ladder runs up the left side, symbolizing the sadness of my impending departure. It is signed in Tifinar, the Tuareg alphabet. The piece is a poem about friendship.

It has one notable weakness. The necklace, a leather cord that's used to loop a camel's nostril, is not worthy of it. Brizot suggests replacing it later.

"Will it hold?" I ask him.

"It should."

I'm delighted. Abda and I stand in the courtyard saying long good-byes. After you shake hands, you put your fingers to your chest as a way of saying you've received the person into your heart. I do, and my fingers land on the talisman. Then Brizot takes me to the airport, where the plane, alas, is delayed, so we go back to town for lamb couscous and Cokes.

"It's an amazing piece he made," Brizot said. "It's museum quality."

"I've never had a piece of jewelry that I cared about," I say. "This really has meaning to me."

I put my hand to my chest to take it out. Only…it's gone. We look everywhere. I'm bereft, worse than when I learned that I had no clothes. Brizot lights a cigarette and philosophizes Frenchly on the meaning of what's happened.

"A blacksmith might say the spirits wanted you to learn something," he says. "Maybe it's something that'll be in your story."

"I'd rather just have the *tcherot*." I'd like the moment back to tuck the talisman into my pocket. I never had an object for such a short time and felt its loss so keenly.

❧ ❧ ❧

Todd Pitock has written for numerous publications, among them Discover, National Geographic Traveler, The New York Times, Continental, *and* ForbesLife, *where he is a contributing editor.*

PAMELA CORDELL AVIS

~≈ ~≈ ~≈

Philomen and Baucis

A modern tale of metamorphosis.

I WAS AT ONE OF LIFE'S CROSSROADS, YOU KNOW, THE
kind that either can or cannot divert you to a journey
down an untraveled road.

To move from L.A. to a tiny farming village in France
was not an option, it was not even an idea. It often happens, however, that the things we don't plan are more
likely than those we do, and the smallest, most insignificant event, can open up a path where there was none
before. In this case, it was a detour on the way back from
the supermarket. I was in France at the time visiting an
American friend-turned-Parisian at her house in the
country. Our shopping out of the way, we drove through
a village she thought I'd like to see—an ordinary sort of
meander on a lazy summer afternoon. It was indeed a
pretty village, but it was so small we were in and out of it

in less than two minutes. As we made a sharp right turn at the end of the Grande Rue and rolled out onto the narrow country road, I looked back over my shoulder and saw a For Sale sign.

Once back home, I found myself talking to my friends about the house. I hadn't even liked it when I went to see it, a quick cursory look and I was off, but somehow it had entered the back of my mind and stuck there. One day I called the real estate agent—let's just see where this goes, I said to myself without much conviction. It would be a miracle of biblical proportions if the French gave me a mortgage and only divine intervention would persuade my employer to let me work in France. I had no experience with miracles, divine intervention, or, for that matter, even exceptional luck.

It's the surprises that change our lives. The mortgage got itself arranged by fax, as did arrangements with the seller with respect to certain pieces of furniture that were too big and too heavy to be moved. Eda, my friend who'd shown me the village in the first place, signed the closing papers as my proxy, and I moved to St. Aubin in time to put up a Christmas tree. The stay would be short, I was due back in L.A. after the holidays—the deal with my employer was that I would show up regularly to meet deadlines and see to it that everything was actually printed and out the door before leaving again. Instead of using the Santa Monica Freeway to get to work, I would be using international airlines. Mortgage payments and consolidator flights, I figured, added up to about the same cost as an L.A. apartment. I'm not absolutely sure of that calculation, but that's the way it looked in rough on a yellow pad. In any case, it was close enough. I'd lived in France before, and its call to me was always there, like an undertow. I could make it work, I reassured myself, and, as I would be pinching pennies most anywhere, better to do it in a country where even the most modest of restaurants serve three courses and the wine is cheap.

On New Year's Eve a neighbor appeared. It was dark as the edge of space outside and raining. My house, an old farmhouse of fieldstone, sat behind a high wall, just like all the others on the Grande Rue. That somebody was inside the wall and outside my house was signaled by a shrill, off-pitch sound that sent currents of ice water through my arms and legs. I stopped what I was doing and stood still, not daring to move. It came again, and again. Then with a flash the lights went on outside in the courtyard, my front door flew open with the force of storm wind, and a man walked in.

"*Bonsoir,*" he called at the top of his voice.

I had moved into the hall at the top of the stairs, my hands holding tightly to the railing as I looked down at him. "*Bonsoir,*" I replied tentatively, not sure whether he should be welcomed or not.

"You didn't answer your doorbell."

I decided to go downstairs and have a better look at him. Offering my hand, I spoke the truth, "I didn't know I had a doorbell."

Raymond introduced himself as my neighbor and thrust a bottle of excellent champagne at me. He began to say something about a woman alone on New Year's Eve, but broke off in mid-sentence to bend over and sneeze explosively, twice, into a pressed white handkerchief. "I'm sorry I can't stay longer," he wheezed, "I have a very bad cold." With that he was gone, and I didn't see him, or anybody else, until I returned in the spring.

It was the first day of May when I next landed in Paris, picked up a rental car and headed south—direction Joigny-Auxerre. My mood was very much different this time. I'd had time to get used to what I'd done. This was now *home.* The car windows were down, the air smelled like *France,* and I was exhilarated by *life.* When I turned off the autoroute and picked up the country road that led to St. Aubin, I was greeted by an amazing expanse of yellow. All the way to my tiny perched village, the gently rolling hills were patched with geometrically shaped fields of bright yellow flowers, their borders separated by rows of tall dark evergreens and lush shrubs. It was the most stunning thing I'd ever seen in my life.

It wasn't very long before I met Philomen and Baucis. In fact, it was probably longer than you would expect, as they could not be missed, but I was discovering there was a lot more to the house and the land I'd bought than I had realized. The house was huge, and I had thought it small. Around the corner from one of the stables, I found a small garden, and one morning while chatting with a neighbor, whose name I learned was Marie-Thérèse, I mentioned that I might put in some tomato plants. After lunch a tall man showed up with a basket of plants and a hand plow. He introduced himself as Jean, the husband of Marie-Thérèse, and said he was there to turn the soil of my garden. When he was finished he asked me if I liked the view from the orchard. We opened the little garden gate and walked out on the slope. From there we could see the entire valley and its geometric shapes of color, crops that had already rotated to another hue and grain since my arrival through fields of startling spring yellow. In the orchard, Jean pointed out which trees were cherries, which were pears, apples, and walnuts. He then spoke of how I should care for them. I looked around the orchard and then at him, "Is this part of my property?"

A single-lane road ran along the side of my house and my orchard, and dead-ended at an old cemetery. In front of the cemetery wall were two enormous trees. One was a linden and the other an oak. They were very old, even ancient, and as they had grown over the years they had begun to lean toward each other, tangling their branches in such an intimate way that I thought of Philomen and Baucis the first minute I saw them.

Philomen and Baucis are the devoted couple from Ovid's *Metamorphoses*, generous farmers who offered hospitality to strangers, two men who happened to be gods in disguise. The gods rewarded them by granting their wish to be together for eternity, thus morphing them into oak and linden that would forever live side by side.

> *Two travelers once, it is said, appeared in*
> *modest disguises that hid their glory, for Jove*
> *and Mercury were the two. They knocked on*
> *door after door seeking a bed for the night, but*
> *over and over again were turned away. In the*
> *end, in one they found a welcome—*

The villagers welcomed me in thoroughly surprising ways. To use a French term, they embraced me. I met them all at once (we were 480 at peak season, which is to say when the Parisians were in residence) at the Feu de Saint Jean, an annual big deal, which, near as I could tell, was a community outdoor cookout to celebrate the first day of summer. Raymond, Marie-Thérèse, Jean, and I would walk down to the plain below where the commune had bought an old mill and its grounds for occasions such as this. It began more or less as I expected, but after we'd eaten the grilled this and that (sometimes it is better not to be specific), drunk quite a few bottles of local burgundy, and it had grown quite dark, some men fired a haystack which was big as a barn. Lighting a fire outdoors, of any sort, can be a terrifying sight to someone from Southern California, but these people seemed to know what they were doing. As the flames roared to the sky we all— men, women, children, and the American—got up to hold hands and dance in a circle around the fire. This was a pagan ceremony old as the time man first stood up straight and recognized the summer solstice. And in St. Aubin, generation after generation had passed down the secret of staying upright on treacherously slippery grass as the dance gained momentum. It got faster and faster as the circle changed direction, and then again, and again. The villagers held securely to my hands, then my wrists, then my arms, and I to theirs.

By mid-summer my failed efforts at gardening had become evident. Maybe too much water, maybe too little. It turned out that it didn't matter at all because every time I went out someone thrust a bowl of strawberries at me, a bag of tomatoes and cucumbers, or a dozen ears of corn. Also, I was often invited to lunch, feasts that progressed through course after course, rituals that lasted for hours and were accompanied by bottles of wine that never seemed to be empty. Is it any wonder that I began to see Philomen and Baucis, known since antiquity for their generosity, as symbols of St. Aubin?

Baucis set out a plate of olives, green ones and

*black, and a saucer of cherry plums she had
pickled, and an endive and radish salad. She
had cheese and some roasted eggs...*

Afterward,

*Baucis served her cabbage and pork stew. For
dessert there were nuts, figs, dates, and plums,
and baskets of ripe apples and grapes...*

When Philomen went to refill the wine bowl,

*He picked it up but felt that it wasn't empty.
Instead, as much as they drank, the wine had
replenished itself, and the bowl was as full as
before.*

There was no way I could reciprocate such generosity. I
couldn't even give my neighbors fruit because everybody
else had orchards too. My orchard had turned out to be a
big producer, and a big pain. I couldn't keep up with the
picking, the eating, or the preserving, and overnight the
grass had grown high as an elephant's eye. It was a village eyesore, but I was in no mood to go out there with a
scythe, nor did I want to pay somebody to tackle it with
a tractor—we're talking a couple of acres.

Nothing went unnoticed at St. Aubin, and anything
that happened at my house spread like wildfire: by telephone, over the fence, and among the women who lined
up every morning for their baguettes. The American, as
I was known to most, was a source of intense curiosity.
This I knew from Raymond. He was quite a well-known
singer who traveled the world but had a solid foot in the

country and understood the mind-set of the neighbors far better than I did. He also had a wacky sense of humor and delighted in telling me what others were saying about me. (Clearly he would only know if he had participated in the gossiping!) Just because they had embraced me didn't mean I was immune to criticism.

When I first moved in several households devoted their late afternoons to watching reruns of *2000 Malibu Road* on television, which went against me in some circles. Most people in the village had not seen foreigners since the German occupation of France during the Second World War, and as far as Americans were concerned, nobody could remember ever wanting to know one. Down below, a farmer's daughter, who was mute and heavily pregnant (the father, a young itinerant with curly red hair, spent his afternoons on a wooden bench in front of their farmhouse eating raw onions as if they were apples), went so far as to sign to the postmistress that The American was going to turn her house into a hotel. What's more, it would have a flashing neon sign in front. And one day when I was shopping at the open market in the next village over, a woman dressed in black and bent with age—widows of the war still dress in mourning—approached me with, "Ah, so you are The American." When I confirmed it, she said she hadn't seen me in church, and when I told her I was Protestant, she replied with, "*Alors, on est Chrétien ici.*" Well, we're Christian here. I simply let it pass. My ancestors were French Huguenots—heretics to some, victims to others. I thought to bring that up would only make things worse. None of the gossiping, or even the confrontations, were mean-spirited, it was just the way it was. After all, I—a foreign woman living by herself—was the odd one.

It is hard to say how many people discussed the condition of my orchard before I had a visit from a couple I hadn't yet met. They came in a pickup with five young sons, who spread out in as many directions to explore everything hidden behind a closed door above ground and below. The couple asked if I would like to have a pair of donkeys in my orchard. They would eat the grass and keep me company.

No donkeys had appeared before I left for California. The snow had taken care of the grass problem. When I returned in May, a pair of donkeys was there, along with a foal. The baby donkey was only marginally younger than the yellow Lab I'd just let out of the car. My puppy was already known as Lincoln. He'd been given to me when he was barely nine weeks old. I could have refused him, but I didn't. I picked him up, held him near, he kissed me on the cheek, I kissed him on the top of his small head, and that was that. We boarded a plane together the day he turned three months and was entitled to travel papers. By bringing a dog to live at St. Aubin I knew I'd crossed a bridge that I hadn't yet come to. It was a bit like buying the house—I'd first do it and then figure out how to make it work.

The news that Philomen and Baucis might be cut down reached me on my first day home. It struck like a thunderbolt. These beautiful old trees had been planted as seedlings in front of the stone wall that enclosed the cemetery at about the same time the ground was consecrated. It was under their budding leaves that my neighbors paused to take in the breathtaking expanses of yellow colza in the fields below the village, announcing the arrival of spring. In deep summer, their shade cooled the footpath, and people sat there on the wooden bench to chat while watching tractors cut through the tall wheat. Even when autumn rains began the change and when snow fell, people took their dogs up there, to pause and to reflect on the meaning of life. It was the most hospitable place in the village to admire the changing seasons, and no one ever, ever went there without feeling the presence of its ancient sentinels. However, the roots of Philomen and Baucis had grown too long and spread too far. They were rattling the bones of the dead.

As the cutting-down process was not yet definite, I quickly became distracted by the imminent arrival of *my car*. I didn't yet know what kind it might be or even what color it was. Eda, my resourceful American friend-turned-Parisian, had found it for me. I'd sent a check, and *voilá*—instant car owner. No more expensive rentals. It was being driven down from Paris by Anne, Eda's daughter and my favorite young lady of all time. I'd known her since she was two, when I was a struggling (read perpetual house sitter) artist and she kept me company in the atelier that belonged to her parents. This night she would stay to meet Lincoln, and the donkeys.

Anne was the first of what would be a procession of houseguests. I'd acquired certain necessities like furniture, plates, knives and forks, wine glasses and picnic baskets—that sort of thing. Marie-Thérèse had given me bed linens—the kind that float over your body like a cloud—from her own trousseau and her grandmother's. They'd been packed away for years as too good to be used, only to be deemed as utterly useless by her daughters who wanted only polyester blends. I was thrilled. My houseguests were varied and many. Several old boyfriends showed up, and one old husband. Some people I didn't know—an overflow from Eda's house. Then came a woman, the friend of a friend who was the clandestine friend of a female friend who would be horrified to know that I'd met this woman (these things *do* happen), and just about everybody I knew in Los Angeles plus some from London, and some new friends from Paris. I love people, especially those I know, and they wouldn't have come if I hadn't invited them, but I soon realized that a lunch, drinks, or dinner relationship is much different from a visit by a fish out of water. There were those who couldn't sleep, wouldn't sleep, because it was too quiet. Others were speechless to learn that there was no air conditioning in my little second-hand French car and cranky the same evening when the house turned chilly and they had to go find a sweater (cranky, because they wanted me to close the windows and turn on the heat), and others were outraged that the part-time employee in the post office didn't speak English. Some never picked up the rhythm of the house or of the place: they ate breakfast at nearly noon and wanted to go out to eat in the late afternoon, even though there are virtually no restaurants in the French countryside that serve lunch after two, which meant that after emptying the refrigerator they were not hungry again until after all the restaurants had long since finished taking evening sitters. Grocery stores closed at noon, didn't open again until four, and closed again at seven. These hours absolutely flummoxed people who were used to 24/7. France has a lot of rules that have been embedded in the culture for a very long time, and they have a lot of attitudes that do not graciously accommodate people who do not think—and eat—like the French. Those travelers who don't believe it, or think a smile will get them into a restaurant after closing hours, are wrong. Those people grow to hate France, and unfortunately some of them were my friends.

The year-of-the-houseguest resulted in an inevitable thinning out of friends and acquaintances. It also marked a change in me. All the griping had pushed me solidly into the French camp. Between visits I'd often sit on the veranda in the evening (wearing a sweater) and sip a glass of wine while trying to figure out what it was about this place that I liked so much. It was beautiful, but lots of places are beautiful. I'd left one of them to come live here. At first it had been the nineteenth-century character of the village. Virtually nothing had changed since then, and I found living in another century a riveting experience. Also, I loved the challenge of functioning in another language. As I got used to the time warp and as my French got better, I became part of the weave. The small friendships of village life became numerous and more important. Most of the early frustrations—like the orchard—had been resolved. The family that came twice a day to feed the donkeys was also picking the fruit and delivering it to the mobile distiller who came every once in a while and set himself up in front of the church on the main square. There, aided by volunteer tasters, he produced barrels of liquid lightning. While the village was literally in the middle of nowhere, I was by no means isolated. Within an easy thirty minute drive I could cast my eyes over a ridge of medieval fortified castles and their pastoral grounds where fat white sheep graze when the grass is at its greenest, listen to Gregorian chants in the Cistercian abbey at Pontigny or hear Bach in the basilica courtyard at Vézelay. More towns than not were ancient works of art, and it was there in the midst of living museums that I bought lipstick and new shoes, shopped for food, and went to first-run American movies. At home, the braying of donkeys got me out of bed with the sunrise (they wanted carrots), and, after a stand-up breakfast of French roast and local croissant that heaped shame on Starbucks, I could step into a state-of-the-art office that instantly connected me with the outside world. Of course I couldn't use any of that modern technology at midday because everybody was cooking lunch and there was not enough electric power to go around. If that got to me, Paris was an hour and a half away.

When the ultimatum came—and I knew it would—to spend more time in the Los Angeles office, I bit the bullet. I'd felt it coming when I accepted Lincoln. I knew he would grow too big to travel back and forth, and I knew I would never leave him in a kennel for months at a time. The bullet was a tough one. Residence permits for foreigners are only for those who can prove that their income is earned outside of France. Work permits for non-Europeans are rarer than McDonald's. There was no way around it. I'd always said a writer could live anywhere in the world. It was time to test the theory.

I managed to stay there, in St. Aubin, for a little over ten years. I never got tired of it, and when I left it broke my heart.

In the end Philomen and Baucis were cut down. The villagers and farmers took it far better than I did—they, of course, were on more intimate terms with nature's life cycles than I could ever hope to be. Just as Philomen and Baucis bid a poignant final farewell to each other when the gods transformed them into trees, I began saying farewell to my friends and neighbors while preparing to transform myself back into an American. Lincoln, at ninety-two pounds, would travel in an airline cage the size of a studio apartment and Gatsby in the cabin with me. Gatsby had appeared on a soft June morning in the rafters above the veranda. One of six tiny kittens, he was the issue of a cat that visited regularly to eat, but not for a caress. Shortly after the morning debut, the mother cat walked five of her litter across the roof, never to return, and left Gatsby behind. There was nothing wrong, no reason to abandon him—he was clearly a parting gift.

Returning to the States was a decision whose time had come; the problem was deciding where. I was exploring cities on the internet like a holiday traveler trawls airfares and becoming more befuddled with each day. Again, it is the surprises that change our lives. One day when having lunch with an American artist who lived close to Paris, and whom I had not seen for a very long time, I learned she had a house for rent in a small American town. "Stonington?" I asked. "Where's that?"

⤖ ⤖ ⤖

Pamela Cordell Avis was born in Colorado and has since lived in many places. Once having finished her undergraduate work in art history and studio art, she painted in Provence until she was hired during a Cannes Film Festival to market feature films, which took her to New York, then Los Angeles, and then all over the world. Later, while living in St. Aubin, the subject of this story, she discovered a film in a neighbor's attic, which sent her back to school to get a graduate degree in Holocaust Studies. She is currently writing a book about the hero whose story was hidden in that attic. "Philomen and Baucis" was a Grand Prize Winner for Best Travel Story of the Year in the second annual Solas Awards (BestTravelWriting.com).

ROLF POTTS

❧ ❧ ❧

Death of an
Adventure Traveler

No doubt he has a special page
in the Akashic Records.

MATTHEW, THE SMALL BURMESE KAYIN MAN WHO worked the front desk at the Lotus Guesthouse, was the first one to suggest that Mr. Benny might be dead. "Benny went back to Burma so he could die near his family," he told me, his eyes fixed on the TV set as flickering Shiites danced in the streets of Iraq. "He was too sick to live in Thailand anymore."

I had just returned to the rainy border town of Ranong, Thailand after an absence of five months. It was April 9, 2003, the day U.S. tanks rolled into central Baghdad. Matthew had been squatting in the guesthouse lobby, translating BBC commentary for the other hotel

311

workers—all of them illegal migrant workers from
Burma. Deciphering the images from Iraq proved to be
a difficult process, since even the BBC commentators
didn't seem to know what was going on. Had Baghdad
fallen or not? Were the U.S. soldiers welcomed or reviled? Nobody knew for sure, but when a soldier on the
TV flung an American flag over the head of the Saddam
Hussein statue in Firdos Square, the Burmese workers
had let out a cheer, as if Rangoon's junta would be next.

When the BBC cut to a commercial, Matthew finally
looked over at me. "How did you know Benny?" he
asked. Matthew's eyes were dark, fringed by faint yellow; he wore a crisp oxford shirt, and his black hair was
just beginning to show gray. A devout Baptist like many
ethnic Kayin, he was painfully earnest in his beliefs—a
quality that would eventually get him fired from the
guesthouse.

"Mr. Benny was my barber," I said. Benny had also
been my best friend in Ranong, and one of the most remarkable men I'd ever met. He'd evaded death so many
times in his life that I found it hard to believe that he
would submit to a quiet end back in Burma. "Are you
sure he's dead?"

Matthew shrugged. "I didn't even know him. You
should talk to Phiman. He'll know if Benny is still
alive."

Phiman was a Thai man who owned the dusty TV repair shop where Mr. Benny slept at night. Since I didn't
speak enough Thai for Phiman to understand me, this
meant I had to get translation help from Ezio, a barrel-
chested Italian who lived with his Thai wife on the other
side of Ranong. Since I'd sold my motorcycle when I'd
last left Thailand, I headed off to Ezio's place on foot,

skirting the hot, murky puddles that choked the streets after heavy rains.

Of all the places in the world where I'd lived for more than a couple months, Ranong was by far the most obscure. A frumpy border town of thirty thousand people in the rainiest part of Thailand's isthmus, it held little appeal for tourists—apart from its proximity to the southern tip of Burma, where backpackers enamored with Thailand's meditation retreats and full-moon parties could get a cheap re-entry visa in a couple of hours. Besides fishing and tin mining, timber poaching and amphetamine smuggling seemed to be Ranong's principal industries, and scores of refugees from Burma's repressive dictatorship lived in squalid huts at the edges of town. Heavy rains resulted in power blackouts that could last for days, and the sour-fresh scent of rainforest competed with the fishy smell of the port. Though just four hours by motorcycle from the tourist resort of Phuket—and ten hours by bus from the modern hum of Bangkok—Ranong felt years away from the rest of Thailand.

I'd first arrived in Ranong two years earlier, while writing about the Moken sea gypsies who lived in the islands on the Burmese side of the sea border. I'd been trying to build my career as an adventure-travel writer, and a Major American Luxury-Travel Magazine had underwritten my journey to investigate recent tourism ventures into Moken territory. I didn't have a permanent address at the time, so I'd rented a studio room at the Lotus Guesthouse to write the sea gypsy article. When it was finished I decided to stay in the sleepy town to work on my first book, a philosophical how-to primer about long-term travel.

Writing my book required long stretches of isolation, and I didn't socialize much during my stint in Ranong. I tried to get out of my room to explore the town from time to time, but even six months into my tenure, Thai kids who lived just a few blocks away from my guesthouse would shout "*farang!*" at me as I walked past, as if I was just another random backpacker in town for a visa run. The word, which means "foreigner," was a reminder of how little I really knew about the daily workings of Ranong, or of Thailand in general.

Besides Ezio and Matthew, the only person I saw regularly when I lived in Ranong was Mr. Benny, a thin, sexagenarian Burmese émigré who worked at a humid storefront barbershop in the center of town. His haircuts cost 40 baht (about U.S. $0.90 at the time), and afterwards he'd invite me to a dim café next door and spend most of his fee on coffee thickened with condensed milk. As we sipped from dented aluminum cups, he would tell me stories about his younger years, when he would make ends meet for his family by smuggling tin to Malaysia, or diving for pearls off the coast of Burma. Sometimes he'd invite me to join him for Sunday services at the local Catholic chapel; other times, he'd ask me to meet him at his cramped bunkroom in the TV repair shop to practice English vocabulary. When he learned that I hailed from the prairies of North America, he told me that his favorite English-language book was an old cowboy novel called *The Big Sky*. I'd found a used copy of the novel when I was back in the U.S. on my book tour, and one reason I'd returned to Ranong was so I could present *The Big Sky* to Mr. Benny.

The other reason I'd returned to Ranong was to find some isolation so I could finish a magazine article that was weeks overdue. The adventure stories I'd written two years earlier for the Major American Luxury-Travel Magazine had attracted the attention of a Major American Adventure-Travel Magazine, and I'd been discussing possible assignments with an editor for months. Unfortunately, no story I proposed—exploring fishing villages along the upper Cambodian Mekong, mountaineering in Turkish Kurdistan, visiting the isolated tribesmen of the Andaman Islands—seemed quite right for him. We'd finally settled on a how-to feature about "classic adventures" in Asia. I'd spent much of the previous three years adventuring through the distant corners of the Asian continent, but this experience had put me at a weird disadvantage in reporting the story. "You're giving us too much geography," my editor would tell me every time I submitted a new list of destination summaries. Readers of Major American Adventure-Travel Magazines, he told me, didn't want to read about journeys that were obscure or complicated; they wanted exotic challenges wherein they might test— or, at least, imagine themselves testing—the extremes of human experience.

For weeks, I had trouble understanding exactly what this meant—and my increasingly irritated editor returned my story drafts marked with comments like "Is there a helicopter service that can get you there faster?" and "Would you recommend some cutting-edge outerwear for this kind of trek?" and "Can you think of any celebrities who've visited the region recently?" In time, I discerned that adventure itself was far less important to the magazine than creating a romanticized *sense* of adventure—preferably with recommendations on where to buy a cappuccino and a Swedish massage afterwards.

The Major American Adventure-Travel Magazine, it seemed, wanted me to create a tantalizing recipe for the exotic and the unexpected—but only the kind of "unexpected" that could be planned in advance and completed in less than three weeks.

It took me less than half an hour to walk the damp streets to Ezio's house. Pong, his slim, shy Thai wife, answered the door. At twenty-three, she was exactly half his age; he'd met her when she was still a student in a country village across the isthmus in Chumphon Province. Before Pong, Ezio had a previous Thai wife—an ex-bargirl who had borne him two daughters and twice tried to kill him before their marriage ended. Once she had stabbed him in the back with a kitchen knife; another time she'd dumped poison in his soup. He had recovered unshaken both times, but their marriage fell apart after a few years, and he rarely saw his daughters anymore. Newly remarried, Ezio was teaching Pong how to help him with his website-design business, and they were successful enough to employ two Burmese girls to cook and clean for them.

Ezio teased me about my latest magazine assignment as he stood in the kitchen, his hulking mass bent over a tiny espresso pot. "These American magazines don't even know what adventure is," he said. "They want you to write about camping toys and sports vacations. They want you to make people think adventure is something that costs $8,000 and lasts as long as a Christmas holiday. They want you to make rich people feel good for being rich."

I didn't argue with him. Twenty-five years ago Ezio had left Rome for a winter holiday in North Africa, and he'd never returned. He'd taught himself Arabic in

Algeria, learned to live in the desert, bought a few camels, made a living as a tour guide. Intrigued by wars, he eventually wandered on to Uganda, and then Lebanon, and then Sri Lanka, picking up languages as he needed them. He eventually landed in Southeast Asia, where he fell in love with Thai women—all of them, from the way he described it—and he'd been based in Thailand for over ten years now. What Ezio had done with his life was unusual, but not unique. Every out-of-the-way province in Southeast Asia, it seemed, had a few guys like him—aging expats who'd lived remarkable lives, enjoyed their anonymity, and had no plans of going home. Whenever I talked to Ezio I was reminded of how the storied travelers of history invariably discovered they were not alone in their wanderings—how William of Rubrouck arrived in Karakorum to find Ukrainian carpenters, Greek doctors, and Parisian goldsmiths; how Marco Polo encountered Lombards, Germans, and Frenchmen in the streets of Cambaluc. These people's stories were never told because they never went home.

I took my espresso and moved on to the living room. Ezio brought out a package of cigars he'd bought during his latest run to Burma. We lit up, and Ezio caught me up on the local gossip—how local gangsters were turning the island of Koh Samui into the Sicily of Thailand; how an influx of Burmese girls had turned Ranong into one of the cheapest places in the country to buy a prostitute. When Ezio ran out of news, I asked him about Mr. Benny.

"I didn't know him; Pong cuts my hair. Did you ask at the barbershop?"

"He had to stop working there," I said. "He was getting sick, and his hands were too shaky. Last time I saw him he was helping Phiman at the TV repair shop."

Repairing televisions and cutting hair were just two of
Mr. Benny's many callings in life. Born to a Portuguese-
Kayin mother, who met his Chinese-Thai father in
southern Burma during the Japanese occupation of
Ranong in World War II, young Benny was trained in
English by Irish priests at the local mission school. When
finances got tight for his family, his unique language
skills led to his first job at age fourteen: fighting com-
munists with a regrouped Chinese Kuomintang army
in northeastern Burma. At a time when the average
daily income for a Burmese soldier was 15 kyat, Benny
made 150 kyat a day carrying ammunition belts and
translating intelligence information for American CIA
advisors.

Mr. Benny deserted the Kuomintang army when the
CIA funding dried up, and he returned to the Burmese
south convinced that risking danger was the most ef-
ficient way to make a living. Against his mother's pro-
testations, he crossed the border and used his newfound
skills to detonate explosive charges in an illegal tin mine
owned by a Thai general who was said to have twenty-
two wives. When his father forced him to return home,
Benny found a job diving for oysters in the Mergui
Archipelago, each day donning a weight belt and a hose-
fed air-helmet to the bottom of the sea ("You couldn't
just bend over and get the shells," he'd told me, "or else
you could fall out of your helmet and drown; you had to
squat and feel for the oysters with your hands").

Marriage to a local girl took Mr. Benny out of the sea
and into a barbershop, but the arrival of children left
him in need of a better income, so he took up an offer
from a group of wealthy Taiwanese men who needed a
guide and translator for a rhino-poaching excursion in

the Burmese jungle. Dodging the Burmese army along the Thai borderlands, the expedition party dragged on for six months, surviving on deer and monkey meat before they managed to bag a rhino; Benny came home with his hair "long, like an Indian," and his young children didn't recognize him.

After the Burmese military coup in 1961, English was officially regarded as a "slave language," and Mr. Benny was forced to toss out his books, including his favorite, A.B. Guthrie's *The Big Sky*. The local economy nose-dived, and Benny increasingly found it necessary to cross into Thailand and do construction work to keep his family fed. For a while he managed to make as much as 800 baht a day smuggling tin across the sea border to Malaysia—until one winter day a group of pirates posing as policemen seized his boat and tossed him overboard. Mr. Benny swam the three miles back to shore and returned to cutting hair. On the side, he taught himself how to fix radios, and, later, TVs. It was a skill he returned to in his old age.

Ezio seemed skeptical that a man who was too sick to cut hair could work on televisions. "You can't do that kind of thing with shaky hands," he said.

"Mr. Benny used to joke that without steady hands he was just a nurse in the TV shop," I said. "He would locate the illness, and Phiman would do the surgery."

Ezio chuckled and stubbed out his cigar. "Let's go and see what Phiman knows," he said.

As I rode into central Ranong on the back of Ezio's motorcycle, it occurred to me that I didn't even know the exact nature of Mr. Benny's sickness. His shaky hands implied Parkinson's Disease, but he also had increasing trouble keeping his food down. On a couple occasions I suggested that he visit a doctor, but he always waved me off. "This is just what happens to old men," he said.

Mr. Benny didn't like talking about his health, and it was only at my urging that he elaborated his memories of Malay pirates and Kuomintang mercenaries. To him, smuggling tin or tracking rhinos were merely jobs—better paid, but not entirely dissimilar to cutting hair or pouring concrete. Usually, he would steer our conversation to the small, charmed moments he remembered from his life, like the first time he learned what garbage was ("before, everything was reused or fed to the animals"). One of his favorite memories was the time a fisherman brought him a bottle containing an English-language letter from a seven-year-old Dutch boy named Donald, who became Mr. Benny's pen-pal for the next five years. He also loved to recall his friend's failed attempt to make an airplane using wood planks and a 120-horsepower motorcycle engine. He asked me countless questions about what it was like to live on the American plains; in his mind, I think, my home was inseparable from the pages of *The Big Sky*.

The last week I saw him, all Mr. Benny could talk about was an article he'd read about Sudan's "Lost Boys." He kept telling me how forty years of war and repression had left Burma with countless refugees of its own, and that maybe Americans would care more about Burma if he could think of a name as clever as "Lost Boys."

Ezio and I found Phiman in the back of his shop, his white hair tousled, his glasses hanging on the end of his nose as he soldered a wire into the back of a television. He frowned as Ezio spoke to him in Thai, then set down his soldering iron. "Mr. Benny left two months ago," he said, Ezio translating. "He's in Rangoon now, with his wife and grandkids. It's better for him to die there."

"But are you sure he was going to die?" I asked.

"Yes. But if he comes back, I'll be the first to know; I still owe him some money." Phiman laughed soberly. "He was good at fixing TVs, you know. That even saved his life once."

"How's that?"

"Sometime in 1979 Benny got word that you could make a lot of money getting gems in western Cambodia and taking them across the border to sell. Back then that area was mostly lawless, except for the Khmer Rouge. He camped out there for a couple of months, digging for rubies, and trading food for raw stones from Cambodians. One day a Khmer Rouge patrol found him, took him back to their camp, beat him up a little, took his rubies. They probably would have killed him, too, but he heard them complaining about how they missed their Thai soap operas. He fixed their TV, and they let him go. They kept his rubies, of course—but they let him go."

Phiman picked up his soldering iron and resumed his work. "Come back in a week," he said. "I'll let you know if I've heard anything new."

I went back a week later—and the week after that—but Phiman had no new news about Mr. Benny.

I stayed on at the Lotus Guesthouse and struggled with my article for the Major American Adventure-Travel Magazine. Every time I researched some upscale mountain trek in the Nepal Himalayas or two-week scuba diving excursion off the coast of Papua New

Guinea, I couldn't help but ponder how pointless it all was. I began to email my editor pointed questions about how one should define the "extremes of human experience." How was kayaking a remote Chinese river, I asked, more notable than surviving on its shores for a lifetime? How did risking frostbite on a helicopter-supported journey to arctic Siberia constitute more of an "adventure" than risking frostbite on a winter road-crew in Upper Peninsula Michigan? Did anyone else think it was telling that bored British aristocrats—not the peoples of the Himalayas—were the ones who first deemed it important to climb Mount Everest? My editor's replies were understandably terse.

Things changed as Ranong slipped further into the rainy season. Ezio and Pong decided the power black-outs were bad for their internet business, so they moved upcountry to Chiang Rai. At the guesthouse, Matthew made the repeated mistake of assuming Western back-packers were as excited about the fall of Baghdad he was. It didn't help that he was an unrepentant Baptist, given to salting his conversations with cheery Gospel references. More than once this led to bizarre scenes in the lobby, where sunburned Germans and Canadians and Californians angrily lectured Matthew about the pacifistic merits of Buddhism while the Kayin desk clerk tremblingly tried to explain how Burmese Buddhists had murdered his brothers. It was as if the backpackers didn't know what to do with this meek little brown man who, with his love of Jesus and affinity for George Bush, didn't follow the accepted narrative of how Southeast Asians were supposed to act. Less than a month after he translated the defeat of Saddam Hussein for his co-workers, Matthew was fired and replaced with another

Burmese migrant—a serious young Buddhist kid who fetched keys, kept his mouth shut, and garnered no complaints.

Eventually I finished the last rewrite of my article for the Major American Adventure-Travel Magazine. I emailed it to my editor, requesting that it run without my byline.

After checking out of the Lotus Guesthouse, I slipped a self-addressed envelope into my copy of *The Big Sky* and left it with Phiman in the hope that Mr. Benny might one day come back.

Then I did something Mr. Benny never had the option of doing: I headed back across the ocean, to a place where "adventure travel" was not a way of getting by in life, but a whimsical, self-induced abstraction—a way of testing our limits so that we can more keenly enjoy our comforts.

❦ ❦ ❦

Rolf Potts is the author of Vagabonding: An Uncommon Guide to the Art of the Long-Term World Travel. *The former Salon. com columnist is best known for promoting the ethic of vagabonding—a way of living that makes extended, personally meaningful travel possible. His work has appeared in* The New York Times Magazine, National Geographic Traveler, The Best American Travel Writing, *several Travelers' Tales books, and on National Public Radio. Visit his web site at www.rolfpotts.com.*

ACKNOWLEDGMENTS

"Red Lights and a Rose" by Joel Carillet published with permission from the author. Copyright © 2008 by Joel Carillet.

"Ice Ghost" by Cameron M. Smith published with permission from the author. Copyright © 2008 by Cameron M. Smith.

"The Unquenchable Sea" by Matthew Link published with permission from the author. Copyright © 2007 by Matthew Link.

"Holy Land Blues" by Peter Wortsman first appeared in *Encounters with the Middle East*. Published with permission from the author. Copyright © 2007 by Peter Wortsman.

"I Read Walden Once" by Sarahlee Lawrence published with permission from the author. Copyright © 2008 by Sarahlee Lawrence.

"The Skeleton Coast" by Clive Crook appeared in *The Atlantic* in May 2007. Published with permission from the author. Copyright © 2007 by Clive Crook.

"The Winding Road to Joshua Tree" by Deanne Stillman excerpted from *Joshua Tree: Desolation Tango* (University of Arizona Press). Published with permission from the author. Copyright © 2006 by Deanne Stillman.

"Castles in the Sky" by Jennifer Baljko published with permission from the author. Copyright © 2007 by Jennifer Baljko.

"Heroes of the Caribbean" by Kevin McCaughey published with permission from the author. Copyright © 2007 by Kevin McCaughey.

"Flamenco Form" by Nancy Penrose published with permission from the author. Copyright © 2007 by Nancy Penrose.

"Key to the City" by Catherine Watson originally appeared as "Unlocking Beirut" on World Hum on December 29, 2006. Copyright © 2006 by Catherine Watson. Reprinted with permission from the author.

ABOUT THE EDITORS

James O'Reilly, publisher of Travelers' Tales, was born in England and raised in San Francisco. He graduated from Dartmouth College and wrote mystery serials before becoming a travel writer in the early 1980s. He's visited more than forty-five countries, along the way meditating with monks in Tibet, participating in West African voodoo rituals, living in the French Alps, and hanging out the laundry with nuns in Florence and penguins in Antarctica. He travels extensively with his wife, Wenda, and their three daughters. They live in Palo Alto, California, where they also publish art games and books for children at Birdcage Press (www.birdcagepress.com).

Larry Habegger, executive editor of Travelers' Tales, has been writing about travel since 1980. He has visited almost fifty countries and six of the seven continents, traveling from the Arctic to equatorial rainforests, the Himalayas to the Dead Sea. In the early 1980s he co-authored mystery serials for the *San Francisco Examiner* with James O'Reilly, and since 1985 their syndicated column, "World Travel Watch," has appeared in newspapers in five countries and on WorldTravelWatch.com. As series editors of Travelers' Tales, they have worked on more than 100 books, winning many awards for excellence. Habegger regularly teaches the craft of travel writing at workshops and writers' conferences (www.larryhabegger.com), and he lives with his family on Telegraph Hill in San Francisco.

Sean O'Reilly is director of special sales and editor-at-large for Travelers' Tales. He is a former seminarian, stockbroker, and prison instructor who lives in Virginia with his wife Brenda and their six children. He's had a lifelong interest in philosophy, theology, and travel, and is the author of a groundbreaking book on men's behavior, *How to Manage Your DICK: Redirect Sexual Energy and Discover Your More Spiritually Enlightened, Evolved Self* (www.dickmanagement.com). His travels of late have taken him through China, Thailand, Indonesia, and the South Pacific, and his most recent non-travel project is redbrazil.com, a bookselling site.

TRAVELERS' TALES

A Sense
of Place

Great Travel Writers
Talk About Their
Craft, Lives,
and Inspiration

with MICHAEL SHAPIRO

Bill Bryson

Frances Mayes

Paul Theroux

Isabel Allende

Pico Iyer

Simon Winchester

Peter Matthiessen

Redmond O'Hanlon

Jonathan Raban

Arthur Frommer

Tim Cahill

Jan Morris

Rick Steves...and many more